D1448013

11·5·79

HOW TO GET
THE BEST
HEALTH CARE
FOR
YOUR MONEY

HOW TO GET
THE BEST
HEALTH CARE
FOR
YOUR MONEY

The Family Guide to
New Choices in Health Care

Edited by Lori Breslow

 Rodale Press, Emmaus, Pa.

Library of Congress Cataloging in Publication Data
Main entry under title:

How to get the best health care for your money.

Includes bibliographies and index.
1. Medical care—United States. 2. Medical care,
Cost of—United States. 3. Medical innovations—United
States. 4. Consumer education—United States.
I. Breslow, Lori.
RA410.53.H68   362.1′0973   79-9309
ISBN 0-87857-251-1

Printed in the United States of America on recycled paper
containing a high percentage of de-inked fiber.

2 4 6 8 10 9 7 5 3 1

Contents

Acknowledgments

It was Charlie Gerras, a Rodale Press editor, who first came up with the idea for a book on new health care options. And although I stamped into his office many times complaining, "Look at this mess you've gotten me into," he deserves a thank you for realizing it was an idea worth pursuing.

And if Charlie Gerras provided the original inspiration, then it was Sara Ebenreck who kept the project going. Besides contributing two chapters, which in many ways served as the prototype for the rest of the book, Sara was available to consult with and to lift sagging spirits.

Peggy Schneck and Carol Stoner also provided valuable assistance. Peggy served as the liaison among all the contributors and Rodale Press, and Carol gave us all a broader perspective with which to judge the book.

In addition, the following people helped with specific chapters: The Health/Policy Advisory Commission (Health/PAC) was the source for most of Cynthia Driver's research on the home health care chapter; Sharon Faelten served as research assistant for the chapter on ambulatory surgery; and Kay Matthews read and commented on the childbirth chapter.

Finally, thanks go to Paul Camp, who, as always, was a source of expert editorial guidance—and moral support.

Introduction

What This Book Can Do for You

You have heard, no doubt, that our health care system is in trouble. Costs continue to rise as consumer satisfaction with the quality of health care continues to fall, and no one seems to be able to do anything about the problems.

In fact, if you read the newspapers, listen to the radio, or watch television, you've probably been bombarded with statistics and information telling you how bad things really are. For example:

The total cost of health care in this country is approximately $200 billion—a nearly threefold increase since 1970.

Hospital costs have been going up by more than 15 percent annually—and the average cost of a hospital room is now close to $200 a day.

Doctors' incomes rose over 9 percent in 1978—a higher rate than in any other occupational group. Since 1950 the increase in the cost of doctors' services has been nearly double the increase of other prices.

Chances are you don't need any of these gruesome statistics to convince you that our health care system is in critical need of doctoring. Hours spent waiting in a physician's office, medication that treats the symptom but lets the cause of your illness run rampant, and those depressing monthly medical bills are proof enough.

Taking Control of Your Health Care

You may feel that there's nothing you—or anyone—can do to get better health care short of wiping out the entire system and starting from scratch. But don't despair. Across the country health care professionals and consumers are teaming up with one another to help you get better health care right now. These people believe that there are at least partial solutions to the problems of high cost and poor service.

One of the ways they are doing this is by making improvements in our basic, or primary, health care system. Most of the time we don't go to the doctor because we have a severe illness or a serious injury. We usually go to the doctor because we need help with a minor complaint like a cold or a sprained ankle.

Yet much of the health care in this country is oriented toward serious disease. While medical technology has been successful in developing miracle cures to treat some of our worst diseases, it has shortchanged us in providing good basic, or primary, care.

The situation may now be changing, however, as we begin to develop new alternatives for dealing with the variety of minor complaints we all have.

For instance, the number of health maintenance organizations (HMOs) is growing. These organizations offer primary care (as well as the services of specialists and hospitalization) for one prepaid membership. By providing a place to get most of your health care under one roof, HMOs not only give continuity of care, but also help in cutting costs.

Other centers are being developed to answer the primary health care needs of certain kinds of people. Feminist and adolescent clinics provide health care that is uniquely suited to women and teen-agers. And holistic health centers are bringing about an entirely new concept in medicine by treating you as a whole person. With their belief that body, mind, and spirit must be integrated for optimal health, holistic centers are moving us away from the idea that a body is something to be worked on the way a mechanic works on a car.

New health care professionals are also arriving on the scene to provide basic care. Midlevel health practitioners (MHPs) are trained to do many of the routine tasks a doctor often does, leaving the MD to do more complicated diagnoses and treatment. Thus, if you've ever been embarrassed to go to the doctor for fear your problem was too trivial or "uninteresting," MHPs are welcome news.

Similarly, we are seeing the return of the family doctor—the GP of old, complete with new knowledge and understanding. And other health care professionals like midwives, wellness doctors, and paramedics are now available to help you with the whole range of health care needs you and your family might have.

For the treatment of more serious illnesses and chronic health problems, home health care and ambulatory surgery facilities are helping people avoid unnecessary hospitalization.

Over and over again health care analysts come to the same conclusion: hospitals are one of the foremost contributors to the runaway inflation in our health care system. The statistics are overwhelming: Secretary of Health, Education, and Welfare Joseph A. Califano, Jr., has charged that hospital costs are rising at the rate of $1 million an hour; the average cost for a hospital room on a daily basis is three times what it was in 1967; and, perhaps most important, many people who are hospitalized don't need to be. (According to New York City's Health Services Administration, 500 people are hospitalized unnecessarily in that city alone on any given day.)

Home health care is an old idea made new. At one time, all our health care took place at home out of necessity. Now we are trying to build a new structure that combines care given by the family with support from professionals, agencies, community groups, and friends and neighbors. A wide variety of help is available to the family that wants to take care of one of its members at home—from medical services given by nurses and therapists, to personal care delivered by home health aids, to social services like homemaking and transportation. All of these mean that institutionalization may not be absolutely necessary.

It has also been found that many minor surgical procedures don't require hospitalization, and in particular don't require an overnight stay in the hospital. Thus the growth of ambulatory surgery facilities, places where you can check in in the morning, have your surgery done, and go home again that afternoon to the comfort of your own home. Not only are ambulatory surgery centers convenient, but they also save time and money.

Similarly there are efforts to move birth and death out of hospitals and to make them more humanizing experiences. In recent years, critics have charged that the medical establishment has divorced birth and death from their natural human connections. By taking them away from the family and home, and placing them in the hospital to be managed by machines, tubes, and medical technologists, we have lost our intimacy with these two natural experiences.

Today, people are trying to regain control over them. Parents are demanding family-centered maternity care, a personal birth experience which puts the needs and desires of mothers, fathers, and their babies first. Family-centered maternity care is happening in three places: the home; maternity centers, homelike places set aside solely for normal labor and birth; and hospitals, where innovative staff are joining with parents and childbirth educators to produce changes in hospital births, including the creation of birthing rooms.

We also are learning about new ways to handle death. Hospices, centers of care for the dying and their families, are springing up across the country. Providing supportive services for the terminally ill, both within and outside of the home, hospices are a sign of hope for people who do not want to spend their last days in an institution. Community support groups are also making it easier for people to have humanizing, personal deaths—and for families to support their loved ones during this time. With the support of hospices and community groups, more people are choosing to remain at home to die. Finally, hospitals are trying to improve their care for the dying through special programs and services.

There are a number of alternatives, options, and new programs you can take advantage of to get the best possible health care for your money. You simply need to know what they are — which is the aim of this book — and how to use them.

Becoming a Discriminating Consumer

Throughout this book, in various ways and at various times, you will get the same message: be a discriminating health care consumer. Although many of these options are exciting, challenging and innovative, you must decide if they are right for you and your family.

Obviously, it would be just as silly to have open heart surgery at an ambulatory surgery facility (assuming you could have open heart surgery there, which you can't) as it would be to have warts removed in the hospital. Similarly, if you are perfectly satisfied with the care you're receiving from your doctor(s), then there's no reason to switch. But if you are looking for better sources of health care, then there are several things you should do to help guarantee that you'll be satisfied with your choices.

The first thing you need to do is read, read, read. Don't use only this book, but look at other books and articles that discuss the particular kind of health care help you need as well. Find out how procedures are usually done. Become aware of the advantages and disadvantages of these new options. Do your homework. Study. Check the facts. (Obviously, this advice holds true for more conventional health care routes, too. However, since this book is about new health care choices and since other books are good guides to conventional health care, we've primarily included methods for assessing these new alternatives.)

Talk to other health care consumers and health care professionals. Ask for their opinions of the programs or people you are considering using. Talk to others who have already used the alternative. Find out if they were satisfied, what problems they encountered, and if they would do the same thing again. Talk to the people who will be providing you with the health care. Visit the places you will be using. Do cost comparisons that measure the new alternative against established routes.

Make up lists—questions to ask, benefits versus drawbacks, points to cover. Often, people get flustered talking to medical professionals and they forget to ask the questions that are foremost in their minds or they become so intimidated that they are afraid to pose questions at all. Something written down on a piece of paper will help you become and stay organized.

We have tried to get you started on the road to making health care choices. At the end of each chapter, you will find lists of books and articles for further reading, lists of people and organizations to contact for more information, and consumer notes which review and highlight the points made in the chapter. There are also stories of people who have actually used whatever option is being described within each chapter. Not all of the stories are wildly successful because problems can arise even under the best circumstances.

But all this is only a start—the rest is up to you. In the last analysis, your time, money—and health—depend on you.

Finally, a note on how this book was put together. All the contributors are laypeople—health care consumers themselves. We have tried to provide you with the most up-to-date information on each program or option described, but happily so much is occurring so quickly in many of these fields that you will need to do some exploring on your own to get the most current information. (Unhappily, this is especially true about prices. Inflation will no doubt cause whatever figures we've quoted in this book to rise rapidly.) Also, you need to be aware that systems change from place to place. We have provided you with general guidelines. Again, research in your own area is advised.

The options we've described here won't solve all our health care problems. They are only a start. But hopefully they will serve as a catalyst for still other improvements in our health care system. Thus, this book will not only tell you about choices that are available to you, but it will also provide ammunition and ideas for those who are agitating for change by demonstrating the feasibility of new directions—both those already in use and those that are evolving.

New Ways to Get Basic Care

part one

chapter one

New Places to Go

Sara Ebenreck

New ways to get basic health care are rapidly evolving across America. Health maintenance organizations are trying to cut costs while offering care in a one-stop setting. Women's centers are teaching women how to take charge of their bodies by understanding how they work and participating actively in their own exams. Along with physical checkups, adolescent clinics are counseling teens about the food they eat and problems they face with sex, drugs, and developing personal identities. Holistic centers are experimenting with team approaches to care and involving patients in setting up "wellness plans" that emphasize the relationship of diet, stress, emotions, and lifestyle.

This chapter takes a look at those centers, describing what goes on in them and how you might benefit from the ones in your area. It focuses on alternatives to the single doctor operating from his private office, because some of the most exciting developments in health care are happening where groups of interdisciplinary professionals get together in a team. As part of a team, no one doctor or other health worker has to be godlike, knowing all aspects of the complex person that is you. Doctors can provide one aspect of your health care while counselors, nutritionists, or physical therapists pitch in for others. Information from all these sources can be linked together for a whole-person approach to your health care.

Even if you have a family physician you treasure, some of these alternatives may provide you with valuable supplements to that care. And, if you're one of the growing number of Americans who rely on a hospital emergency room when a bone breaks or a virus hits, you'll want to look even more closely at these improved ways to get health care. Emergency rooms are notorious for long waits, impersonal care, and limited crisis-oriented treatment. No one there is going to have time to really help you see how to grow healthier.

If you read this chapter, become interested in making new choices, and then find that the center you like doesn't exist near you right now, have some hope. Such centers are growing in number and may be available to you in the near future. At a minimum, under-standing what these centers do may give you some ideas for improved health care with the options you have at hand now.

Health Maintenance Organizations

The fastest-growing alternative to getting your health care at a private doctor's office is getting it through a group health center known as an HMO (health maintenance organization). HMOs across the country often offer a broad range of services for less money than traditional insurance plans. Being a member means you can get as many checkups and as much care as you or your children need for the same set fee — a terrific bargain for families with kids who fall off bikes or get winter wind earaches and chicken pox. HMO member-ship may also mean getting basic eye exams or dental services for that same fee, and having the chance to attend programs on how to deal with hypertension or diabetes. And all the services are offered in a medical center where gynecologists and pediatricians operate as a team with internists or family practice doctors.

HMOs have been around for a long time. One of the largest, the Kaiser Foundation's Health Plan, was established in the 1930s for workers building the Grand Coulee Dam on the West Coast. Dr. Edward Hinman, director of Washington's Group Health Associ-ation, claims the concept can be traced back to a merchant seamen's health plan created by Congress in 1798. But until the last several years only a handful of people working for companies like Kaiser were part of them.

One major reason for the slow growth of HMOs was opposition from the medical community itself. Private doctors understandably saw group health plans as competition. Some doctors felt that a prepaid plan just didn't offer quality medicine. In the 1930s, the American Medical Association went so far as to refuse hospital admission privileges to HMO doctors. A 1943 court decision removed that obstacle, but grudging support from the medical community kept the idea from gaining strong momentum until recently.

In the 1970s, government, business, and labor leaders are realizing that it's possible to cut health costs while still providing good health care through the use of HMOs. They are combining forces with doctors who do see the advantages of group medical plans, and HMOs are finally blossoming. There are now 203 in the United States, which represents a 23 percent increase from 1977. In Washington, D.C., home of three HMOs, over 200,000 people have chosen to get their health care through these plans.

How HMOs Work

What exactly is an HMO? It's an organization which agrees to provide medical, hospital, emergency, and preventive health care in return for a prepaid membership. Instead of paying for an insurance plan which will then repay your private doctor or hospital for some specified health expenses, you pay in advance to be a member of an HMO. The group will have a center where you go for checkups with such doctors as an internist, family physician, or pediatrician.* Members will be asked to choose a center, if the HMO has more than one, and in that center to choose a primary care doctor from among the staff. That way you and the doctor get to know each other, a relationship which should improve care.

This physician will be your link with other staff doctors when needed and arrange referrals to specialists or hospitals. For some people, that may mean following up on medical care you'd neglect if you had to pay for the specialist out of your pocket. "Many patients we see had symptoms for years, but didn't have care until they came to our group plan," says Dr. Isadore Alpher, the adult allergist at Group Health Association's Maryland Center. Maybe such patients felt they

*There is an alternate model for an HMO called an individual practice association (IPA). Here doctors link together for prepayment but give medical services in their private offices. Most rural HMOs work this way, since not having to build a central clinic cuts back on expenses for a group which will always have a small membership.

One HMO

"Look! Love Is Here to Stay," says the sign posted just behind the information desk at the entrance to 110,000-member Group Health Association's (GHA) eight-floor medical center in downtown Washington. The sign suggests that a big medical center in a big city doesn't have to be impersonal. And a walk through the center confirms that fact. The adult medicine floor has two moderately sized, comfortable waiting areas with tan sofas, soft lighting, and bright pictures. Individual doctors' offices for consultations and examining rooms open off a hallway that looks much like the space in any private doctor's office except for the multiple doors.

The Ob-Gyn floor, which draws a high number of regular patients, is divided into three areas, each with its own small waiting space. You find your doctor or nurse by checking a color-coded name plate over the main information desk and following red, blue, or yellow marking lines to the right space. A nursery cradle in each space offers a place for a very young child. And a sign "No Smoking, Fetal Growth in Process," reflects the organization's interest in health education and a healthy environment.

"Checking in with a member's card that looks like a charge plate is the only strong reminder of the size of this HMO," says Karen Freer, a young woman who signed up with GHA when she first came to Washington as a free-lance writer. Karen sees her nurse-midwife for regular gynecological checkups. "She's a compassionate woman, comforting when I'm in pain and reassuring when I'm frightened," Karen

couldn't afford allergy shots or thought testing for allergies would be a long and confusing process. In either case, the allergy treatment center at that HMO has grown from one staffer to three and one-half in response to the demand.

Since HMO services usually include a social worker, some short-term counseling is available for situations that warrant it. "I had a 14-year-old who called saying she was pregnant and wanted to have the baby," said one HMO nurse. "Then her mother called to say she wanted the girl to have an abortion." A social worker helped them sort through feelings and thoughts and come to the best possible decision.

said as she talked about the nurse's help with birth control methods. Seeing a nurse-midwife instead of a doctor is a choice provided by this HMO, one that Karen made after being unhappy with the insensitivity of the first doctor she was assigned to. Karen's doubts about whether or not she was safe with a nurse for her exams were resolved by the nurse's competence and her quick consultation with center doctors when questions came up.

Karen is particularly pleased with the amount of self-help information her nurse gives her. She learned the right way to do a breast exam and is able to use a mirror to check her own cervix when she gets a pelvic exam. The waiting rooms have pamphlets with information on birth control methods and VD, and bulletin boards in the center post articles on problems with the Pill. Information is put out where consumers can read it — something that often gets neglected in a private doctor's office.

There have been some snags in the system. Karen suffers chronically from eczema, a skin disease. When she tried to get a referral to the center dermatologist she faced a six-month wait. Since her eczema hurt, she chose to go to a private doctor, paying her own way, rather than wait. And the primary staff can also get caught under the pressure of patient loads, she feels. You need to make a checkup appointment well in advance.

Karen Freer pays about $33 a month for her individual health care. That's the entire cost of the care since she's self-employed and doesn't have an employer chipping in. "But that's a bargain for good regular care in Washington," Karen insists.

The group approach to health care can also give members continuity of care. Doctors in the same organization may find it easier to talk with each other and with the other health professionals there. All your health data is kept in a central file so each doctor can read your whole medical history. That means you won't get a repeat of X-rays, EKGs, and lab tests as you go from office to office — another way to cut health costs.

HMOs cover emergency care, sometimes in their own centers, sometimes by prearrangement with a hospital clinic. "That's really comforting to people who want to know a doctor is there when they suddenly need him," says Ralph Gallo, vice-president of Georgetown

University's Community Health Plan. He's the father of two children and a member of the HMO where he works. Along with getting quick emergency care, you can also easily get a second opinion from within the group, he points out.

If you need hospitalization, you'll be admitted to a hospital which has payment arrangements with the HMO and your plan will cover most expenses. (Exactly how much is paid varies with the plan and is something you should check carefully.) Because of the HMO-hospital linkup, you should check on which hospital the group uses when you consider membership. How good and how convenient the hospital is could be an important factor in crisis health care.

HMOs do emphasize outpatient care instead of hospitalization whenever possible. That means you may get diagnostic testing, a D & C, or a tubal ligation done in the HMO center. If you like being able to have a procedure done during the day and going home that night, it's an ideal setup. Across the country, HMO members spend 30 to 50 percent fewer days in the hospital than a comparable group under traditional insurance coverage.[1]

There are good reasons for this lower rate of admissions. Along with having centers to use instead of hospitals for some procedures, many of the usual incentives for hospital admission are missing with HMOs. HMO doctors don't have to admit a patient to the hospital to get the treatment covered by insurance, as do many private doctors. And, unlike the private doctor who is highly paid for surgery, the HMO doctor who is on a salary receives no extra compensation for a hospital procedure. HMO members had only one-third as many gynecological operations and tonsillectomies as comparable patients with private doctors.[2] Those operations are precisely the ones which medical critics charge often benefit doctors more than patients.

Regular health care may itself result in lowered hospital admissions for crisis health problems. A California study showed that 58 percent of men in one HMO plan had a yearly checkup, compared to 43 percent of those with traditional insurance policies.[3] That increases the chances that medical problems such as hypertension, glaucoma, or cancer will be caught at any early stage, before hospital care is needed. That may save even more than money because, as HMO director Edward Hinman quipped, "It's dangerous to be in a hospital. You can get sick there."

An HMO member can get some home care services if an illness or recovery can be handled there instead of in the hospital or a nursing home. That may be comforting knowledge for a patient who doesn't like institutions, and it's a money-saving strategy for the group plan. Services may include a doctor's visit, although several HMOs admitted this was rare. The plan will usually include payment for a visiting nurse, but it doesn't cover home care help such as private duty nursing or homemaker aids.

HMOs for the Family

Ron and Sue Neble along with their children, Alex and Ann, are members of a suburban Maryland HMO center. They joined when Ron got the option through his job. Sue's first hesitancy about not having a choice of doctors has changed after a year's experience with the plan. "You have some choices within the system, and you can get referred to specialists," she says. Sue and Ron use their center frequently. They've all had checkups, including eye tests. Alex and Sue both get allergy shots and Ron used the sports clinic at the downtown office when his knees began to bother him after playing soccer or riding his bike to work. Alex was examined by an orthopedic specialist at the main center after he fell on the basketball court. And when Ann fell off her bike last summer and knocked out her front teeth, their plan covered the emergency room treatment — although there is still a debate about who should pay for the oral surgery which came later and was done by a private doctor. For their monthly payment of $20 (Ron's employer pays the rest), that's a lot of care.

"You do need to take the responsibility of asking for what you need," said Sue. Once, when Ron was stunned after being thrown from his bicycle by a sideswiping car, their doctor ordered only an X-ray for his wrist. They insisted on having Ron's head checked, too, and they got the action they wanted.

Overall, Sue and Ron Neble have been satisfied with their group alternative to the conventional health care route. They feel freer from worry about unexpected medical expenses than they might with a usual insurance plan. The HMO's low cost and good basic care are especially valuable to them.

Problems with HMO Care

All the advantages of an HMO don't come without some limits. First of all, as an HMO member you must use doctors at the group center if you want the plan to pay your expenses. You can pay for consultation with another doctor, but the plan covers only HMO care or specialists to whom the HMO refers you. That could be a problem if you're already seeing a doctor you like.

HMO doctors do come in a wide variety of ages and personalities, however, so there's a good chance you can find one you think is competent and to whom you can relate well. A new HMO may have mostly young staff since it's easier to recruit beginning physicians than doctors with established practices; older plans will often have doctors who have grown with the group in age and experience. To be sure about getting a competent doctor, ask the HMO for staff credentials and experience. Ask if specialists are board certified to practice in their areas. Any group with competent staff will be glad to give you information on the training of their doctors and nurses.

A second problem with HMOs is that you may have to wait to see some nonemergency specialists like dermatologists or allergists. Teen-agers with skin problems, for example, are referred to a dermatologist *if* they can get an appointment, said a staffer in one clinic. A consumer in another clinic who faced a six-month wait for an appointment chose to pay for her own specialist. Ask about the patterns for nonemergency referrals in any HMO you may consider.

Another area to look into is your relationship to a specialist like a gynecologist whom you will need to see regularly. Find out if you will see only one gynecologist or simply be assigned to whichever doctor is on duty when you come. Continuity in a doctor-patient relationship can make a big difference in getting good care.

There are some limits on HMO payment for medical care given away from home, so if you travel a good deal you'll want to check that out carefully. HMOs usually will cover payments for emergency care received away from home, but most won't pay for nonemergency care you could have gotten from the HMO while you were home. Some HMOs may cover only a limited amount of out-of-area hospitalization.

Mental health services get only slight coverage in many HMO plans. Better plans offer up to 20 outpatient visits for nervous or mental disorders, but other plans may offer less or none. Some plans pay hospital costs for treatment of mental illness; others don't, even as an added payment option. The reasons for this omission are tied directly to the main intent of HMOs — cutting costs while offering quality basic care. Mental health costs can be high since such illness often demands lengthy treatment or repeated hospitalization.

Although HMOs are generally praised for preventive care, this is generally no more than traditional physical exams along with the opportunity to take some educational programs. Georgetown University Community Health Plan in Washington, for example, offers programs on diet, diabetic nutrition, childbirth preparation, hypertension, and cardiac risk factors. These are free for members and provide a good way to get accurate information that can be tied in with your doctor's advice on your health needs.

You ought not to expect detailed attention to or advice on nutritional or stress factors from your HMO doctor or nurse, however. The need to cut costs to keep membership fees low does limit the amount of time a doctor can spend with any patient. Obvious factors such as overeating, complete lack of exercise, heavy smoking, or drug or alcohol abuse will get attention. But the typical HMO isn't equipped, any more than most private doctors are, to help you with an individually balanced nutritional program or to analyze and propose solutions to stress problems in your life. For those kinds of services, you'll need to choose a supplementary program. (See the section on holistic health, pages 27–35.)

As an HMO member, you'll need to be aggressive in seeking out what you think is good preventive care. An HMO won't automatically schedule you for a physical. Indeed, some HMO staffers admit that low prices depend on the assumption that not everyone will come in for an introductory physical, for example. So ask for those services that you would like to receive.

The need to take responsibility for your own health carries over into other areas also. One HMO nurse said that the center referred abortion cases to a local women's clinic, but admitted that nobody checked on whether the patients got follow-up birth control counseling or even information on the possible adverse effects of multiple abortions. You're on your own to dig out this sort of information.

HMO Costs

Monthly payments for a family plan range between $60 and $100, with variations from state to state and plan to plan. The Public

Health Service in Washington has 1977 figures which show Hawaii with a low of $52 and Michigan with a high of $116. An individual membership may be about one-third of that amount.

There are several things to remember as you look at those figures. One is that your employer may pay part of the cost. Another is that the cost covers all basic care. You won't be writing a check each time you head for the doctor's office. (In 1976, the average American family spent $450 for medical services not covered in their private insurance plans.) So the $87 average monthly figure is a bargain in many ways.

You'll need to compare costs between an HMO and a regular insurance plan in order to figure out actual savings in your case. Because both costs vary widely, it's not possible to draw conclusions that fit every case. An HMO membership in one Pennsylvania county, for example, costs slightly more than Blue Cross and Blue Shield insurance, while a comparison in Washington, D.C. shows a lower price for the local HMO.

If your local HMO costs less than a major insurance plan, the HMO itself probably will have drawn up a chart comparing costs and benefits of the plan. Likewise, a major insurer like Blue Cross and Blue Shield may have local figures you can analyze. A call asking for that information can save you a lot of time in figuring out actual cost-benefit factors in your case.

If there are several HMOs in your area,* it's worth checking for the best buy. Government-qualified HMOs, for example, must charge all members of a community a common rate regardless of the health status of the particular person or group. A nonqualified HMO may be able to offer a lower rate. (According to the federal office of HMOs, most groups apply for federal qualification to gain the up to $2 million in grants available to newly formed plans. Federal qualification in itself doesn't mean an HMO is giving better care than a nonqualified HMO, although it does mean the group has to offer a broad range of services and have a mechanism for insuring that quality medicine is practiced.)

Within HMOs, you should also check on high- and low-option plans. With a low option, you might get a cheaper membership rate

---

*You can find local HMOs by calling your local medical society or a toll-free number for the federal office of health maintenance organizations in Washington, D.C. (800-638-6686).

and pay $2 each time you visit the office or get a prescription filled. If your health doesn't take you into the center often, that may be a bargain. High-option plans may cover all your visits and prescriptions as well as services such as dental care.

Most members of an HMO get into the plan because they're employed by a company which offers that option. A 1973 federal law requires that all employers of more than 25 persons in an area where a federally qualified HMO operates must offer this plan to their employees as a possible choice.

But you can enroll in an HMO even if you're self-employed or work for a very small business. Plans may accept individuals. Federally qualified HMOs with more than 50,000 members must accept up to 4 percent of their membership base from anyone who applies, unless they can show their financial capability is strained by this. An HMO may argue that it is financially pressured by taking on a person who needs kidney dialysis or an aging person with acute health care needs. Some HMOs will take Medicare members into their plan; others will not. Some will take the members for services supplementary to the Medicare benefits.

If you do come in as part of a group to a federally qualified HMO, the plan can't limit services or cancel your membership because of your past or present health status. Nor can the group ask for a waiting period for maternity coverage as do many private insurers. But these terms don't apply to nonqualified HMOs, so check those details out carefully.

The Last Three Questions

Almost anyone thinking about an HMO ends up with three other questions: Why are qualified doctors attracted to a group which limits their income and makes them employees? Doesn't the desire to keep costs down make it likely that medical care will be skimpy? And isn't care in such a large center going to be impersonal?

Ralph Gallo, of Georgetown University's Community Health Plan, answers the first question by pointing to the positive factors in HMOs that attract doctors. They start practice with salaries in the low forties and with significant privileges: a month's vacation, HMO payment of malpractice insurance, time off for study, work in a center where staff and equipment are provided free of cost and effort to them, work with a peer group which provides professional contacts and learning experience, a working schedule that makes a more normal family life possible.

Since quality doctors are the core of any HMO team, however, this general answer shouldn't keep you from looking hard at the HMO you consider. If doctors' salaries are low, especially competent staffers may leave the plan. Then you're stuck with changing doctors or leaving the plan yourself. A pointed question about the turnover of staff is in order as you talk about pros and cons with the membership staff of the HMO.

The second question, about how quality care is insured, gets an emphatic response from HMO spokespeople. A money-hungry HMO could limit care, they admit. But skimping may mean more hospitalization or even malpractice suits — both counterproductive to the desire to keep costs low. Marketing departments in HMOs know that their best advertisements are the word-of-mouth references given by satisfied members, and they also know how fast criticism spreads. So there are internal reasons for maintaining quality.

These reasons are backed up by mechanisms for getting action on complaints. A small complaint about waiting for appointments or a brusque nurse may get results from the first person you mention it to. But if it doesn't and you feel strongly about it, most HMOs have a system for reporting grievances. At one center, a complaint box gathers notes for the consumer board. Over the months, complaints at this center focused on telephone calls. Callers were put on hold for a long wait or told that they'd get a return call which never came. The board decided that complaints were both common enough and strong enough to warrant hiring a special receptionist whose entire job would consist of taking telephone calls.

Quality care is more than an issue of convenience, however. You should check on any formal programs for review of medical work at your HMO. Some groups have a medical committee which reviews patient records; others send a team from one center to another to check cases. Ultimately, even this can't assure you of high-quality care. Getting a personal evaluation from a present member may help. And finally, you'll have to remain alert to quality-care issues yourself if you do join up.

The final question, about impersonality of care in a large center, may well depend on the individual HMO. If you establish a good relationship with an HMO doctor or nurse, seeing him or her in the center may be little different from a private office experience. But some factors can cut down on personal care. If your HMO is growing quickly, new members (sometimes thousands of them in one year) can grow faster than the staff and create pressures on staff time. Waiting time for routine care such as physical exams can be lengthened in such a situation. And inevitably a doctor who sees more and more patients can spend less and less time and energy with any one of them. A visit to the HMO you are thinking about joining and some specific questions about typical time allowed for an appointment and waiting times for services should help you figure out if that's going to be a problem for you.

HMOs are going to grow in size and number, partly due to the decision of the federal government to stimulate their birth. Along with providing initial funding, Washington planners are visiting cities across the country to push the cost and health values of HMOs to local business, labor, and medical leaders. The high rate of inflation in health care, 40 percent of which is traceable to hospital care, is making HMOs look better and better to more people. So even if you haven't yet had the option, you may soon. And armed with some good questions about care, you can analyze a plan to find out if it will meet your own health care needs.

Women's Health Centers

"Every woman has a right to feel good about the amazing creature she is," says Barbara Mayo of the Vermont Women's Health Center in Burlington. That includes feeling good about yourself while you're getting your annual gynecological exam and knowing enough about your body to be an active partner in that exam.

Convinced from experience that health care from most male doctors doesn't help women gain responsible control over their own bodies, women's groups around the country have begun organizing their own health centers. Most of the roughly 40 centers that have sprung up since 1971 got their start as abortion clinics shortly after state and federal laws made abortion legal. But many have branched out to offer further "well-woman" services: gynecological exams, birth control counseling, pregnancy testing, and general education about women's health issues. Women are choosing these clinics not just for one-time crises like abortions, but also for ongoing health care.

Participatory Exams

Looking at what happens during a gynecological exam in one center shows how care can be different in a women's clinic. If you come to the Women's Health Center in Burlington, Vermont, for an exam, you'll first see a counselor to talk over your health history and any current problems. That conversation will cover topics such as whether you've been exposed to hormones or drugs that could affect your body, whether you have pain with your monthly menstrual period, and whether your lifestyle is heterosexual, lesbian, or celibate. The atmosphere of the discussion tries to reinforce the idea that you're not there just as a passive patient with a pelvic area, but as a responsible person seeking knowledge for taking charge of your own health needs.

Counselors at the Burlington Center will talk about your "fertility cycle" rather than your "menstrual cycle." This focuses on ovulation as the key point in the monthly cycle during which hormonal changes lead to emotional and physical changes, including the discharge of blood. Centering on ovulation means a difference in the way a woman thinks about herself, one staffer says. "It means thinking of yourself as a fertile woman rather than a monthly bleeder."

Discussion about methods of birth control will involve a frank pro and con look at alternative methods in the context of your lifestyle. Problems with the Pill and the IUD can be discussed, as well as the effectiveness of foam or condoms. Many women find that talking with a woman who herself has to face the risks of birth control choices helps make the discussion more honest than a conversation with a male gynecologist.

Along with chemical and mechanical forms of control, the center also offers classes in natural birth control. (One such method, for example, is based on observing the quality of cervical mucus that is discharged from the vagina.) You're also likely to hear about herbal tea remedies rather than drugs for menstrual cramps.

Natural methods take longer to learn than chemical or mechanical controls and are ideally taught by women who have used them. That may explain why women's centers are starting to offer information on these options. And since these methods also frequently demand cooperation from a sexual partner, the center encourages men to come in to learn about them, too.

Whether it's for birth control or not, learning about the structure of and changes in your body can help deepen your sense of respect for yourself, women who know the process say. Understanding your natural rhythms and working with them, not against them, leads to a joyful awareness whether you're sexually involved or celibate, fertile or going through menopause.

After a thorough discussion of birth control methods, a woman seeking a gynecological exam at the Burlington Women's Center meets with the woman doctor on the staff. The emphasis during this physical exam is on learning and participation. If the woman wants to, she can watch in a mirror held between her legs while the doctor does the exam, talking quietly about the external and internal parts of the body. Most women haven't seen their cervix, the center finds. So once the speculum is inserted to stretch the vaginal opening for the doctor to check the cervix, the woman will be invited to look for herself in the mirror. If her uterus can be felt through the lower stomach area, the woman can touch it herself, getting another experience in understanding just what her own body is like.

Women who've had bad experiences with insensitive gynecologists reach out to a center with participatory exams like this. If your doctor has discouraged your questions, handled your body roughly, or generally treated you as an object, then the personal approach of such a center is especially appealing. But even if you've had a fairly sensitive gynecologist, points out one center staffer, that doesn't mean you were given an explanation of what was going on or the choice to see and learn about your own body. One aim of the women's center is helping women learn to make their own judgments about their health. The doctor is a skilled consultant, not somebody who observes and then tells the passive patient if she's OK or not.

Such an introductory exam with counseling takes about two hours and costs $30. Since the center uses a sliding fee, women with low incomes pay less for the exam. Giving you so much time for the same amount of money as you spend for ten minutes with a regular gynecologist means that the center normally operates on a break-even basis and pays its staff a fairly low salary. The doctor who works there two days a week earns $12 an hour, and a counselor takes home about $5.50 an hour. For the women involved, the shared commitment and atmosphere of learning about health seems to make up for the low salaries. But the situation does point to one structural dilemma of alternate health care: it takes personal sacrifice to offer personalized, competent care while keeping fees affordable.

The Group Approach and Self-Help

The desire for self-help in health care led women at the Feminist Women's Health Center in Los Angeles to develop the technique of participatory group exams. Women coming to that center are scheduled to meet with a leader and several other women who are all there for the same purpose, for example, pregnancy testing or abortion counseling. For the Los Angeles women, the group concept was a natural development from the consciousness-raising groups of the 1960s. Being part of a group forces a radical sort of reorientation in itself. In a society where women are conditioned to passively receive health care from a doctor, just meeting with a group for that care is a clear statement that the whole process is being rethought.

In these groups health counselors present information verbally and with slides. In a vaginal infection group, women learn what causes these infections and what the vagina and cervix look like when they're inflamed. In a pregnancy screening group, women learn to do their own urine pregnancy tests and see the results right away. (Blood tests have to be sent to a lab for processing.) They discuss other signs of pregnancy, too, such as the slight opening and darkening in color of the cervix. Abortion counseling groups discuss all aspects of the abortion procedure and testing. Questions that a woman might forget in a hurried exam with a single doctor are often recalled and brought up during the group discussion. And usually one woman's question will spark many others.

Part of the feminist self-help group's approach to care is helping women learn how to do their own self-examination with a plastic speculum. A health worker shows the women how to insert the speculum and use a light and mirror to view their own cervixes and vaginas. In some of the self-help learning groups, women may practice doing exams with each other. For many women, being able to do for themselves what they'd always thought they could only "have done to them" is a major step in freedom from the mystification surrounding their health care. After a demonstration from a Los Angeles clinic leader, one nurse wrote about her sheer joy at realizing you could get into a "direct dialogue with your innards." Most women experience a sense of awe and excitement when they see an inner part of their body for the first time, wrote another woman after talking with many participants.[4]

Responsible participation, health education, and personalized care are the common themes of women's health centers, but exactly how they are implemented varies from center to center. The seven Feminist Women's Centers around the country all stress the group approach to health care. Other centers, like Vermont's, choose private counseling and exams. Some offer a broad range of services, including discussions on topics like menopause. Others are mainly abortion clinics with only a small effort given to other health concerns. Still others are information and counseling centers which provide referrals for actual physical care.

Some of the centers are staffed by radical feminists dedicated to the end of male-controlled health care. Others have chosen to have male doctors on their staffs after being disappointed by insensitive female doctors. Most centers are directed by lay women, reflecting a belief that women, not doctors, should be in control of women's bodies. Whether that structure leads to a better doctor-client relationship depends on the individual situation.

With all these differences, a visit to a women's center near you* and a talk with some women who go there will be major factors in a decision about using the center. If you do decide to take an introductory look, there are a number of questions you should ask along with usual ones like hours and cost.

Since staffing patterns differ so much, ask whether gynecological exams will be done by a doctor or other staff members and what their training is. If you're interested in learning how to do a self-exam, ask if that's possible. Find out how much education is done in the course of an exam. In contrast to the Vermont Center, for example, a male doctor at a women's clinic in Washington, D.C., gave an exam much like any other routine gynecological checkup — quickly and without educational commentary. Ask if the doctor is male or female, if that matters to you.

Check on whether you can get an appointment or if it's a matter of "first come, first served." Faced with loss of income from "no-shows," some centers have moved away from giving any appointments. That can mean a long wait. Also ask about who comes to the

---

*Local medical societies and chapters of the National Organization for Women are likely to know of women's health centers in the area. Also see the reading guide at the end of this chapter for a source book listing many of them.

center. If you're going to get involved with a group discussion, you may want to know something about the ages and backgrounds of the women likely to participate.

You'll also need to check the extent and limits of services the center offers and whether the doctor who sees you will function as your personal doctor. Some centers are ready to act as continuing health centers. In others, although you may see a doctor initially, there's no guarantee that when you come back you'll see the same doctor.

Staff doctors don't necessarily have admitting privileges at a hospital. That means you might need referral to another doctor if you face hospitalization. The center should have a good relationship with doctors who will take referrals from its staff. Knowing about how that works is important or an emergency could leave you stranded.

Although most women's centers offer pregnancy tests, abortions, and childbirth education, few offer childbirth services. Some have developed referrals to midwifery services, local obstetricians, and hospitals. If you're planning to have a baby or wouldn't choose an abortion for an unplanned pregnancy, you'll need to check on obstetrical services.

Finally, it's important to remember that care in almost all women's centers is focused on reproductive concerns. That means you'll need a general doctor when you've got any other problem, from a virus to suspected cancer.

Whether or not you choose a women's center for your reproductive health care, you may want to share in some of their programs. Being part of a self-help discussion and experience group may help you deal more knowledgeably with your regular gynecologist. If your doctor usually talks with you when you're naked, draped, and flat on your back on his table, a women's group can help you gather the courage to insist on some discussion time during your appointment.

Since most doctors are pressed for time and consequently cannot share educational information, health education at a women's center can be an important supplement to your regular medical routine. Learning about your body functions and rhythms, alternate birth control methods, and about natural ways to lessen menstrual pain can fill a big gap left by the usual medical preference for fast, efficient action.

A Major Alternative?

Whether women's centers are going to grow into a major alternative for health care is still an open question. They're new: the first Women's Health Conference and first clinic both came on the scene in 1971. In the short time since then, women have organized over 1,000 information centers and over 40 clinics — strong growth for so short a period.

But acceptance by at least some parts of the traditional medical community is the key to referral services and hospital privileges, and that acceptance is still uncertain. Some centers have built supportive relationships with local doctors and hospitals. Others fill a vacuum through their roles as abortion clinics and self-help information centers and are accepted as such by other health care groups. One group health center in Washington, D.C., for example, regularly refers its abortion patients to a local women's clinic.

Other centers have been surrounded by controversy and opposition from the traditional medical community. When the Los Angeles Feminist Women's Health Center developed a technique for removing the contents of the uterus (to lessen menstrual pain but also for very early abortions if conception had taken place), the medical community was strongly opposed.[5] In 1972, two staffers in that clinic who fitted diaphragms and taught women to insert speculums were arrested and charged with practicing medicine without a license. Carol Downer, who chose to stand trial rather than pay a fine, was acquitted. But her acquittal doesn't mean doctors have accepted the right of lay women to examine their own or other women's bodies, and that nonacceptance has an effect on the growth of some centers.

Along with the rough road to gaining medical acceptance, women's centers face some economic obstacles. In order to offer longer sessions and broader services for a competitive or smaller fee than other gynecologists, they usually pay low staff salaries and depend on the commitments and energies of women with strong views on participatory health care. How many women are willing to commit time and effort to this kind of health care is an unanswered question.

Whether or not women's clinics prosper and become part of the normal medical scene of the future, their decade of question-raising is producing a new approach to women's health care. Medical schools and gynecologists are responding to the fact that women are asking more questions and want to understand exactly what goes on in their treatment. And it's clear that whether you choose to use a women's center or not, getting acquainted with the questions such centers raise about your health care can help you to a greater awareness of "the amazing creature you are."

Adolescent Health Centers

Ann, at 17, has had her first sexual experience and is frightened that she may be pregnant. Luke, a 15-year-old, is having a tough time going to his gym class because he's still the same height he was at 13, while all his friends are growing quickly into masculinity. He's worried that he may never grow at all. Susie, a 12-year-old who just changed schools, has stomach pains and headaches along with a budding record as a shoplifter. What these kids have in common is a health-related problem — and the likelihood that if they go to a doctor he will see only what's physically, and superficially, wrong with them.

If, by a lucky choice, they end up at one of the more than 80 adolescent clinics across the country, they'll receive some health care that focuses on them as whole people. Ann may get a chance to talk about her sexual feelings along with finding out if she's pregnant. In addition to hormone tests and other physical exams to see if there really is something wrong, Luke may be able to wrestle out loud with his feelings about starting puberty late. And Susie may get some help in seeing that her shoplifting and headaches are related to having had to leave behind a whole group of friends. Coming to terms with those feelings may help her get rid of the aches without aspirin.

Adolescent clinics are a growing answer to the health needs of teen-agers. Mostly located in larger cities now, they're a model for what adolescent health care can be: care that helps teens look at themselves as whole persons, talk about the stresses that are pressuring their lives, relate those to physical sickness when necessary, and — most important of all — get health care in an atmosphere that treats them as individuals with both dignity and a capacity for self-responsibility.

The Need for Teen-Age Health Care

Traditionally, teens have fallen between the cracks in the health care system. Up to about age 12, they may have regular checkups with a pediatrician. But even though a children's unit might treat adolescents, most teens would rather face lions than sit in a waiting room with babies and 4-year-olds. A possibly pregnant girl of 14 doesn't want to see a children's doctor or her mother's gynecologist because she fears that whatever is discussed will be passed on to her parents. A family doctor often hasn't had the training necessary to establish the rapport with teens that will let him move beyond the physical complaints. Even if he does, he may feel obligated to obtain parental consent for any treatment or relegate the teens' psychophysical problems to the bottom of his priority list. And lack of money or private access to insurance coverage keeps teens from choosing doctors on their own.

Ordinary health problems — whether minor matters like earaches or major ones like suspected cancer — usually do get channeled through a family doctor. But our society has a growing number of teens with other health problems which traditional medical help may not meet.

More than 2 out of 13 first births in the United States are to girls so young they are biologically at risk in childbearing because their own physical growth hasn't been completed.[6] Pregnant adolescents have higher rates of toxemia, prolonged labor, pelvic disproportion, and Cesarean section than older women, and precisely because of this, they need intensive maternity care. But they're exactly the people who may wait the longest before seeing a doctor or discontinue care if it doesn't relate to their deeper psychic needs.

The rise in sexual activity among teens has meant a marked increase in venereal disease. Some health professionals talk about an "epidemic" of gonorrhea and syphilis occurring among teens. Drug and alcohol abuse is a major health problem for adolescents, and the rising rate of teen-age suicides points to the need for mental health services for this age group. All of these are areas where a young person is unlikely to reach out to the family doctor for help.

Even teen-agers who don't have these dramatic health problems experience stress about their developing sexuality, changing sense of personal identity, and growing need to be respected as individuals. Adolescence is a time when a person can learn how to achieve independence, control moods of depression, and gain self-respect. If a health care system meets these needs, teen-agers are more likely to develop good health practices that they will carry with them into adulthood. If the health system "turns them off" through its lack of respect for them as people and insensitivity to their emotions and needs, then they are likely to turn off good health care. They'll avoid doctors, get only crisis care, and miss chances to learn about living in a healthier way.

Adolescent clinics aim at meeting these special needs of teenagers. A look at several will show how they do it.

Mount Sinai's Adolescent Center

A separate one-story building down the street from other parts of the hospital houses the Adolescent Health Center at Mount Sinai Hospital in New York City. In a small waiting room where rock music is playing, a young receptionist registers teens as they walk in, giving them membership cards for the center and making appointments. Kids come from all over the city because other teens have told them it's a good place for health care. Some may be referred by school counselors or other agencies. Nobody is turned away, and teens don't need a parent's consent to be treated. That can be especially important if the issue is drugs, VD, or pregnancy. Often teens will share their health concerns with their parents, of course. And if there is something the parents would need to know about — like a diabetic condition or cancer — then the staff will contact them after having talked about it with the teen.

Because it's easier for young people to talk about having physical problems than about having emotional ones, they often use medical issues as a ticket into the center even if they hope to talk about another area of their lives. So most visits start out with a physical exam. The teen can choose a man or woman doctor — already a step in making decisions about how to handle her own health care. The physician then talks with her about her life, gently pulling out information about home, school, sex, and work. The keys are respect, understanding, and warmth — no value judgments which could imply condemnation are made. "It's an ideal situation," says Leslie Jaffee, a doctor on the staff. "We can see a patient for a longer time — a half hour or more — and really have a chance to develop rapport."

If there's a physical problem which needs treatment, the teen will meet regularly with the doctor who becomes her primary care physician. The doctor and staff respect the confidence of their patients, relating to them first, even if parents choose to come with them to the center. Nothing is so devastating to a teen's ability to grow in self-respect as a parent who insists on "talking for his child" and a doctor who listens primarily to the parent.

The staff emphasizes nutrition and general health education. If the doctor finds a teenage junk food addict, the teen will get an appointment with the center nutritionist and perhaps a social worker will help work out an alternate food pattern as well as changes in lifestyle that will reinforce the new choices. "Our goal is helping teens know what first-rate health care is," says Sue Cohen, social worker at the center.

About 50 percent of the teens do take a referral for some form of counseling service. A pregnant teen-ager with no way to pay for her prenatal care needs help from the social worker as well as the doctor. A teen who comes in asking for some medication for depression will get a referral to the staff psychiatrist rather than pills. Because the psychiatrist and primary doctor are in the same small building, they spend 45 minutes a week together and can share information that will help each of them help the patient they're working with. That way the teen's care is unified, not fragmented as it might be if he were running between two doctors, neither of which knew what the other was really doing.

The center has access to specialists: ophthalmologists, neurologists, surgeons, gynecologists. If there's an emergency and hospital admission is needed, the center uses a 15-bed adolescent unit in Mount Sinai Hospital and the primary care physician stays in touch with the patient to give continuity of contact.

The staff's concern about the teens they work with runs through the whole center. Dr. Jaffee goes jogging with kids to help them catch the exercise habit. In the center court garden, Sue Cohen and others share work with volunteer teens, digging, planting, and finally eating some of the good food they've grown. That sharing helps break down some of the mystical ideas about medicine, says Sue. The kids can see that being healthy is part of being human, something the staff has to work at, too.

That sharing turns into outreach when it's needed. If a teen is under a lot of pressure at home, a social worker may visit the home to see what can be done to help. One teen was left to babysit with her younger brothers and sisters in an apartment where the lights had been turned off because of an unpaid utility bill. Sue Cohen worked on getting the utilities functioning again, along with helping the teen return to the health center.

Counselors find that many major problems are related to school failures. A 16-year-old who can't read is ashamed and acts rebellious to create an image of independence, ultimately weakening his chances for success. For teens like him, the center began a nongraded alternative school which can give regular high school credits within the New York City school system.

Who pays for all this? Dr. Joan Morganthau, founder and director of the center, is good at getting grants to help with some innovative areas of the work. But adolescent patients also pay, on a sliding scale determined by family income. If they have access to insurance or Medicaid, the center helps with reimbursement. If they don't and if there is no support from parents, the teens can work off the bills themselves. A teen can come in and pay $5 a week on his bill until it's paid — another important symbol of self-help in health care.

The Door

Downtown from Mount Sinai on 18th Street, in a large building that used to be one of New York's fanciest department stores, is an adolescent health center in which "total person care" breaks through to a whole new meaning. The Door — Center of Alternatives describes itself on its poster as a "Place to Get It Together, A Place to Get Help, A Place to be Together." For many young people, it fulfills all of these goals.

A deceptive warehouse-looking entrance from Sixth Avenue opens into a bright yellow orange gymlike space subdivided with low walls and groupings of sofas or chairs into counseling, educational, and activity spaces. Rhythmic music blurs the noise of conversation and activity. A counselor may be sitting in an open space talking intensely with a teen. The message is that emotions don't have to be hidden away, nor does the kind of help offered here. Seeing one teen dig into his problems and sort them through is an incentive for others.

Farther back are grouped eight private rooms for physical exams, with a waiting space outside where counselors talk informally with teens in groups about common problems in sexuality, skin disease, or food while they wait for a doctor. Right next door are offices for nutrition counseling and a lab with windows where teens can see what goes on with their blood or urine samples.

Back farther and to the left are a group of snack tables and then a dining room where a nightly dinner, with a vegetarian menu choice and lots of organically grown food, is served for 40¢. On the way is a gallery with paintings done by teens in a workshop. Another room off the side is for babysitting — free for teens while they're involved at The Door. And back one more jog in the labyrinth of space is a grouping of larger rooms: a martial arts space, dance studio, pottery shop, and jewelry-making center. The smells of sweat, silver solder, and earth mingle with the sounds of dance and pottery wheels. From crisis intervention to lessons in growth through art — The Door is an entrance to learning about achieving total health.

Two hundred to 400 young people a night come to The Door, between 80 and 100 of them for strictly medical help. They get membership cards, which are needed for entrance, and are channeled first to a house meeting led by other young people who explain the services and activities and answer questions. Next come individual talks with counselors about their specific reasons for being there as well as about what's happening with family, friends, drugs, school, home, food, exercise, work. Counselors, often young graduate students who themselves were once teens coming to The Door, help new people make some choices about which services they'll want to use. If a young man comes in to see the doctor about potential VD, he'll be asked if he wants to get into a rap group also, or get some legal advice if he's had a run-in with the law.

Concern about drugs, VD, or pregnancy is what most often brings teens in for medical help. Some are afraid of seeing their parents' doctor. Others come from places where nobody has access to medical help. A few are relatively calm, but most come with degrees of confusion and ignorance which need sensitive counseling along with medical exams. During an examination, a doctor can pick up on missed immunizations, poor nutrition, hypertension, bad diet, or other more serious problems. The team will act as a primary care unit, with one member always available for contact.

Donna, a 13-year-old, was one of the frightened and confused teens who came to The Door. Her relationship with her boyfriend left her afraid of pregnancy, although she hadn't had intercourse. Mostly she was filled with guilt about her sexual feelings and was struggling with a negative image of her own body. "Her poor hygiene was a reflection of her body image," said the nurse who coordinates the medical unit, "and she had a bad image of her body partly because she thought she was a bad person." A nurse and woman doctor helped Donna deal with acne and a vaginal rash. Using models of the reproductive system, they helped her understand the functioning of her own body. Four months later, Donna was on the way to more self-confidence. Now she volunteers to watch the children of other members when she comes to the center. And on her own she's become an outreach worker, telling other teens about what's happening at The Door.

Donna's quiet success story is a source of pride for the staff at The Door. Michael O'Shea, director of operations, talks about how learning the discipline of dance helps teens move toward better treatment of their bodies and more integrity in their whole approach to life. Street kids who come in to learn martial arts so they can come out on top in their alley fights emerge from the classes with enough confidence to feel they don't have to fight anymore, says O'Shea. That may be one of their best tickets to health.

Anybody who comes to the center for one of the physical arts classes is encouraged to have a checkup as part of admission to the group. That's another way in which the total health concept gets reinforced — helping out your body through karate should also get you involved in health on a larger scale. Problems with school might be connected to anemia, poor eyesight, or malnutrition. At The Door, a teen can get remedial tutoring, a medical checkup, and sessions on better ways to eat. A total picture of the teen is gathered in his "medical record," creating a new image for that often abstract and partial chart of body health.

Doctors at The Door have admission privileges and a good working relationship with the specialists at a nearby hospital. When an emergency like a drug overdose comes through their doors, they can cut through all the red tape and get the teen to emergency care fast.

The Door was originally established as an experimental approach to total health care for teens, and it's been able to attract significant grant money and volunteer help from many professionals. As a result, it offers all its services free to teens who come. In this unique case, money isn't an obstacle to getting good health care.

It's hard to think of any reasons for not using services like The Door or Mount Sinai's Adolescent Center. Both offer competent, professional medical care. And the activities which supplement that care allow teens to develop a vision of really healthy living.

Adolescent Centers Nationwide

Adolescent health centers across the country come with many faces and structures. In Minneapolis, for example, a network system is used to link a drop-in clinic with counseling and educational services. The Door in New York City is unique right now, although a group on Long Island is thinking of starting a similar center. Places like Mount Sinai are more widespread, often as adjuncts to children's hospitals. The adolescent unit at Boston Children's Hospital was the first when it was started in 1952.

Government funding, which totals $14.4 million, may help spur adolescent centers within the network of community health centers across the country. And some health maintenance organizations are considering setting up such units. A quick way to find out if one is located near you is to call the nearest children's hospital, since adolescent units are often part of that system. You can also get a list of adolescent health centers from the Society for Adolescent Medicine. (See the resource list at the end of the chapter for an address.)

If you're looking at an adolescent clinic and want to know if it's for you or someone in your family, there are basic questions you should ask — questions which will help you compare that center with the ideals of Mount Sinai or The Door. Find out if the center is accessible so teens can get there by themselves. Ask about fees and whether a teen can pay the bill. Ask about confidentiality — when parents are informed about treatments. Find out what sort of educational work goes on along with the physical exams and counseling, whether nutritional and preventive health education is also provided, for instance. Visit the center and notice attitudes and feelings. Is it people-centered? Do teens seem involved in their conversations with the staff? What happens during waiting times and how long are they? What emergency services are provided and what link is there to specialists and hospitals? Getting answers to these questions should help you decide — and a first visit will let you tell for sure.

Holistic Health Centers

Imagine a health checkup during which you don't list simply physical complaints, but rather share your feelings about food, consider what parts of your body you like and dislike, discuss whether you've been under stress in the past weeks, and whether you feel you're meeting your goals in life. Imagine yourself getting a thorough body massage by a therapist trained to pinpoint places of muscular tension. Picture a conversation with a nutritionist which includes a thorough look at what you eat and when. And finally envision yourself sitting down with the staff to examine your total health picture and put together a "wellness plan" for what you can do day by day to make your life healthier.

The Holistic Approach

What you've imagined gives you a quick look at a holistic approach to health care. Holistic medicine emphasizes your personal responsibility for your own good health. It also sees that your body, emotions, mind, and spirit are all interacting parts of the whole you that needs to be healthy. (The word "holistic" itself comes from the world "holism," which means an emphasis on the relationship between parts and wholes.)

The holistic emphasis on personal responsibility means accepting the fact that there are limits to what any health expert can do for you. Medical experts are often superb at diagnosis and treatment of acute illness — the heart attacks, advanced cancer, kidney failure, broken bones, or other illness that demand surgery or highly technical treatment. But many of our ailments are chronic — the ongoing diseases like hypertension which result from the chemical, physical, and emotional stresses on our lives.[7] Making good choices about how to deal with these demands medical advice, but the patient is the one who must work with them on a daily basis. Helping such patients see what they can do to become healthier is a major goal of holistic health centers.

While hypertension or emphysema usually sends us to a doctor for help, we often suffer from other "minor" ills that we simply learn to live with: gas pains, lower backache, diarrhea, or sleeplessness. "We adjust to our aches and pains and settle for mediocre health," says Jill Raiguel of New York's East-West Holistic Health Center. Few of us have a well-thought-out plan for increased wellness, let alone a plan for "superhealth," which is an optimal state of ease, comfort, and high energy.[8]

Holistic health centers aim at helping their clients set up a wellness plan. They do it by using a team approach to analyzing a problem and suggesting approaches to its solution. By combining a doctor's skill with that of a physical or massage therapist, a nutrition-ist, counselor, or nurse, they can take a look at the whole you.

Washington's YES Wellness Center

At the YES Wellness Center in Washington, D.C., for example, the team consists of a doctor with 20 years of around-the-world expe-rience as a family practitioner, a nutritionist who is also experienced in psychology, and a massage therapist with 17 years of work in "seeing patients with her hands."

If you come to the center for a "wellness checkup," you begin work with a short questionnaire that will explore areas where atten-tion might be needed. Along with asking about the physical symp-toms that brought you to the center, the form also asks about stresses. These can be "positive" events like marriage or a promotion as well as "negative" ones like getting fired or having trouble with friends. Changes by themselves stress our lives.

The form also asks you to make a 24-hour food-intake inventory as a quick check on eating habits. It asks about your favorite foods and any you associate with a particular place or person (like choco-late chip cookies with your mother or crab cakes with the time your romance broke up). Getting you to identify some of these associations helps you begin to understand how you use food, react to stress, and create a lifestyle for yourself.

After the staff has looked at your form, you'll meet with all three for a conversation about what brought you to the center. For one client that led to a blood check by the doctor that showed anemia, a talk with the nutritionist that traced those eating habits which led to lack of iron, and a session with the massage therapist that showed an empty small intestine — another sign of malnutrition. A conversation with the doctor uncovered the reasons why this client generally thought of herself as healthy despite her symptoms — she was pres-sured at work and afraid to get sick. All those facts fit together to produce a health plan focused on better eating habits and help with handling stress.

"It's really valuable to have different points of view on the whole situation," says Dr. George Keeler, the MD on the Wellness Center staff. It helps get a good diagnosis and helps convince the patient that the diagnosis is valid. That's important if the result is going to mean a change of lifestyle for the client.

The psychological factors in disease get attention. "What I've gotten out of 20 years of medical experience is that there is a definite relation between stress and the illness you have," says Dr. Keeler. If you want to understand illness, you have to understand its function in the life of the person who is sick. One client in her twenties, for example, noted that she usually got sick when she was home with her family. Eventually, she was able to connect that with her need to get attention from them by doing something dramatic. Remembering that you probably got attention when you were sick as a child helps you see why that pattern can happen again.

After you've had individual interviews with the staff at YES, the four of you meet together to create a plan of action for your near future. That might include counseling to help with stress, exercises to loosen up a tight back, or some massage that will help your headaches. The goal is that you will learn to catch your own signs of stress and illness and do as much as you can about them. Exercises, for example, are a way of learning about your body and feelings as well as toning up muscles.

Your plan might include better ways to eat. "Americans are so used to eating processed food that they've lost the concept that fresh food is closer to being alive and has more energy," says Richard Power, nutritionist at YES. Power often recommends that clients eat more raw fruits and vegetables or meats from animals raised organically, without the hormones and drugs injected into usual supermarket meats. He can suggest diet changes that help pinpoint allergies or relieve symptoms such as fatigue.

The YES staff emphasizes that they are a primary care center. Dr. Keeler deals with viruses, cuts, and all the other ills that usually take us to a family doctor. But the staff also wants to help people who are well look for "more wellness." So along with stitches or a prescription, you'll find new, dynamic ways to better health.

Fees at the YES Wellness Center are roughly comparable to ordinary doctor's fees. The initial health assessment by the team takes about an hour and a half and costs $85. Follow-up care is figured on the basis of $50 an hour for the doctor, $30 for the nutritionist, and $25 for the massage therapist. Blood or other tests are extra. The center is new and in the process of working out arrangements for insurance coverage, so right now you're on your own for insurance reimbursements.

Holistic Centers Nationwide

Holistic centers exist in scattered spots across the country, with more in California than any other state. Each has a unique organization based on the particular vision that inspired it.

In the Midwest, four Wholistic Health Centers,* which are based in churches, offer family practice medical care. There each team is composed of a doctor, a nurse, and a pastoral counselor. People come to the centers with sore throats, ulcers, fear of failure, marital tension, backaches — "for the full range of personal health concerns in which we human beings seem to be good at getting ourselves trapped," writes Dr. Donald Tubesing, founder of the centers.[9] Patients are individuals, couples, and families from all income levels. They may get anything from lab tests, to support in a crisis, to a nudge for getting out of a dead-end life situation.

Integral Health Services in Putnam, Connecticut, is another clinic which offers family practice medicine in a whole health setting. There the team includes yoga and meditation instructors along with doctors, nutritionists, a chiropractor, and others. Clients who show signs of stress are likely to get instructions on relaxation or a tape on meditation as part of their health plans. "Yoga meditation is like an antistress tablet — it helps you keep your center and not get depressed or anxious," says Dr. Sandra McLanahan, medical director of the center.[10]

In addition to clinics which offer a direct alternative to the usual primary care routes, there are two other sorts of holistic centers: larger ones which offer a live-in experience and smaller ones which focus on educational and counseling efforts.

At St. Helena's Hospital and Health Center in Deer Park, California, for example, most programs involve a short stay at the 76-bed hotel with swimming pool and tennis courts. There the health assessment and planning may stretch over several days. A typical client may be in his thirties and experiencing stress and depression along with physical complaints. A check may show heavy smoking, high alcohol intake, minimum exercise, gastrointestinal tract distress, and a marriage problem. The center is a one-stop place for planning stress relief, marriage counseling, exercise, and ways to lower the craving for alcohol and cigarettes. The cost of a workup is between $300 and

*Some centers use the spelling "wholistic" to emphasize the "whole person" idea.

$750, making it a relatively expensive choice in the spectrum of centers we've considered here.

Smaller holistic centers offer education and counseling with group and individual sessions. At East-West Holistic Health Center in New York, for example, the program includes evenings with leaders in the human potential movement aimed at helping people understand the body-mind-spirit connection and ways to healing. Nutrition courses show how what you eat affects your mood, energy level, sex life, and health. Sessions on eyesight explain how to improve yours through exercise and relaxation techniques.

East-West is staffed by a counselor, massage therapist, and nutritionist who offer a wellness assessment aimed at checking for stress points. Lacking a doctor, they're building a referral list of physicians who cooperate with their "whole health" approach to care. But even without a doctor, there's plenty to be gained from such a center because they are dealing with crisis symptoms that most doctors don't get to. If you suffer from continual shoulder or back tension, the center can suggest exercises — and help you realize that maybe the problem erupts when you've taken on too much responsibility or are pushing yourself too hard. Strengthening the body and learning to catch signals of stress before they become physical problems pays off. East-West charges $35 for a health assessment, making it available to a broad group of people.

Is a Holistic Center for You?

Finding out whether there is a holistic health center in your area is a little tougher than locating an HMO or adolescent clinic. There is a national association for holistic health (see resource guide for address) which is putting together a list of centers. Your local medical society may be aware of doctors practicing with a holistic approach. And there is a 1978 resource guide, *Wholistic Dimensions in Healing* by Leslie Kaslof (see reading list), which gives a number of centers. If those sources fail, you might try talking with staffers at a natural food store in your area. People who eat organic foods are likely to know of medical professionals interested in nutrition, and that can lead to a contact.

If you do find a holistic center and are trying to decide whether to use it for part of your health care, there are a number of evaluative questions to ask. First, check on the staff, asking if there's a doctor.

That will let you know whether to expect primary or supplementary care. If there is an MD, ask about credentials, hospital affiliations, and health philosophy. With any primary care doctor, you'll still need connections to other specialists and a hospital, so be sure the center has a good working relationship with other parts of your community's health care system.

Some holistic centers, like the ones described here, are innovative largely because they bring together pieces of health care for a total person approach. Others are moving into experimental approaches to health such as using acupuncture or iridology (the diagnosis of disease based on signs in the iris of the eye). You should talk with the center staff about their methods and health beliefs to be sure you're comfortable with them.

Because holistic centers use teams, try to sense whether the team is working smoothly together. If assorted professionals are each pulling for their own sort of diagnosis and treatment, then the entire point of being at a holistic center is undermined. Also, even holistic health advocates admit some of their number are unabashed salesmen. If you're being talked into an expensive series of nutritional counseling sessions, for example, you'll want to make a serious evaluation of their worth to you and the credentials of the nutritionist. "Buyer, be aware" definitely applies here.

With these cautions in mind, making a connection with a holistic health center may be a great step toward moving your own health care from "sickness care" to "wellness help." A good center can help you understand your health needs, design actions to meet them, and embark on your unique journey to a healthier life.

Still More Places and Ideas

The centers we've looked at here are major points of the evolving health care scene in America, but they're not the only ones. Some phone calls and digging for information may help you turn up others to complete your own health care plan.

Some senior citizen centers are organizing health care programs along with their usual exercise, craft, and other continuing education activities. At Senior Citizen, Inc., in Nashville, Tennessee, for example, a full-time nurse leads exercise programs, gives vitamin B_{12} shots, and takes blood pressures regularly. A doctor comes in one morning each week to see patients, and a yearly clinic day gathers physicians and technicians from around the city to give a complete physical to anyone who wants one. The center is supported by the local United Way, so services are free to the elderly who participate. Care at such a center is regular, convenient, and tied in with easy access to the staff nurse.

Planned Parenthood centers, with a network of clinics in most cities across the country, are stepping into a new primary care role for men and women interested in contraceptives. Most centers do basic gynecological care and offer good information on birth control choices. The use of volunteers allows these centers to give more time to each client than a gynecologist would. That means people can really work through questions about birth control and sexuality. And most centers have a sliding scale in fees, ranging from about $15 to $45 for exam, tests, and chosen method of contraception. Some clinics have special teen sessions with rap groups where problems such as how to tell your parents about your sexual activity are discussed.

Another part of the medical clinic scene is the network of Neighborhood Health Centers. Although fairly traditional in the care they give, they were originally innovative in design. Begun in the 1960s, they attempted to provide family-oriented, walk-in health care service to low income neighborhoods. These centers were to be accessible, staffed by people from the neighborhood when possible, and inexpensive. Although original plans projected 1,500 centers, as of 1979 there are only about 150, and federal funds for those are being squeezed tightly. If you're having a tough time making ends meet and live in an urban area, you might consider using one of these centers. The quality of care you'll get varies greatly, depending on available funding and the quality of local management.

A call to a local senior citizens' group or a government office on aging or human resources should put you in touch with any senior citizen health centers near you. Contact with the public health service of your local government will give you a list of neighborhood health centers. And the phone directory will list Planned Parenthood clinics.

Creative people in the basic health services are projecting still other ways to better meet our basic health needs for the future. Dr. Robert Rushmer, author of a study on alternative futures for medicine, suggests the idea of neighborhood health information centers to bring people quickly into contact with the health help they need. Such a center would make emergency contacts with doctors or ambulances and hospitals. It could share information about available health services with new residents, and could even organize volunteers to provide transportation for people caught in emergency situations. That's a lot better than the yellow-pages approach to community care that many of us must use.

With imagination, solutions to our health care dilemmas do appear. The alternatives in this chapter hopefully have provoked your own imagination into creating a better basic health plan for yourself — one that is affordable, health promoting, and whole-person care.

2072255

Notes

1. U.S., Department of Health, Education, and Welfare, Office of Health Maintenance Organizations, "Questions and Answers on HMOs" (Rockville, Md., 1978), p. 8.

2. "HMOs: Are They the Answer to Your Medical Needs?" *Consumer Reports* 39(October 1974):758.

3. Ibid.

4. Sheryl Ruzek, *The Women's Health Movement* (New York, 1978), p. 53.

5. Ibid., p. 56.

6. Hilary Millar, *Approaches to Adolescent Health Care in the 1970s* (Washington, D.C., U.S., Department of Health, Education, and Welfare, 1975), p. 17.

7. C. Norman Shealy, "Holistic Health: The New Medicine" (Unpublished paper from the East-West Holistic Health Center, New York, 1978), p. 1.

8. Jill Raiguel, "Roadmap to Superhealth" (Unpublished paper from the East-West Holistic Health Center, New York, 1978), p. 1.

9. Donald A. Tubesing, *Wholistic Health* (New York: Human Sciences Press, 1979), p. 97.

10. As quoted in Dominick Bosco, "The Clinic Where Love and Medicine Go Hand in Hand," *Prevention* 29(December 1977):141.

For Further Reading

Ardell, Donald. *High Level Wellness.* Emmaus, Pa.: Rodale Press, 1977.

Boston Women's Health Book Collective. *Our Bodies, Ourselves.* New York: Simon and Schuster, 1973.

Freese, Arthur. *Managing Your Doctor.* New York: Stein and Day, 1974.

*Grimstad, Kirsten, ed. *The New Woman's Survival Sourcebook.* New York: Alfred A. Knopf, 1975.

Harris, Marlys. "Medical Care on a Monthly Fee," *Money* 7(July 1978):65-69.

"HMOs: Are They the Answer to Your Medical Needs?" *Consumer Reports* 39(October 1974):756-62.

*Kaslof, Leslie J. *Wholistic Dimensions in Healing.* New York: Doubleday, 1978.

Millar, Hilary. *Approaches to Adolescent Health Care in the 1970s.* Washington, D.C.: U.S., Department of Health, Education, and Welfare, 1975. (May be ordered from the U.S. Government Printing Office, Washington, D.C. 20602 for $1.50. Order number 107-031-00012-1.)

Pembrook, Linda. "Adolescent Clinics: A Vital Step in Solving Problems of Teenagers," *Parents' Magazine* 47(July 1978):70.

Shealy, C. Norman. *Ninety Days to Self-Health.* New York: Bantam Books, 1978.

Tubesing, Donald. *Wholistic Health.* New York: Human Sciences Press, 1979.

Ziegler, Vicki, and Elizabeth Campbell, eds. *Circle One: A Guide to Self Health and Sexuality.* (May be ordered from P.O. Box 7211, Colorado Springs, Colorado 80933 for $2.)

*Lists clinics across the country.

Resource Guide

Office of Health Maintenance Organizations
Department of Health, Education, and Welfare
12420 Parklawn Drive
Rockville, Maryland 20857
800-638-6686 (toll-free number)

This federal office has lists of HMOs, information from its survey of HMO costs and services across the country, and publications such as "Questions and Answers on HMOs." Call the toll-free number listed above for questions.

Your local medical society or government health department will usually be able to tell you more about HMOs in your area. If you work for a company employing more than 25 people and there is a federally qualified HMO in your area, your employer should have information on membership.

Society for Adolescent Medicine
Box 3462
Granada Hills, California 91344
(213) 368-5996

This national organization has a list of adolescent clinics. They appreciate a prestamped envelope if you send for the list.

A call to the nearest children's hospital would locate any clinics in your area.

Feminist Women's Health Center
1112 Crenshaw Boulevard
Los Angeles, California 90019
(213) 936-6293

Feminist Women's Health Centers are located throughout California and in Tallahassee, Detroit, and Atlanta.

Local medical societies and local chapters of the National Organization for Women and Planned Parenthood are also likely to know of women's health centers in your area.

Association for Holistic Health
P.O. Box 33202
San Diego, California 92103
(714) 275-2694

The association maintains a list of members and is compiling a directory of holistic health clinics.

Brian Bouton, M.D.
Center for Holistic Health
2120 Ivy Road
Charlottesville, Virginia 22901

Dr. Bouton has compiled a resource guide including holistic organizations, books, journals, and newsletters on holistic health.

Consumer Notes

HMOs

1. If you're considering membership in an HMO, visit the center where you're likely to get care during regular hours as well as during an open house if possible. Find out where you'd go for children's care, gynecological care, regular family physicals. Visit those areas and notice the size of waiting groups and rapport of staff with patients.
2. Ask about waiting times to get an appointment for physicals or specialist services and also about typical waiting times once in the HMO center for an appointment.
3. Find out about how you will be assigned to a doctor. Will you be able to choose a man or a woman? Can you ask for a change if you're not happy with the first assignment?
4. Find out if nurse practitioners or midwives do some of the services in your center. If you prefer to work with one of those, can you? If you prefer not to, can you make that choice?
5. Ask about the training and experience of the staff. If the HMO is new, its staff may be relatively young and you'll need to decide if you're comfortable with that. Will one doctor act as your personal physician? Will a specialist whom you see regularly (like a gynecologist) be "your doctor"? Or will you be assigned to the specialist on duty when you need one?
6. Check out emergency procedures. Does the HMO have its own emergency room or will you use a local hospital? Ask for names of doctors who can tell you about the quality of the hospital's service.
7. Ask about coverage when you're out of town. Find out about limits of coverage for mental health services. If dental work is covered, check to see if that includes dental surgery. Are prescriptions covered?

8. Finally, in comparing expenses with regular insurance coverage, ask for levels of membership. Low-level coverage, in which you may pay a small amount for visits or prescriptions, may be economical if you don't use a doctor often. If you've a family with children, full coverage may be better. Remember that with insurance, you need to pay many out-of-pocket expenses. So count them in as you compare the costs of an HMO with a traditional insurance plan.

Women's Centers

1. Call the women's center you're interested in and arrange to talk with someone there about their services. Find out about group discussions and lecture programs as well as regular services.
2. Ask about the history of the group and about any political activities. This may tell you about the working relationship the group has with the rest of the medical community. That relationship is important for referrals to specialists or other services outside the center. And you'll want to be comfortable with the general attitude in the center.
3. Ask about the training and experience of the doctor who works with the center and about the staff. Find out what services the doctor performs and which are done by other staff members. If there's more than one doctor, ask about whether you will relate to one as your personal physician or whether you'd simply see whomever was on duty. Find out how long the doctor has been associated with the center and if there is a high turnover rate among staff.
4. Discuss the usual process for physical exams. How much education goes on? Will you have time to ask questions and discuss your feelings? If you're interested in learning how to use a speculum or in seeing your own cervix, ask if that's possible at the center.
5. Find out who will be discussing birth control options with you and whether discussions are done in a group or individually.
6. Check on whether the center has admission privileges at a hospital should you need emergency care. With most centers, you'll need connection to a gynecologist for operations such as a hysterectomy or sterilization. So you should have some link between the center doctor and a gynecologist for more serious treatment.
7. Many of the women's centers do only pregnancy tests and abortions. Find out how much of your center's work is devoted to primary care. If it's only a minimal amount of primary care, that may mean that you will have to go elsewhere for basic care.
8. Finally, do check on the cost. Most women's centers offer care at a lower rate than a typical private doctor's office. But don't assume that. Ask about costs for tests also.

Adolescent Clinics

1. On a visit to the center, talk with the staff about available services and costs. Adolescent clinics vary widely in their funding, staffing patterns, and services so you'll need to know the details of the one you're looking at.
2. Ask what happens during a typical physical exam. Will the doctor talk about nutrition and related psychological issues along with doing a physical check? Does the doctor have special training or background in adolescent medicine?
3. Is there a nutritionist who will cover diet planning with the teenager? Is there follow-up help such as group discussions on feelings about food?
4. What is the attitude of the center toward adolescent sexual experience and pregnancy? Will birth control information be freely given? What is its policy regarding abortion? Will there be individual or group discussions on sexual problems?
5. Is the teen seen as the primary person or as "a child of the parent"? Which information goes to parents and how? Does the teen need to consent for information to be given to parents?
6. How is payment handled? Is part of the costs underwritten by grants or donations? Can the teen pay directly? Or are all costs billed to the parents?
7. How are emergencies handled? Is there a 24-hour telephone service to center staff? Will the doctor admit the teen to a hospital and continue to follow his care? If not, will he refer to another doctor?
8. Finally, notice the atmosphere of the center. What is being done to reach out to teens? Music? Posters? Rap groups while waiting for appointments? Do members of the staff talk with teens in a way that respects the individuality of the person?

Holistic Centers

1. Visit the center to talk about services, staff, and costs. Ask for the names of people who have used the center before and check with them for an evaluation.
2. Ask about the medical philosophy of the doctor and staff. What is their theory about the relationship of stress, nutrition, and disease? What does the center do to help you locate stress points and deal with them? Do they teach you techniques you'll be able to use yourself?
3. If there is a nutritionist at the center, what is his or her background? If there is a tendency toward vegetarianism or the use of vitamin and mineral supplements, be sure you understand the reasons why you're asked to change your diet in these directions.

4. Find out what hospital the doctor is affiliated with and what the procedure will be for emergency problems or referral to specialists. Check the reputation of the hospital and notice whether it is convenient to use.

5. Ask about any unusual methods used at the center for diagnosis or treatment. You should know ahead of time if the staff is committed to acupuncture, for example.

6. Find out about supplementary programs like discussions or lectures on holistic topics that may help you learn more about health at less cost than individual consultations.

7. Talk frankly about costs for health assessments and what those cover. At some centers, the assessment cost doesn't cover items such as blood or urine tests. Ask about whether insurance plans cover costs at the center.

chapter two

New People to See

Loralee Wenger

At one time, if we were asked to conjure up our vision of the perfect health professional, we probably would have described the kindly family doctor who came at all hours of the day or night to nurse our ills and offer comfort and sympathy. Several decades later, asked the same question, we might depict a white-coated specialist with ten years of medical education behind him and a slew of technological equipment at his disposal to combat and cure even the most dreaded diseases.

Both kinds of professionals have their advantages — and limitations. The kindly doctor of yesteryear always may have been ready to hold your hand and offer words of sympathy, but medical knowledge wasn't his strong suit. The medical expert may be well versed in sophisticated techniques, but he can be cold, brusque, and unwilling to recognize that healing can take place without CT scanners* and laser surgery.

---

*Formerly called the CAT scanner, this sophisticated machine works by sending an X-ray beam through a cross-sectional layer of the body or brain, allowing physicians to "see inside" the body or brain to detect tumors and other abnormalities.

Today, however, we are finding a new kind of health professional on the scene: a person who combines sympathetic, humanizing care with all the current knowledge medicine can offer.

Midlevel health practitioners (MHPs), for instance, with one or two years of medical training, are capable of doing many of the basic jobs a physician does. That means you can go to someone who is trained and has the time to offer you advice on taking care of that awful cold or dealing with a cranky baby. By relieving the physician of some duties which do not require sophisticated training, midlevel practitioners are performing a valuable service for the consumer while leaving the specialist to do what he or she does best — treat our most severe medical problems.

We are seeing, too, the return of the family doctor. Family practitioners, the GPs of old, are another source of basic health care. This is good news for people who are tired of seeing one doctor when they've sprained their wrist and another one when they have an earache. It's good news, too, for health care consumers who have been forced to receive primary care in hospital emergency rooms because no other option has been available.

Many other health professionals are either enjoying a renaissance (midwives, for example), or are being trained specifically to meet certain health care needs in the community (like paramedics). Wellness doctors, hypnotherapists, acupuncturists, nutritionists, and chiropractors are all part of the new community of health care professionals.

In this chapter, you'll find out not only who these people are, but also how they can help you, the advantages and disadvantages of using their services, and questions to ask them to guarantee that you receive top quality care.

Midlevel Health Practitioners

Jan May glances up at the clock from the desk where she is filling out an emergency room sheet. It is nearly midnight, and she has already admitted five patients to the Coulee Community Hospital in Grand Coulee, Washington.

A two-car accident along a road winding between the Columbia River and the parched, sage-covered hills left three persons injured. One suffered bumps and bruises. The second had a few lacerations.

Both were treated and released. The third received a broken collar-bone, a bad bruise, and a laceration over his left eye.

Shortly after dinner, an old man in the nursing home adjoining the hospital was admitted for severe cramps and nausea. Around 8:00 P.M., a worried mother came in with her eight-year-old daughter. Tonsillitis and perhaps a strep infection, May diagnosed.

And then about 10:00 P.M., a man brought in two of his buddies who had beaten each other in a local bar. Friendly talk developed into a heated discussion; an argument ensued. The results were a knife wound in one man's shoulder. The other was beaten severely about the head and chest.

As each patient arrived, May took a patient health history and gave initial treatment for the emergency.

Finally, she picked up the telephone receiver, dialed a number, and waited for the physician with whom she works to answer. For although up until that point Jan May had done nearly everything a physician would do, she is not a medical doctor. She is a physician's assistant, a new kind of health professional who works with a doctor, assuming many of his or her routine tasks.

Answering a Need

Physician's assistants (PAs), nurse practitioners (NPs), and nurse clinicians (NCs) are the names given to the new professionals, which number about 20,000 nationally. Although PAs, NPs, and NCs often find themselves doing very similar tasks, there are some differences among them. Physicians (and their assistants) focus on the medical and diagnostic areas of patient care; thus, PAs tend to spend more time on surgery and emergency care. Nurses (and nurse practitioners and clinicians) do more well-patient care, psycho-social counseling, and health maintenance.

The concept is so new — training programs started only about 15 years ago — that educators and professionals are still trying to come up with a satisfactory name for the group as a whole. "New health professionals" is one term; however, most will agree the professional will not be "new" for long. The other term, which will be used here, is "midlevel health practitioner" (MHP).

MHPs came into existence for several reasons. To begin with, poor geographic distribution of health care providers has produced a shortage of services in rural and inner city areas. MHPs have helped fill the gap. We have also found ourselves with an overabundance of specialists, and a corresponding lack of doctors to whom we can go with a case of the flu or a child's sprained ankle. (By 1963, only about one-fourth of all medical doctors in this country were general practitioners.) One of the MHP's most important functions is to provide this basic primary care. Finally, we have begun to see that disease prevention, health maintenance, and patient education are all areas in which the medical consumer needs guidance and help — in other words we have come to realize that health care is more than simply getting pills to cure the diseases we already have. MHPs have shown that prevention, maintenance, and education are areas they can handle with competence.

Between 1955 and 1960, Thelma Ingles, R.N., attempted to set up a program at Duke University in Durham, North Carolina, to train nurses to take over some of the routine tasks usually done by doctors. The program was denied accreditation by the National League for Nursing, which said that medical tasks performed by nurses were inappropriate and possibly dangerous.[1]

The need for assistance in the delivery of medical care finally gave birth to two training programs in 1965. The first nurse practitioner program was instituted by Dr. Henry K. Silver and Loretta Ford, a nurse, at the University of Colorado. The program trained nurses as pediatric assistants. The same year, on the East Coast, Dr. Eugene A. Stead, Jr., launched a two-year program at Duke to train physician's assistants to help overworked general practitioners.

Then in 1969, Dr. Richard A. Smith started a one-year Medex* program at the University of Washington. It was designed to train returning service medics for placement in rural, underserved areas of the Pacific Northwest.

There has also been federal involvement in the training of MHPs. All three branches of the armed services have developed PA programs, and several congressional acts have authorized funds for educating PAs and NPs. At present, there are about 198 nurse practitioner programs graduating 1,800 students a year. There are about 55 physician's assistants programs accredited by the American Medical Association. Nationally, there are approximately 12,000 NPs and 7,000 PAs compared with 350,000 physicians and 800,000 nurses. But

*Medex comes from a French phrase meaning "extension of a physician."

their numbers are growing, and it is likely that in the next several years, you may have the opportunity to utilize their services.

Accessibility, Understanding, and Education

If you go to your doctor for a physical examination, with a minor injury or illness (like a bruise, sprain, cold, or tonsillitis), or to have some simple lab work done, you may find yourself in the hands of an MHP. Along with these responsibilities, MHPs are also qualified to obtain patient histories, make simple diagnoses, prescribe certain drugs, respond to common emergency situations, and make hospital rounds.

This is not the first job many MHPs have had. In many cases, they have worked as nurses, medical technicians, paramedics, or in a variety of other areas. Somewhere along the way, something made them stop, change directions, and head for MHP training. Often that something was a chance to have greater influence on patient care, to gain additional knowledge, or to find more challenging work. As Kathy Fernau, one of eight MHPs at the walk-in clinic at Harborview Medical Center in Seattle, explained, "I was an RN with a B.A. and an M.A. I had three years of primary care and two years of teaching experience before I went back to school. It was seeing the limits of what nurses could do that got me interested in changing directions."

Some MHPs specialize in certain fields like pediatrics, geriatrics, or psychiatry, working with specialists in those fields. Some practice in outpatient clinics while others are in private practice with doctors. Although most MHPs must work under the supervision of a physician, some states allow NPs and NCs to work independently. (Some state laws also limit a physician to employing one MHP; other states make no such restriction.)

Barbara Boulton Clark, who works with three physicians in an obstetrics and gynecology clinic, has a wide variety of responsibilities. She performs Pap smears and pelvic examinations; counsels patients on birth control, sexual relations, and marital problems; fits IUDs and diaphragms; and treats patients with hormone and/or bleeding problems. She also teaches prenatal classes and speaks on birth control to women's organizations and student groups.

Another PA assists a heart specialist with cardiovascular surgery. For instance, she does all the preliminary surgery for a bypass operation, the surgeon steps in to perform the actual bypass, and the PA finishes the operation.

Most MHPs, however, provide care that is somewhat less sophisticated. Kathy Fernau, for instance, describes how she is the patient's first contact with the health care system: "I go in and get a history, physical, X-rays, and lab work when it's appropriate. I get all the data and if I need medical advice, I present the physician with the patient, either over the phone or in person."

Statistics show that MHPs are capable of providing 70 to 80 percent of the total primary care that's needed, freeing the physician for the other 20 percent that he or she is uniquely trained to do. "And that's not to say that PAs can replace physicians," says Stephen Turnipseed, one of 20 MHPs working in the several clinics of Seattle's Group Health Cooperative, a health maintenance organization. "But it does say that when a patient calls with a problem that he can have access to health care that's as good if not better than the care he would receive if he waited to see a doctor."

Barbara Clark believes that accessibility is her drawing card. "When a patient is here for something routine, a Pap smear, for instance, when a young mother has arranged for a babysitter, taken a day off from work, and made all the necessary arrangements, and she has to sit here for hours and then finds out the physician can't come in — well, I would be furious. That's probably where I help the most — I'm there to fill in when the doctors are called out."

But access to health care is not the only reason MHPs are valuable. The amount of time and attention midlevel practitioners are able to give patients is probably their most significant advantage.

"There has to be interaction between the patient and the provider," says Stephen Turnipseed. "People want to see someone whom they feel they can trust, someone they can confide in, someone they can interact with." Midlevel health practitioners are the people who can spare the time to develop those relationships. As Kathy Fernau explains, "Physicians can be just as compassionate and empathetic, they just don't have the time." It is the MHP who can sit with you and talk about why you're feeling low or what to do about anxiety pains.

MHPs also spend a great deal of their time in counseling and patient education — two areas that are stressed in their training programs. This means MHPs are particularly good in handling

Jan May

Jan May, who was a respiratory therapist, an RN, and a nurse anesthetist, did not go to Grand Coulee, a small rural community in the state of Washington, with the idea of working as a physician's assistant. The hospital there was trying to build a surgical team and she went to become part of it. But after two years, there still weren't enough cases to keep her busy, and in her spare time she did everything from health screening to remodeling the surgical unit.

"Finally," she says, "I realized I wasn't contributing medically and so I decided to go to school to become a PA — to work part-time as a PA and part-time as an anesthetist."

May left for six months of study at the University of Washington and returned to Grand Coulee for her six-month rotation with a physician with whom she had made arrangements prior to enrolling in the program.

Now she works in both the clinic and hospital at Grand Coulee. "I work four days a week in the clinic and I see any kind of patient who comes in," she says. "I take walk-in patients and more acute medical cases as opposed to patients with chronic illnesses. I take emergency call two nights a week and every fourth weekend."

When May handles emergencies she sees all kinds of cases — heart attacks, respiratory problems, lacerations, strains and sprains, eye injuries. She admits patients to the hospital and makes rounds with the nurses.

"The physicians have to read all my charts. They have to sign all orders in the hospital and they have to sign my ER sheets. They have worked with me long enough to know what kind of patients I can see. They rely on my physical findings. I call them any time that I have something major — tendon damage, deep lacerations, a vessel or permanent nerve damage — and I'll have them sew it up. Otherwise, I'll handle the lacerations," she explains.

"Any patient who is sick enough to be admitted to the hospital is seen by a physician soon after admission. I always phone communication on every patient who goes into the hospital, and we talk about the case."

chronic illnesses like diabetes or high blood pressure, since people must be educated to learn how to live with these diseases.

When Phillip Furth first became an MHP he was astounded at

She averages eight patients a night in the emergency room. "You're up and down, up and down all night," she sighs. And the long hours have taken their toll — she's had pneumonia twice. May thoroughly enjoys her relationship with her supervising physicians. "They give me a lot of freedom and teach me anything I want to learn," she says. "And after I demonstrate that I'm competent in doing something, they let me go ahead and do it. But if I have someone who's sick and not responding to therapy, I can say, 'Hey, pal, this is all yours.' I don't mean any time I can't think of an answer I automatically turn it over to them, but it's a very secure feeling to know I can get help if I want it."

May makes house calls if the situation warrants it. "I see old people, the poor, and I'll give them free medicine — the samples we receive. If I know they can't afford it, I won't make them come in to the hospital or clinic where they'd have to pay for an office call. The doctors don't really like that, because they have to take over my ER duty when I'm gone. Sometimes when patients can't pay they'll bring me cookies or fresh strawberries. That's one of the nice advantages of rural medicine."

May's biggest complaint is that she doesn't have time for herself because she's on call so often. One of the reasons for this is her dual function as anesthetist and PA. As a PA, much of her schedule depends on the physician(s), the work setting, and the patient load.

Another reason for her erratic work schedule is the growing tendency to use emergency room services for minor ailments and acute discomforts. "It's really irritating to get up in the middle of the night and go to the emergency room for someone who's had a headache for an hour," she says. "Pretty soon you don't feel so dedicated anymore. You get so tired, tired of being called out — people don't realize what it's like to have your sleep interrupted constantly two or three nights out of every week."

Some of these reasons are why Grand Coulee is having a difficult time keeping physicians. In this case, it is the midlevel health practitioner, Jan May, who is the stable medical person in the community. And Jan May is determined to stay.

how little his patients knew about anatomy and physiology. He tried to increase their understanding of their bodies.

"It just appalls me how many people have come into our office after having a heart attack, and they don't even know what a heart attack is," he says. "When I ask them if their cardiologist explained to them what happened, or if they know what kind of medicine they're taking and how to take it, they tell me, 'Well, I have a rough idea.' It's frightening, but this is exactly where the MHP fits in."

A survey of four clinics comparing midlevel practitioners with physicians showed that the MHPs gave greater emphasis to perceptively observing and listening to the patient. (As one MHP said, "If you listen to a patient long enough, he'll tell you what's wrong with him.") The same survey showed that midlevel health practitioners prescribe more nondrug therapy and follow-up care than physicians.[2]

Patient satisfaction seems to reflect these advantages. "I think she's great," said one patient about her PA. "She's not only good in her profession, she's also a really special person to talk to. I was in the hospital with a broken hip for five weeks. Periodically, she would come in and see me. Lots of times when I was really down, she'd sit and talk to me. Not necessarily about myself, but just talk."

Another patient seconds the opinion that MHPs are easy to talk with. "She tells you what to do to help yourself. She tells you what kinds of medicines are good, what kinds of foods to eat. My son had the flu and I didn't know you weren't supposed to eat certain kinds of food, like milk. She told me how to get his fever down."

Should You Use an MHP?

There is often a natural reluctance to use an MHP. The primary issue seems to be the quality of care. Many people feel that midlevel practitioners just can't care for them as well as a full-fledged physician can.

Yet, according to the 1977 *Report of the Physician's Extender Work Group,* "Nurse practitioners and physician's assistants provide at least the same quality care as the physicians with whom they were compared on the same tasks."[3] And other studies show that nurse practitioners diagnose, manage, and produce patient outcomes similar to *or even better than* physicians.[4]

If you do have the opportunity to receive some of your health care from an MHP, give him or her a try. But before doing so, there are some things you should be aware of.

As with all health professionals, find out about the training of the person on whose skills you are relying. Training programs for MHPs range from three months to five years, although the average length is nine months to two years. Study programs take place at a clinic, hospital, or medical school, and include classroom lectures, laboratory sessions, and a 6- to 15-month rotation in which students work in a health care setting with a physician. Rotations are commonly in clinical medicine, surgery, obstetrics and gynecology, psychiatry, and pediatrics.

There are some slight differences in training among PAs, NCs, and NPs. Physician's assistants are trained through Medex programs, university- or medical center-based programs, and programs in nonmedical school settings. The Medex program is usually a one-year program; the others are most often two years. The graduates receive either a certificate or an associate or baccalaureate degree. Nurse practitioner programs are usually certificate programs and nurse clinician training results in a master's degree. National tests are given to certify PAs and NPs, and there are provisions so that the graduates of a PA program may take the NP certifying exam and vice versa.

It may be wise to talk with your physician before beginning care with an MHP to see how the two are working together. Ask what duties and responsibilities the physician has given the MHP. Decide which of those services you feel comfortable allowing the MHP to perform, and which you would prefer to have your doctor continue to do. Find out, too, what means of supervision the doctor has set up for his assistant, and how you can let the doctor know you are happy — or unhappy — with the care you are receiving.

One MHP felt that she and her colleagues were sometimes too available to the physician. "It's quite easy to be used," she said. "It doesn't take long for a physician who's not especially dedicated or who doesn't like office work to push patients on the PA. This is really obvious whenever there's the least excuse to leave — zoom — and there I am left with all the patients." If this is happening to you as a patient, put in a complaint with your doctor. It's important to remember that one of the main advantages of the MHP is that he can spend more time with you than the physician. If you're getting rushed out of his office, it defeats the purpose of having him there in the first place.

Cost is another central concern. Unfortunately, you will probably be charged the same amount for the services of an MHP as for the services of your doctor. As discussed below, this has an effect on the cost effectiveness of the profession as a whole — as well as on your pocketbook.

Insurance reimbursement policies are still in a state of flux. As late as 1977, Medicare did not reimburse patients for MHP services traditionally provided by a physician. Since Medicaid involves state and federal cooperation, reimbursement varies from state to state. Presently, 40 states recognize, by statute, one or more kinds of MHPs as providers of medical services. Medicaid, however, does not provide for reimbursement in all of these states.

The National Association of Blue Shield Plans supports reimbursement for MHP services provided they are under a physician's supervision; however, as late as 1977, some of the member plans were not subscribing to that policy.[5]

The issue of supervision is a central one. Reimbursement has been less frequent for MHP services in satellite clinics, hospitals, and for nursing home visits because the supervising physician is not on the premises. The passage of the Rural Health Clinics Services Act in December 1977, which recognizes MHP services for the purpose of reimbursement, will probably change this situation.

Insurance companies commenting on reimbursement say they fear that expanding eligible providers to include MHPs would escalate inflation of health care expenditures. Some say reimbursement for MHP services should be made at a lower rate than that for a physician. Other companies want to see the effect MHPs have on physician charges for services.

Some MHPs and physicians say they avoid the issue by having the supervising physician sign all forms as though he or she performed the services for the patient.

The MHP's Future

The future of MHPs depends largely on three things: their cost effectiveness, attitudes, and the demand for their services.

One of the most important criteria in judging the MHP concept is productivity. Jane Record has demonstrated that for each MHP used at the Kaiser Permanente Health Plan, there is a cost savings of $20,000. Another Medex study showed that in nine practices, Medex increased the number of patients seen by 40 percent, and a later New England study showed a patient load increase of 37 percent.[6]

Similarly, according to Dr. Robert Harmon, director of the University of Washington's Medex program, the MHPs' training contributes to their cost effectiveness. "First of all," he says, "to train an MHP costs only about one-fourth as much as it costs to train a doctor — about $12,000 to train a midlevel practitioner as compared to the $15,000 per year for four years for a doctor. Then, the doctor has a three- to five-year residency, but with an MHP, you have a practitioner after one year."

Unfortunately, these savings aren't always passed along directly to the consumer. One very simple reason for this is that it is the doctor who collects the fee (remember you pay the same amount for an MHP's services as you do for the doctor's) and pays the PA's salary (which is about one-half to one-third the physician's). The difference between the MHP's fees and her salary sometimes translates into the doctor's profit. Other times, the cost effectiveness of the MHP is reflected indirectly — in overall reduction of office fees or clinic charges, if the MHP is working in a clinic setting.

There is still some physician resistance to accepting MHPs. "Generally, I think it's the older physicians who feel most threatened," says Phillip Furth. "They're used to their practices, they're used to being the absolute authorities." Nurses, too, may feel their place in the health care hierarchy is being threatened by midlevel practitioners. And such obstacles as insurance liability problems and vaguely defined state practicing laws have discouraged some physicians from employing MHPs.

According to Dr. Harmon, "Physician reaction is very positive. Doctors realize that midlevel practitioners will give them the chance to do the kind of practice they want to do. They're relieved of the parts of the practice that are burdensome — everything from physical examinations to routine screening to minor complaints. They may like to deliver babies or do surgery, and now they can devote more time to those things. MHPs also can give them help with night calls. So their practice becomes more controllable and they have more free time."

As the advantages of MHPs become more well known, the demand for them should increase. Not only can MHPs be used in areas where medical people are in short supply, but they could also be used in prisons, state mental hospitals, and clinics in remote areas. Internationally, Dr. Richard Smith, founder of the University of Washington Medex program, has developed programs for MHPs in Thailand,

Pakistan, and Micronesia. But perhaps most importantly, you may find an MHP right down the street — in your own doctor's office.

The New Family Doctors

Remember old "Doc" on the television show "Gunsmoke"? There were few diseases or illnesses he couldn't cure with a few kind words. And when words didn't work, a shot of whiskey would. The weary face, worn leather bag with its ever-present stethoscope, and a compassionate hand on the patient's forehead spelled d-o-c-t-o-r. The man delivered generations of babies, removed countless bullets, and watched patients in the throes of pain as he sewed up gashes and cauterized deep wounds without the benefit of anesthesia.

What old "Doc" lacked in medical training and credentials, he made up for in his personal touch and accessibility, two of the most uncommon, although perhaps most important, qualities among doctors today.

Why is it so difficult to find a doctor who will take the time to understand you as a complete human being? There are a number of reasons, not the least of which is the fact that for the past 50 years, doctors have been trained *not* to perceive you as a whole person, but to focus on your individual organs and ailments. Doctors have been taught that the only way to really succeed in medicine is to specialize. As a result, we have ear, nose, and throat doctors, skin doctors, orthopedic surgeons, children's doctors . . . the list is endless. Trying to keep up with all these specialists can make anyone sick, especially at bill-paying time, when you look back on all the visits and realize that many of your health problems or questions could have been resolved easily by a general practitioner. So what happened to the familiar GP and who has been taking his place?

The Disappearance — and Return — of the Family Doctor

The GP was still a vital force through the first decades of the 1900s. In 1931, there were 112,000 physicians who listed themselves as general practitioners in the American Medical Association's (AMA) annual directory. But by 1960, the number shrank to 75,000, and by 1975, it shriveled to 53,565.

Dr. Merrill Werblun, former director of resident training programs at the University of Washington School of Family Medicine, explains why the family doctor was becoming such a rare breed: "The problem is that, after a report by Abraham Flexner published in 1910, medical education made a big turnaround and became very subspecialty oriented. Eventually, there was the general feeling that the only way you could be successful as a physician was to be in a small box and know everything you could possibly know about what belonged in the box."

Soon after the Flexner report was published, the Carnegie and Rockefeller foundations started supporting medical schools that focused on clinical research. Medical care became more technological, and it moved from the doctor's office to the hospital.

Specialist instructors replaced generalists in medical schools. Students were encouraged to specialize. Status and salary were their rewards. In 1970, the general practitioner averaged $33,859 and saw 139 patients weekly, while an internist earned $40,251 and saw 85 patients. The government contributed to this movement by pouring funds into research programs, paying indirectly for postgraduate training of many specialists.

With all this encouragement, most students elected to take a specialty. More often than not, the little problems patients brought to the doctor's office were seen as uninteresting and trivial. By 1963, less than 25 percent of all physicians in this country were general practitioners and most of these were found in small towns and the suburbs. The wealthy were more than content with specialists and the urban poor were left with emergency rooms for their health care. As is still the case, many rural and inner city communities were without doctors and adequate medical care.

Concern about the vanishing family doctor started in the mid-1940s when the AMA set up a special panel to study general practice. Dr. Wingate Johnson, chairman, called for the return of the generalist. "Those who would substitute the family doctor with specialists, even group practice, overlook the fact that 85 percent of the ailments for which people consult doctors can be cared for by a competent general practitioner," he said.[7]

Within ten years, the cry for the resurgence of the generalist was translated into a demand for a new kind of specialist — the family practitioner (FP) — who would focus on a continuous doctor-patient relationship. By 1960 medical students could choose one of four ways to become general practitioners or family practitioners, although the number and percentage of graduates entering these fields continued to decline.

In 1965, the push for family practice became stronger; several AMA studies on health needs in the United States called for a change in the direction of medical education. These reports basically said that while modern medical schools were turning out excellent specialists and highly trained scientific clinicians, what people needed were personal physicians.

So in 1969, the AMA officially added family practice as its twentieth medical specialty. At the same time the American Board of Family Practice was established to certify physicians in the field. In 1976, the number of doctors in family practice increased for the first time in many years. By 1977, the number of family practice residency programs increased from none to 325; the number of residents went from zero to 5,421; and more than 80 percent of the medical schools in this country developed departments or divisions of family practice where there had been none before.

Now that you may be able to receive care from a family practitioner more easily, you need to know when and how you can best use his services.

What Is a Good Family Practitioner?

As with all health care choices, you must exercise your responsibility to ask questions and make the demands that will insure the best health care for the money. Not every family practitioner (FP) is a great one. Familiarizing yourself with the responsibilities, schooling, advantages, and disadvantages of the profession can help you make an intelligent choice.

The main characteristic — and advantage — of the family practitioner is that he or she is qualified to handle a wide range of ailments. In fact, FPs maintain that they can treat 95 percent of all the problems that are brought to them. That means that your family doctor can set the broken leg your son got falling from his tree house, suggest an exercise program to help you lose weight, and give you tips on the care and feeding of your newborn baby.

The FP is the first doctor you see when you have a medical problem. She will either take care of that problem herself, or recommend another health professional for you to see. Even if you do need additional medical help, she should continue to have an interest in your case, acting as a leader in the health care team that is taking care of you.

But there is one more unique characteristic of the family practitioner. As the title implies, the FP is concerned not only with you as a person, but sees you as a member of your entire family. This is particularly important because an illness you have could affect other members of your family, or stresses within your family could produce physical illness. Because family practitioners have adopted this wider perspective, they can be much more effective in providing you with good health care.

Thus, besides repairing broken bones, delivering babies, or giving advice on tennis elbows, family practitioners also find themselves working with alcoholics, counseling patients whose emotional problems are leading to physical symptoms, or even trying to mend broken hearts. You may want to discuss marital or sexual problems with your family doctor, or if a catastrophic illness like heart disease or cancer should strike, the doctor can help you and your family learn to cope with it. And, of course, you will always be directed to more specialized care if you need it.

Family practitioner programs preach continuity of care so that physician and patient have an ongoing relationship. That allows family doctors to do more health maintenance, prevention of disease and illness, and patient education. As the AMA definition of FPs states, "The family practitioner is a personal physician, oriented to the whole patient. . . ."[8]

There is perhaps one crucial difference between the new family practitioner and the GP of old: FPs are rigorously educated and monitored. After graduating from medical school, family practitioners have to complete three-year residencies. During that time, they are required to have a minimum of 12 months of internal medicine, 6 months of pediatrics, 2 months of psychiatry, and 2 months of obstetrics and gynecology. Months not spent doing required rotations are often spent in electives such as orthopedics. Before they can be certified by the American Board of Family Practice, they must pass stringent exams. Then every six years they are reexamined to make sure they have kept their medical knowledge up to date. Finally, within that six-year period, they must have had at least 300 hours of medical education.

Cost is another advantage of using an FP. A patient seeing a specialist will probably pay higher office visit and/or consultation fees than a patient who sees a family practitioner. The broadly trained physician, who has a continuing relationship with you, will also have a better knowledge of your medical history and problems than a specialist. That may cut down on lab tests and X-rays.

Another important aspect in cost consideration involves hospitalization. "We don't like to put people in the hospital," says Dr. Werblun. "Most specialists function in hospitals, and if you look at the breakdown of health care costs, the vast majority are in the hospital, not the traditional office." The emphasis on preventive medicine — catching a problem before it gets serious — could also save money.

Of course, no profession is without its problems. Dr. Vicki Black, an FP in Washington, complains, "I'm not able to spend the time delving into family problems that I would like to. I really can't get very close to my patients." Black believes this is partly because her patients don't want that closeness, which brings up an important question you should ask yourself. Do you really want a doctor who is going to be concerned about more than your bodily functions? "I want a doctor who is a good technician," says one health care advocate. "I don't particularly care if he's got the warmth and understanding of Marcus Welby, as long as he solves my health problems."

Some specialists have also charged that FPs lack the know-how to handle serious problems. Dr. David Van Gelder, president of the American Academy of Pediatrics, is quoted as saying, "When a pediatrician is available, children are better off with a pediatrician."[9]

In part his statement reflects the fact that FPs have sometimes been poorly accepted by the medical community. This has resulted in some family practitioners having difficulty obtaining hospital privileges to care for their patients. (For the most part, the trouble has been in pediatrics and obstetrics.) Check with your doctor to see where he has admitting privileges and if there are any restrictions on those privileges.

Finally, you may find that the FP you choose is in a group practice with several other physicians. (As Dr. Werblun explains, "The day of the solo practitioner is pretty well gone.") That means you will want to check the credentials of the other doctors in the group practice since you may find yourself being treated by them.

They Even Make House Calls

One aspect of general practice that is experiencing a resurgence is the house call.

A house call might be appropriate for the home-confined elderly patient, the physically disabled person who can't travel easily, or the patient in a rural area who is seriously ill or injured.

Dr. Werblun emphasizes the benefits of some house calls. "We'll often make a home visit if there's a family problem, and we need to make a judgment based on the environment of the home." Alcoholism, family stress, and adolescent problems are some situations that might call for a home visit.

"You learn a great deal by going into the home," contends Dr. Werblun. "You have a depressed lady who comes into the office looking like a slob. But you visit her house and find it's immaculate. Now that's an important piece of data to the doctor. What's really going on? What's the message? Why does she look awful when everyone else in the household is neatly dressed and clean and she's a great housekeeper? It gives you more to go on."

Dr. Werblun also cites the case of an elderly woman who visited her doctor, complaining of depression and an inability to function in her daily life. Her physician decided this woman needed to be put in a nursing home. But the woman protested vigorously.

A social worker visited the woman in her home. She discovered the old lady had many family heirlooms and antiques and she was upset that she could no longer clean them and take care of her apartment. Now a home health care worker cleans the apartment once a week, and the lady is content.

"She's living there and she's happy. Well, how would we have known that?" Werblun asks. "She couldn't tell us what was wrong with her. It was the home visit that revealed the problem."

For all the good that a house call can do, Dr. Werblun still believes that in most cases, "requests for house calls are inappropriate. Diagnostic abilities in someone's house are difficult," he says, "and besides the child with a 104° fever who appears to have a cold will not die by being taken out in the fresh air to see the doctor."

Dr. Black also believes house calls are basically an inefficient mode of operation. "Certainly, it takes more time than seeing patients in the office." But, she concludes, "There's a lot you can learn by seeing someone in his or her own home."

Find out, too, how easy it will be to schedule appointments with your particular doctor, and if the practice has any other health professionals associated with it.

The Trend Will Continue

In answer to the swelling number of cries for more family physicians, Congress began to invest heavily in family practice training programs. But then internal medicine, obstetrics and gynecology, and pediatrics personnel argued that they were also providing primary care. Their voices were loud enough that they were included in the next round of funding.

Some medical schools still harbor ill feeling toward family practice and probably will never offer it. Others have given in grudgingly. Some medical schools have accepted family practice out of necessity — the necessity being an influx of federal funds for the training of family physicians.

Yet in spite of these negative feelings, it looks like family practice will continue to grow and thrive. The goal of the Ad Hoc Committee on Education for Family Practice, which was first established in 1964 and reconvened in 1977, is to have 25 percent of all graduates of medical school entering residency training in family practice by 1985.

A large dimension of the future of family practice and family practitioners depends on how well these physicians can deal with two major problems in health care delivery: escalating costs and health manpower shortages.

Dr. Werblun believes family practice can have a significant effect on both. "We think we can and are cutting costs," he says. "But you have to accept, first of all, that modern medicine is very expensive. We've got all the gimmickry in the world, all kinds of fancy machines. They're expensive and that's going to be a factor no matter who we use for doctors." Nonetheless, as discussed, family practitioners can help individual families save money, and it's not unreasonable to expect that they can do so on a broader scale.

Another potential way to reduce health care costs is through the use of teams of physicians and allied health personnel — MHPs, social workers, public health nurses, clinical pharmacists, nutritionists, and psychologists. With a family physician, who will be knowledgeable in the expertise of each of these practitioners, coordinating the effort, an interdisciplinary health care team should be able to make more efficient use of the professional's training and the consumer's dollar.

Family practitioners are also helping to correct the problem of maldistribution of health care professionals. As of January 1978, 53.2 percent of the 34,000 graduates of family practice residencies settled in rural areas or small towns of less than 25,000 people. Unfortunately, only 3.2 percent settled in inner city areas.

Lastly, the family practitioner may be increasing his or her areas of interest and not limiting it solely to the family. Job-related stress, environmental pollution, carcinogens, food additives, and unsanitary living conditions are not family-transmitted diseases, but instead call for the physician to enlarge his view and responsibilities to the needs of the community. Addressing the health problems patients face today requires the physician to expand his boundaries, allowing the patient's family to be one unit within a social and political community which contributes to or threatens the individual's health.

Other Health Professionals You Can Use

Would you prefer to have your baby delivered by a woman who is trained basically in normal pregnancy and childbirth rather than a male obstetrician whose focus is often on disease? See a midwife. Want a doctor who will tell you how to stay healthy as opposed to one who cures you after you get ill? Try one of the new wellness doctors. Haven't been able to stop smoking on your own? Go to a hypnotherapist who may be able to get you to kick the habit through hypnosis.

There are a number of professionals in the health care field who may be able to help you with the one problem that's been vexing you, or who may offer you a whole new approach to health care. Their areas of expertise and range of knowledge may differ, but together they deliver the same message: you're no longer confined to receiving your health care solely from an MD.

The Midwife Makes a Comeback

Years ago there was no question about it. When a woman was about to give birth, it was the local midwife who came to help. The midwife, often an older woman, was as dedicated to her clients as they were to her. Grandma Hupe, the midwife in a small midwestern town at the turn of the century, "faced the heat, cold, storms, and rain. No night was too dark or stormy for her to make the visits to the expectant mothers, or those who had been and still needed her services."[10]

Midwives may have been extremely important to the women they served, but they were a thorn in the side of the medical establishment. As early as 1830, 13 states outlawed midwives (as well as anyone else who practiced medicine without a license). For the next 100 years, doctors attempted to define pregnancy and childbirth as a disease which demanded the skills of a highly trained obstetrician, and to picture midwives as dirty, old, toothless hags who could do nothing but endanger the health of mothers and their babies. Their campaign proved to be so successful that by the 1930s most states had passed laws making midwifery illegal.

But today, midwifery is enjoying a comeback. As the growth of the natural childbirth movement demonstrates, people are beginning to realize that birth is a natural phenomenon and should be attended by someone who supports that belief. As one obstetrician who works with midwives explained it very simply, "Midwives are trained in handling normal pregnancy and delivery; the obstetrician is trained to handle complications." Each is valuable in his or her own way, and, as this obstetrician enthusiastically pointed out, "Together, the two are unbeatable."

Couples who select a midwife to help them with childbirth generally do so because midwives are committed to providing personalized, family-centered care. Many women also choose midwives because they want to return to the idea that women should help other women with birth. As one mother said, "I just thought having a midwife deliver my baby, having a woman deliver my baby, would make it a more human experience."

Unfortunately, even with this resurgence of midwifery, controversy still surrounds the profession. Specifically, there is a current argument over the relative merits of certified nurse-midwives versus empirical, or lay, midwives.

A certified nurse-midwife is a registered nurse (RN) who has had one year of experience in obstetrics, and who has then gone on to take a one- to two-year course in midwifery. (Twenty-four schools are approved by the American College of Nurse-Midwives to train women — and men — in the profession.) A nurse-midwife must also pass a national certification examination.

There are now about 2,000 nurse-midwives in the country, about half of whom are actually practicing. A little under half of those are employed by hospitals; others are with public health agencies, or in private practice with one or more physicians. (Nurse-midwives are not allowed to work strictly independently, but must be associated at least with a backup doctor or institution.) In addition to providing prenatal care, helping the couple with labor and delivery, and doing postnatal care, many midwives provide gynecological services to non-pregnant women as well as doing sexual counseling.

Empirical midwives have no formal training per se; rather they learn their craft from other lay midwives and by studying on their own. It's hard to estimate how many empirical midwives are practicing today — a 1975 source put the number at 2,500. One reason that estimates are hard to make is that many work "underground" because lay midwives continue to be charged with practicing medicine without a license. Only a handful of states now license lay midwives.

Certified nurse-midwives and lay midwives disagree on several issues. Generally, lay midwives feel that nurse-midwives have been co-opted by the medical establishment. They believe that the current requirement to license nurse-midwives is simply another way for the medical establishment to control alternative health care. They hold that midwives should not have to work in association with doctors, but should be independent practitioners. Nurse-midwives charge, however, that many lay midwives do not have the training, skill, or experience to deliver babies. They say that licensing is one way to help the consumer determine that she is getting quality care.

Whether you are thinking about hiring either a nurse-midwife or a lay midwife, there are several inquiries you should make. Find out about her education and training, how many births she has attended, and with whom she apprenticed, if she is a lay midwife. Determine exactly what services she is going to give you (for example, does she do prenatal care?), and which you are responsible for providing for yourself. If it matters to you, ask what her legal status is, and, if you have insurance, find out if your policy will reimburse midwifery services. Ask, too, what emergency backup facilities she is associated with, if she works with another midwife or other birth attendants, and, of course, what her fees are. You might find out if you can talk to some of her satisfied clients as well.

In addition to the above, the Informed Homebirth Organization also suggests that your birth attendant should have the following knowledge and resources:

- How to monitor labor;
- How to recognize variations from the norm and determine whether they can be managed by her in the home, or if she needs to refer you to an obstetrician or hospital;
- How to handle critical emergencies;
- Has hospital privileges or a doctor who will meet you at the hospital;
- How to help the head deliver without tearing the perineum or vagina;
- How to recognize degrees of tearing and how to deal with them;
- How to check the placenta, umbilical cord, and membranes;
- How to check the uterus after birth;
- How to check the newborn, and, in particular, knowledge of the Apgar scoring system;
- How to instruct you in the care of your newborn, breastfeeding, and your own postpartum experience;
- How to help you have the kind of birth you want.[11]

(See chapter five for more information on midwives.)

Wellness Doctors

Think about when you normally go to a doctor. If you're like most people, it's usually when you have a minor ache, pain, or illness, or when you suspect that something more serious is wrong. But wouldn't it be nice to have a doctor with whom you could consult on staying well? Wouldn't it be helpful if your doctor could educate you to take responsibility for keeping yourself healthy? Wouldn't you like to meet a doctor who could give you tips on good nutrition, ways to handle stress, and exercise techniques?

Well, some doctors are doing just those things. We've called them the "wellness doctors" because they subscribe to the theory of "high level wellness," a concept first developed by Dr. Halbert Dunn in 1961. Dunn put forth the idea that being healthy wasn't just a question of not being sick. He talked about a state beyond just being "OK," a state in which you feel energized, supremely healthy, hap-

One Nurse-Midwifery Service

Maternity Center Associates began in Bethesda, Maryland, in 1975. Certified nurse-midwives practice in cooperation with board-certified obstetricians to provide care to childbearing women, especially those who want to give birth in their own homes.

The two founding nurse-midwives, Janet Epstein and Marion McCartney, had worked as obstetrical nurses and assisted in home births. But, as they write, "The day inevitably came when we 'caught' a baby because the physician was unable to come to the home. It was an exhilarating experience for us. After a few such 'catches', we decided to attend a one-year midwifery course and become certified."

In consultation with the physicians, Epstein and McCartney reasoned that the best way to meet the increasing desire for home birth in their area was to establish a nurse-midwifery service to help "normal" women deliver at home. "This would free the doctors to practice their specialties, particularly with women who were high risks or who had complications of pregnancy," they write. "These physicians would also act as consultants to our service in case we had problems we wanted to discuss."[12]

Maternity Center currently handles about 20 births a month. Besides managing labor and delivery, the midwives do complete prenatal care and offer postpartum follow-up care, including a "parenting service," a series of four sessions on parent education and family development.

They also provide such gynecological services to nonpregnant women as pelvic and breast examinations, health screening such as Pap smears and venereal disease detection, pregnancy testing, and the treatment of common infections. Family planning information and devices are available as well.

The underlying philosophy of Maternity Center is based on the fact that the midwives see themselves and their organization only as resources. "When we help with a labor and delivery, we are guests in our clients' homes, and we adapt our assistance to what they want and what is safe," Epstein says. "We don't want people to be dependent on the medical person — we want them to rely on themselves — to become as self-sufficient as possible."

py, and creative. Wellness doctors try to help you reach that state.

One of the first people to put Dunn's idea into practice was Dr. John Travis, who founded the Wellness Resource Center in Mill

Valley, California. This center specifically does not see anyone who has a physical problem or symptoms requiring medical treatment. The center does not use drugs, doesn't do lab work, conducts no physical examinations, and sees no patients.

Instead, if you go to the center, you will be asked to do an extensive inventory on yourself — your lifestyle, feelings, thoughts, relationships, habits. Then Travis and his wellness staff help you choose one or more groups that deal either with stress control, self-responsibility, nutritional awareness, or physical fitness. You will attend these groups or meet with staff members individually over the following few months. (There is also an intensive ten-day wellness program for people who live away from Mill Valley.) The point of these sessions is to help you learn to work with yourself — to become what Dr. Travis calls, "an expert in yourself." The doctor and his staff help you learn how to take charge of your own life and feel good about yourself. In short, they assist you in moving toward high level wellness.[13]

Rather than establishing a separate center, many doctors are now trying to integrate the idea of high level wellness into their practices. Dr. Walt Stoll of Lexington, Kentucky, is one of these doctors.

Stoll is a family practitioner. As such, he sees people with a wide range of health problems. But along with treating their ailments, Stoll tries to introduce his patients to the concept of high level wellness.

Stoll believes that wellness is a state that anyone can reach. The three basic guidelines he recommends to begin your journey toward wellness are: aerobic exercises (exercises that are aimed at raising your heartbeat); skilled relaxation; and totally eliminating refined carbohydrates (such as white sugar) from your diet. But he also writes that, "Since any change in habits takes effort and perseverance, the change that takes the least effort, and produces the greatest results, should be made first. The skill of the wellness practitioner must be to choose that approach."[14]

Stoll does several other things to help his patients achieve wellness. Perhaps the most important is that he puts them in charge of their own health care — he calls it "returning the patient to his rightful place as the most important member of the health care team." Patient education, he maintains, "is the most powerful treatment or medication available in this doctor's office." In order to stimulate this education process, each prospective patient receives a

"Patient Brochure and Self-Help Manual," which outlines Stoll's wellness philosophy, the objectives of his practice, office policies, and how to handle common complaints. This is supplemented by a wealth of one- or two-page handouts available that tell people how they can treat themselves, how they can avoid problems, and when they should consult a doctor.

Stoll also has other health professionals working with him in his practice. They offer his patients courses in basic relaxation, biofeedback, hypnosis, yoga, and acupressure massage — all of which are designed to help people enrich their lives as they become healthier.

You may not be able to find a wellness doctor in your community yet, but it's important that you question your physician about his feelings concerning preventive care, patient self-responsibility, and the concepts embodied in the idea of high level wellness. Hopefully, you will find a doctor who is sympathetic to all of these goals. If not, take it upon yourself to start your own doctor-education program. Tell the physician how you feel about good nutrition, regular exercise, and ways to reduce stress. You might make him — and his other patients — healthier in the process.

Paramedics Save Lives

When Lee Meisner, a 69-year-old retired resident of Seattle, came home for dinner one warm, sunny evening near the end of June, he had no idea he would die just a short time later.

Meisner had just fixed cocktails for himself and his wife and was rummaging through the refrigerator to see what there was for dinner, when he fell to the floor. He began to breathe heavily and turn blue. His wife ran to the phone to call 911, the number for emergency help.

Suddenly, Meisner stopped breathing entirely. But within two minutes paramedics from Medic I, Seattle's mobile intensive coronary care and emergency rescue squad, were there. They got his pulse going again and transported him swiftly to the hospital. If they hadn't been available, Meisner would have died. "As far as I'm concerned," said Mrs. Meisner, "it was a miracle. Every minute seemed like an eternity, but they were here in such a short time. A miracle, it really was."

Meisner is one of more than 1,000 people in Seattle who literally have died and been brought back to life by Medic I. Founded by Dr. Leonard A. Cobb and Gordon Vickery, then chief of the Seattle fire department, the system was patterned after a program in Belfast, Northern Ireland, where physicians showed that mobile care units could cut the rate of heart attack fatalities. They applied for and received a federal grant in 1968 to develop a rapid response emergency system using fire department vehicles and personnel. In 1969 a group of 15 fire fighters, all volunteers, were given 1,018 hours of paramedic training.

The program started with a single vehicle and those 15 fire fighters. Today, the paramedics, trained almost as much as physicians, number more than 50 and the program has 12 vehicles. Heart attack victims are by no means the only ones benefiting from the rescue efforts. Paramedics have saved persons from drowning; they have rescued people suffering from seizures resulting from diabetes and drug overdoses; they have delivered babies; they have helped psychologically disturbed people; and they have rescued victims of fires and bad automobile accidents.

Medic I was born about the same time that emergency rescue programs were instituted in Columbus, Ohio, and Jacksonville, Florida. The program has proved to be so successful that representatives from more than 200 cities in the United States and abroad have come to see it work, with the hope of implementing it in their own communities. Paramedic emergency rescue systems are found today in most major cities in this country; however, there is a wide variation in funding, training, and backgrounds of personnel.

The emergency squad is beckoned by a call from the patient or someone at the scene of the emergency. The fire department dispatcher is the link to the system. He dispatches the nearest of 12 mobile units strategically located at fire stations throughout the city and at Harborview Medical Center; this process insures the rapid response necessary for dealing with life-or-death emergencies.

Of the 12 mobile units, 8 are first aid units — primary care vans staffed with fire fighters trained in an 81-hour course as emergency medical technicians (EMTs). The EMT course, offered by the state's Department of Transportation, gives training in such procedures as splinting broken bones, bandaging minor wounds, and treating burns. More than half the fire department personnel is EMT trained.

A 1,300-hour course is provided for the advanced-level paramedic personnel who staff four mobile intensive coronary care units. These medic units are really small hospital emergency rooms on wheels. Each carries a portable defibrillator, which generates a high-energy direct current used to resuscitate victims of ventricular fibrillation, a state in which the heart, due to a sudden shock, stops pumping blood.

The van also carries a portable life pack to monitor the heart and transmit information to the physician at the hospital. Equipment for performing an endo-tracheal intubation, inserting a tube into a victim's clogged airway, is also in the unit. The medic unit carries 22 different drugs and fluids necessary for intracardiac injections and other lifesaving measures. Essentially the van is equipped with everything but the physician, who is at the hospital, available via radio or telephone communication.

If the emergency appears to be a life-threatening situation, the dispatcher sends a medic unit, staffed with two paramedics, in addition to sending the first aid van. Sudden collapse, suspected heart attack, major trauma, drowning, obstetric problems, and unconsciousness call for this double response.

"If we know that it's going to take a first aid van more than two minutes to get to your house, and it's a life-or-death emergency, we'll send the nearest fire engine, then the nearest first aid van, and then the nearest medic unit," explains Captain Clyde Neaville, one of the original volunteers in the Medic I program. "Understandably, there are times when two emergencies happen in the same area, so we have to back the system up with fire engines. This is what makes it work. We have EMT-trained people on every fire engine, and we can get that vehicle to nearly any place in the city within two minutes."

Upon arrival, the paramedics evaluate the patient and when appropriate, they talk with a physician via phone or radio. Certain therapy, such as administration of drugs, is carried out under standing orders.

"The most important thing is to administer first aid and stabilize the patient's condition before moving him or her to a hospital," Neaville says. In certain trauma situations, such as when emergency surgery is necessary or when there is serious bleeding, the paramedics must rush the patient to the nearest hospital.

Patients with certain kinds of heart attacks are placed under continuous electrocardiographic monitoring. If the heart patient requires immediate hospitalization, the dispatcher makes the arrangements and the patient is admitted directly to a coronary care unit, avoiding the delay of waiting in an emergency room.

To date, there are about 50 certified paramedics in Seattle.

Paramedic students must first have five years experience as Seattle fire fighters and have EMT certification. They are taught rescue procedures, physiology and anatomy, pharmacology, record keeping, and public relations. They learn to give medication, draw blood, give shock treatments, treat seizures and drug overdoses. They spend about half their training time working and observing in the 14 area hospitals' emergency rooms; cardiopulmonary, orthopedic, obstetric and pediatrics, and psychiatric wards; and in the operating and recovery rooms. Local physicians, emergency room nurses, residents, and certified paramedics train new paramedics.

Paramedic certification is based on two written tests, a final oral examination, and review of internship evaluations. Paramedics also must take a recertification test every two years.

"We have taken advantage of the resources of an existing agency responsible for delivering emergency medical care — the fire department," Dr. Cobb says. "Physicians have contributed in direction, supervision, and training. The county medical society, the area's hospitals, service clubs, and citizens are an integral part of the system's successful operation."

Public support of Medic I has been "just fabulous," Clyde Neaville says. When the program was only 18 months old, there was a funding problem. Administrators launched a drive to collect $100,000, but within a matter of days, Seattle residents contributed $200,000. Service clubs and families of individuals whose lives have been saved have made large donations to the program, even donating a fully equipped medic unit, amounting to almost $30,000.

Check with your fire department or public health department to see what's available in your community. Understanding what the emergency system can and can't do may help you decide how to act if a problem arises. And, if your city or town doesn't have adequate emergency services, you might think about working on upgrading them. As Seattle's Dr. Cobb says, "There aren't many benefits in medicine. This program is relatively inexpensive. It doesn't take too many people who were ostensibly dead — to see them up and walking around two weeks later — to make an impact on people."

And Still More People to See . . .

There is a myriad of other health professionals who can help you with your health problems or lead you to a healthier lifestyle.

Some aren't really "new," but you may be unfamiliar with

them. Chiropractors, homeopaths, and osteopaths, for instance, have been around for quite a while. Each practices medicine according to individual guiding tenets.

Chiropractors operate on the theory that a misalignment of the bones of the spine can produce a number of physical problems. They try to bring about improvements through "adjustments" which put bones back in their proper places. Similarly, osteopaths (DOs) base much of their therapy on manipulation because they believe that many ailments can be helped by correcting imbalances in the neuro-muscular-skeletal system. Osteopaths spend four years in osteopathic school, have a hospital-based internship, and are able to prescribe drugs, perform surgery, and generally provide the same kind of treatment as MDs.

Homeopathy is based on the idea that "like cures like." Its founder, Dr. Samuel Hahnemann, wrote, "If a medicine administered to a healthy person causes a certain syndrome of symptoms, that medicine will cure a sick person who presents similar symptoms."[15] Hahnemann's reasoning may seem a little strange to you, and indeed his principle has never really been thoroughly tested.

On the other hand, acupuncture, a centuries-old Eastern therapy, has been tested and is gaining some acceptance in this country. Acupuncturists insert slender needles at various points of the body to help relieve pain and treat various conditions. No one, including Oriental practitioners, is quite sure why or how acupuncture works.

There are also those people who practice various therapies: oxygen therapists, who treat patients with pure oxygen under high pressure; orthomolecular therapists, who try to create the correct molecular environment for optimal health either by prescribing amounts of certain vitamins or eliminating certain substances from the diet; herbalists, who have maintained and expanded upon the ancient art of healing with herbs; and dance and poetry therapists who seek to help their patients improve their mental health through dancing or poetry.

Finally, there are people who will teach such things as yoga, Tai-chi, biofeedback, or meditation.

It's important to realize that the medical establishment's reactions to these various professionals range from outright criticism (of homeopaths, for instance) to cautious acceptance (as in the case of acupuncturists).

As we have been saying throughout the chapter, it is your responsibility to check on the credentials of all people whom you allow to administer health care to you. Find out what they promise to do. Read up on their specialties. Talk to other patients or clients. Ask the opinion of other health professionals you know. Get recommendations. Ask about fees. Protect yourself — and your body.

Notes

1. Ann A. Bliss and Eva D. Cohen, *The New Health Professionals* (Germantown, Md.; Aspen Systems Corp., 1977), p. 40.

2. Donald W. Simborg, Barbara H. Starfield, and Susan D. Horn, "Physicians and Non-Physician Health Practitioners: The Characteristics of Their Practices and Their Relationships," *American Journal of Public Health* 68(January 1978):1.

3. U.S., Department of Health, Education, and Welfare, *Report of the Physician's Extender Work Group* (Washington, D.C.: Government Printing Office, 1977).

4. Charles Lewis and Barbara A. Resnick, "Nurse Clinics and Progressive Ambulatory Care," *New England Journal of Medicine* 277(1967):1236.
   Walter O. Spitzer et al., "The Burlington Randomized Trial of the Nurse Practitioner," *New England Journal of Medicine* 290(1974):251.
   Evan Charney and Harriet Kitzman, "The Child Health Nurse (Pediatric and Nurse Practitioner) in Private Practice: A Controlled Trial," *New England Journal of Medicine* 285(1971):1353.

5. Bliss and Cohen, *New Health Professionals*, p. 152.

6. Interview with Dr. Robert Harmon. August 1978.

7. As quoted in Joanne Lukominik, "Family Practice: Teaching New Docs Old Tricks," *Health/PAC Bulletin*, no. 80(January/February 1978):25-26.

8. Ibid.

9. "The Friendly New Family Doctors," *Time*, 4 July 1977, p. 72.

10. Lori Breslow, *Small Town* (St. Charles, Mo.: John J. Buse Historical Museum, 1977), p. 117.

11. Informed Homebirth, Inc., "Informed Homebirth" (Boulder, Colo., 1977), p. 9.

12. Janet Epstein, "Setting Up a Viable Home Birth Service," in *21st Century Obstetrics Now!* eds. Lee Stewart and David Stewart (Chapel Hill, N.C., 1977), vol. 2, pp. 329-30.

13. Donald B. Ardell, *High Level Wellness* (Emmaus, Pa.: Rodale Press, 1977), pp. 8-20.

14. Walter W. Stoll, "Patient Brochure and Self-Help Manual" (Lexington, Ky., 1977), p. iii.

15. As quoted in Mark Bricklin, *The Practical Encyclopedia of Natural Healing* (Emmaus, Pa.: Rodale Press, 1976), p. 281.

For Further Reading

Ardell, Donald B. *High Level Wellness.* Emmaus, Pa.: Rodale Press, 1977.

Bliss, Ann A., and Eva D. Cohen. *The New Health Professionals.* Germantown, Md.: Aspen Systems Corp., 1977.

Bliss, Ann A.; Blair L. Sadler; and Alfred M. Sadler, Jr. *The Physician's Assistants — Today and Tomorrow.* Cambridge, Mass.: Ballinger Publishing Co., 1975.

Brennan, Barbara, and Joan Heilman. *The Complete Book of Midwifery.* New York: E.P. Dutton, 1977.

Bricklin, Mark. *The Practical Encyclopedia of Natural Healing.* Emmaus, Pa.: Rodale Press, 1976.

Clark, Matt. "The Supernurses," *Newsweek*, 5 December 1977, p. 64.

"The Friendly New Family Doctors." *Time*, 4 July 1977, p. 72.

Gaskin, Ina May. *Spiritual Midwifery.* Rev. ed. Summertown, Tenn.: The Book Publishing Co., 1978.

Willard, William R., and C. H. William Ruhe. "The Challenge of Family Practice Reconsidered." *Journal of the American Medical Association* 240(4 August 1978): 454-58.

Resource Guide

American Academy of Family Physicians
1740 W. 92nd Street
Kansas City, Missouri 64114
(816) 333-9700

This organization exists to promote and support the family practice movement and to assist graduating residents in finding practice locations.

American Academy of Physician Assistants*
2341 Jefferson Davis Highway, Suite 700
Arlington, Virginia 22202
(703) 920-5730

This organization furthers the interest and education of PAs through continuing education and public education, and insures the competence of PAs.

American College of Nurse-Midwives
1000 Vermont Avenue N.W.
Washington, D.C. 20005
(202) 347-5445

This is the professional organization for certified nurse-midwives. Among other things, it accredits the schools which offer nurse-midwifery programs and degrees.

Association of Physician Assistant Programs
2341 Jefferson Davis Highway, Suite 700
Arlington, Virginia 22202
(703) 920-5730

This organization helps develop curriculum and funding for PA programs.

International Academy of Preventive Medicine
10409 Town and Country Way, Suite 200
Houston, Texas 77024
(713) 468-7851

This is an organization of doctors who are committed to teaching people how to live in a healthy way.

*Consumers can obtain more information about the status and laws regarding the practice of PAs and other MHPs through the state regulatory agencies, state boards of medicine, and state chapters of the American Academy of Physician Assistants.

National Midwives Association
1119 E. San Antonio Avenue
El Paso, Texas 79901
(915) 533-8142

The group publishes a newsletter for practicing midwives and sponsors workshops and conferences.

Consumer Notes

Midlevel Health Practitioners

1. Find out from your doctor or clinic what tasks have been assigned to the MHP. (You should also inquire whether the MHP is a physician's assistant, nurse practitioner, or nurse clinician. This will give you some idea of the individual focus of the person.)
2. Find out about the MHP's training and if she has specialized in any field.
3. The time and attention MHPs give their patients are probably their most important attributes. If you are not receiving those benefits, voice a complaint.
4. Ask what kind of health education and/or prevention programs your MHP may be doing.
5. Inquire about the means of supervision the doctor or clinic has set up for the MHP and how you can provide feedback to the appropriate person.
6. Find out if your insurance company will cover the services of an MHP.

Family Practitioners

1. Talk with the physician you are thinking about choosing to see how she defines her role as a family practitioner: does she provide you with basic care, continuity of care, and referral to specialists?
2. Find out what the FP feels he is not qualified to do. Ask how referrals are made.
3. Does the doctor see herself as interested in you as a member of a family? If so, do you want someone who is going to be interested in things that are not strictly biological?
4. How does the FP feel about patient education, self-help, and prevention?

5. Ask about training and credentials.
6. Compare costs among various primary health care models: using a family practitioner, enrolling in an HMO, using an internist.
7. Ask the doctor about his opinion of hospitalization. Does he perceive hospitalization as the last resort in solving a medical problem?
8. Ask about hospital admitting privileges.
9. Talk about office policies: how are emergencies handled, what are the office hours, are house calls made?
10. If the doctor is in a group practice, find out as much as possible about how it functions. Will you see one doctor or many doctors?
11. Talk to other specialists to weigh the pros and cons of using a gynecologist or pediatrician, for example, as your primary care physician rather than a family practitioner.

Midwives

1. Talk to the midwife about her feelings concerning childbirth: does she see it as a natural event, does she see her role as an assistant rather than a manager, is she willing to help you have the kind of birth you want?
2. The expectant mother should examine her feelings to determine whether she would really prefer a woman to deliver her baby.
3. Find out if the midwife is a certified nurse-midwife or an empirical midwife. In either case, find out what her training is. Speak to satisfied families the midwife has worked with.
4. Determine exactly what services the midwife is going to provide for you (for example, prenatal care) and which you are responsible for.
5. Ask about the midwife's emergency backup facilities.
6. Find out if she has the skills recommended by the Informed Homebirth Organization. (See pages 63–64.)
7. Ask about fees and see if they are reimbursable by your insurance company.

Wellness Doctors

1. Ask the doctor what he means by "wellness." The concept is so new that the word sometimes means different things to different people.
2. Find out exactly what the treatment entails — taking classes, working out a new diet, or getting patient education in addition to regular medical care.
3. Investigate the doctor's credentials.
4. Ask about fees. One criticism of wellness doctors is that their services are really a luxury.

Paramedics
1. Find out about emergency services in your community.
2. If they are below standard, determine what you can do to improve them.

Other Professionals

Generally, there are three rules to follow when dealing with any medical professional:
1. Find out what his credentials, training, and philosophy of health care giving are.
2. Determine specifically what his course of treatment is and what it will do for you. After that has been discussed, read up on the claims and, if possible, talk to other patients or clients.
3. Ask about fees.

Staying Out of the Hospital

part two

chapter three

Getting Well at Home

Cynthia R. Driver

Years ago when a person became sick, he was simply bundled up in one corner and nursed back to health — or else he was taken out of the house in a coffin. There was simply no other choice.

Healers and midwives, our first health professionals, also delivered their care in the home. They were often called in to consult on diseases and offer opinions on possible cures while giving emotional support to the family. Even hospitals, when they began, understood the roles of home and family in health care. The first outpatient clinic, the Boston Dispensary, was founded in 1796 to assure that, "The sick, without being pained by separation from their families, may be attended and relieved in their own homes."

Homes began to be displaced by hospitals and clinics as the primary site for medical care within the last century — but not without a certain degree of reluctance on the part of the lay population. A resident of the town of St. Charles, Missouri, recalled in 1920 that, "Most people in the olden days were possessed of a great fear of hospitals. To be sent to a hospital as a patient was imagined by many to be a positive sign that one would never emerge alive."

That fear no doubt still exists today — coupled with the fear of financial ruin and lack of humane treatment in the hands of the medical establishment. Add to that our inability to financially contain an almost $200-billion health care system and the fact that our population of people 65 years old and older is growing at a rapid rate, and the burgeoning interest in home health care as a full-fledged alternative to institutional care is easy to understand.

Of course, the likelihood of our returning to the "good old days," when grandmothers and aunts helped mother take care of the sick children, or when grown children assumed the responsibility of caring for their elderly parents, is very slim. As the United States Special Committee on Aging reported, "The day of the extended family in which generations live together is disappearing, destroyed by economic pressures which attract young families either to the city and away from the farm, or away from the city to the suburbs. . . ."

What we need to do, then, is to build another home care structure — a structure that relies on a mixture of the family, professional medical help, social service agencies, and informal social support networks. The goal of this home health care structure is to help the patient recover from his illness (or in cases where complete recovery is impossible, to help him gain maximum rehabilitation) in a way that will cause the least possible disruption to his, his family's, and his community's daily pattern of living.

Sadly, home health care has a long way to go to fulfill the promise it offers. According to the Committee on Aging report, the estimated total number of homemaker-home health aids in 1972 was 30,000, but the total estimated need established in that report was 300,000. Similarly, less than 1 percent of the total amount of federal money spent on health care ($272 million of $33 billion) was used in the reimbursement of home health care. But perhaps most important is the fact that many potential home health care consumers are still being institutionalized. A report by the Department of Health, Education, and Welfare estimated in 1976 that 25 to 40 percent of the people who are institutionalized are admitted only because of a lack of home health care services.

As one expert explained, "Home care is the newly found attic antique that has potential value, but no one is yet willing or able to estimate the value and to begin the bidding." Home care may have the potential value of an "antique," but there are so many stumbling blocks in its way that it is virtually impossible for it to reach its full value right now.

The Promise of Home Health Care

Much of the excitement over home health care stems from the fact that it has the potential to respond to two pressing problems in our current health care system: spiraling costs and increasingly ineffective and impersonal institutionalization. Not only can home health care save you money by decreasing the number of days spent in a hospital or nursing home, but it also allows you to heal in a place in which you're comfortable and surrounded by people who know and care about you. Those two characteristics alone make home health care a very attractive alternative.

The Psychological Advantages

"Mother made it very clear at the time she was diagnosed as having terminal cancer that she wanted to be cared for at home. We were worried we wouldn't know how to deal with her, but we did the best we could and I know it was better for her than being institutionalized," explained one home health care advocate.

On the most basic level, the advantage of home care is that it allows people to be in their homes rather than in a hospital or nursing home. It means that you or a member of your family can be in familiar surroundings rather than in a strange, and often terrifying, place. It allows patients to live according to their own time schedules rather than the time schedule of an institution. It means that at a time when someone is under the stress of an illness, he can be surrounded by people who love him and want to take care of him rather than by strangers in starched white uniforms who are paid to be there.

Over and over again studies demonstrate this preference for home care. A survey conducted at Mount Sinai Hospital in Milwaukee showed that 84 percent of all patients receiving home care preferred it to hospitalization. Among patients who did not receive home care, 50 percent said they would have preferred it. In the same study, members of the nursing staff said they believed that both the patient and his family did better at home than in the hospital.[1]

It isn't hard to understand the psychological benefits that come from being at home. Hospitals are anxiety-producing places. Patients often feel helpless and are unable to cope with hospital routine and personnel. More often than not, the food is unappetizing and unnourishing. Roommates can make you feel more uncomfortable than the illness does.

Conversely, the relaxation and security that come from being taken care of in familiar surroundings can help in the healing process. One report on home health care described a man who "was convinced that he was healing faster" at home, and it went on to point out that "many doctors confirm that how a patient feels about getting better affects his/her capacity to heal."[2] Pain, too, is often directly related to anxiety and thus can be lessened when anxiety is reduced.

Home health care can also be of tremendous help to the families of the ill. Hospitalization disrupts normal family routine. It means that a member of the family isn't there to fulfill his normal duties. Children often suffer from being separated from their parents just as spouses suffer from being apart from one another. The physical strain of having to be with the sick person in the hospital worsens an already stress-filled situation.

Similarly, in cases where a person must be put in a nursing home, the family often finds itself in a no-win situation: the decision to institutionalize causes guilt and unhappiness, but without support, caring for an ill or disabled relative at home is inconceivable. Home health care aid gives these families another viable option.

The Financial Advantages

An unfortunate fact of life in this country is that people who face catastrophic illness often face financial ruin. Much too frequently, the two go hand in hand. But since home care means a reduction in the number of days spent in a hospital or nursing home, it also means that the financial burden can be lightened as well.

Many studies have attested to the cost savings potential of home health care:

In a study of 485 patients receiving home care by a Rochester home care association, physicians recorded an average "saving" of 21 hospital days. With Rochester hospital costs averaging $108 [in 1976 when the study was done] and Rochester home care costs averaging $15.61 a day, the total annual savings ran to approximately $900,000.[3]

Upjohn Health Care Services, a home health care agency, analyzed the case of a patient who fractured both legs in an automobile accident. The patient received 29 nursing visits, 16 physical therapy visits, 96 six- and eight-hour visits by a health aid, 3 visits by a social worker, and 4 *deliveries of equipment during his 141 days of home care. In addition, he used an extensive range of rental equipment and was transported by ambulance to the hospital or to a physician's office on 4 occasions. Total cost of his home care, including program administrative costs, was just over $3,500 or an average of $25 a day. Without home care, he would have had to remain in the hospital for at least 74 days at a cost of nearly $8,500.*[4]*

And home health care isn't applicable only in cases of broken bones or other relatively minor injuries or diseases. Recently, there has been an increasing awareness that illnesses which have traditionally required institutional care can also be treated at home.

For instance, in a study at St. Luke's Medical Center in New York City, the costs and outcomes of stroke patients who had home care were compared with similar stroke patients who didn't. Among the advantages of being taken care of at home were shorter hospitalization, fewer admissions for recurring stroke, fewer deaths, continuity of care, the ability to remain self-sufficient in the community, and, predictably, reduced costs.[5]

Similarly, in England, cardiologists have shown that some heart attack patients may do just as well — or better — in their homes. A report appearing in the *Lancet*, a British medical journal, tells of a study on the management of heart attack patients and concludes that, ". . . for the majority of patients to whom a general practitioner is called because of suspected infarction [i.e., heart attack], hospital admission offers no clear advantage."[6] In fact, according to the author of the study, Dr. H. G. Mather of Bristol's Southmead Hospital, ". . . in uncomplicated cases the essential need is to relieve pain, to relieve anxiety, to make the patient comfortable."[7] If this can be done at home, so much the better. Work in England has also included the treatment of kidney dialysis patients in the home.

Naturally, the importance of the cost savings potential[†] of home health care will continue to rise as hospital costs continue to rise —

---

*Currently the average length of time for which home health care services are given is a little over 52 days. The National League for Nursing's Council of Home Health Agencies' yearly review for 1978 shows the average cost for a nursing visit to be $26.07, for physical therapy $20.92, and for home health aids $6.79 an hour.

†While most home care enthusiasts argue its cost savings potential, it should be noted that there are those who doubt the long run savings, if broader factors are taken into account. These include: (1) that we do not yet have sufficient data to determine the cost of developing and upgrading the services which are not now adequate or available; and (2) the current wages of home care workers do not reflect their real value.

and there is every indication that it will be impossible to *stop* hospital costs from increasing under our present health care system. Add to this the fact that our country's population includes more and more

Home Health Care: It Can Work

Tommy, at age five, was active, lovable, and as hopelessly mischievous as most other children his age. With his parents and two sisters he lived comfortably in a newly built, middle-class home in rural Indiana.

It was a shock to his family, then, when Tommy suddenly became very ill. His parents took him to the local hospital, where he was admitted by his pediatrician. The diagnosis was Reyes' syndrome, a viral infection of the central nervous system. Within 24 hours it became apparent that his condition was deteriorating: increasing intracranial pressure (characteristic of Reyes' syndrome) demanded the more specialized care available in a large medical center nearby. At the medical center, Tommy's specialists found his condition to be serious. At one point, his breathing became so difficult that it was necessary to insert an endo-tracheal tube — establishing a free passageway from mouth to windpipe — which could be connected to a ventilator to breathe for him.

Slowly, Tommy began to show signs of improvement. At the end of a long three weeks, he appeared able to breathe on his own and his doctors decided the endo-tracheal tube could be removed.

Following the surgery necessary to remove the tube, Tommy's mother, Ann, could tell immediately that the news was not good. "They told me there had been a complication," she remembers, "and that they had to do a tracheotomy." That was necessary because Tommy's endo-tracheal tube had irritated his windpipe so that when it was removed the sensitive mucous lining began to swell shut. The tracheotomy, a surgical opening into the windpipe through the front of the neck, was done to continue to help him breathe.

"I remember the doctors telling me that they hoped the tracheotomy would be temporary, although it would be impossible to tell for several weeks or months," Ann continues. "The doctor also told me at the time that we could probably take him home in a few weeks and return for weekly examinations. My reaction to that was, 'What? Take him home with a hole in his neck? How can we handle that?' The cost and strain of Tommy's illness on our family was already nearly unbearable."

The day after the tracheotomy, the hospital's home care coordi-

people 65 years old and older (the elderly with chronic or long-term disabilities like cancer, arthritis, or cardiovascular disease are the primary recipients of home health care today), and it becomes clear that

nator visited Ann in Tommy's room. Together they discussed Ann's fears and questions. The hospital's representative assured Ann that they'd have plenty of time to teach her all she needed to know about Tommy's health needs, equipment, and home treatments before Tommy would leave the hospital. They also promised to contact the family's county health department so that a visiting nurse would be assigned to help them make the transition from the other end.

Such was Ann's first encounter with home health care. "I'd heard about public health nurses, but I never dreamed of them in terms of my family," she says. Yet Tommy's and his family's experience is fairly typical of the way in which some 2½ million Americans each year first experience home health care.

In the days that followed, both Ann and Tommy's father, Bob, learned that Tommy's "trach" required a humidifier, regular suctioning, and cleaning in order to rid the passageway of mucus. And there was the list of danger signals to look for: the amount and color of mucus, noisy respirations, temperature. It seemed endless. Meanwhile, Tommy had learned that by placing a finger over the "trach" opening momentarily, he could use the force of an outward breath to say a few hoarse words.

As arranged, the visiting nurse came to visit Ann and Tommy in the hospital. She reviewed his chart with the nurses and received a copy of the physician's home treatment plan. She assisted Ann and Bob in locating the necessary equipment to make home care possible. They rented a suction machine and a humidifier; the nurse ordered a large supply of sterile gloves, suction tubes, and sterile water.

Shortly after the family returned home the visiting nurse pulled into the driveway. "I was so glad to see her!" remembers Ann. "And the first week she came every day because she knew we were frightened. She did so much." The nurse realized the family needed more support than she alone could provide. Together they slowly established a support network: a neighbor was taught basic care in order to "babysit" occasionally, the local fire department was instructed on assistance in case of emergency, and, later, even Tommy's preschool teacher became involved in plans for his future return to school. This support continued for almost two years until the family was able to function independently. Within a year after that, Tommy's tracheotomy was repaired and he was completely recovered.

we are in urgent need of developing a good home health care system.

But even if our home health care system has not yet reached its full potential, through a careful (albeit often frustrating) search, there are still ways you can make use of what is currently available. The trick is to determine your particular home health care needs and then to find the people or agencies who can best help you fulfill them.

Plugging into the Home Health Care System

Plugging into the home health care system requires a series of decisions, the most basic of which, of course, are whether or not the patient wants to be taken care of at home and whether or not her family is able to cope with illness or rehabilitation there.

George Madden is blind. But at 70, George is still very active and able to get around alone. He never married and still lives in the house where he was born.

"When I started losing my sight, I knew I just couldn't do it myself," he said. "I wondered how I would ever make out. I'd have horrible nightmares about having to go to a nursing home. One of my older sisters is in a nursing home. When I'd visit her there I thought it would kill me to be in her place."

There was no doubt in George Madden's mind that he wanted to stay home. "I know every inch of this house," he continued. "Having to depend on others, including my family, is a heartache. Giving up driving is a heartache. So, it really wasn't hard to ask for help from a home care agency. Some women from the old age group told me about a home care corporation. They've been lifesavers for me."

Indeed, Dr. Mather's Bristol study showed that the patients most likely to benefit from home care were those who had no qualms about being treated outside the hospital. On the other hand, if being away from potentially lifesaving medical equipment and professionals makes the patient nervous or uncomfortable, then home care may not be the best course of treatment.

It's probably safe to assume, however, that the majority of people in this country who face illness, if given a choice, would prefer not to be in a hospital. The next question that needs to be answered, then, is: Can my family take care of me in our own home?

Physical factors must be taken into consideration. Will the setup of the house allow for the care of the sick patient? Are there physical barriers that might make it difficult for the person to get from place to place, assuming he's not bedridden? Is there a place where the person is far enough away from the family to get needed quiet and rest, but not so far away that she feels cut off? Similarly, the distance between your home and a backup hospital needs to be taken into account. Are you close enough to a hospital, if it were needed in an emergency? Do you have adequate transportation to the hospital?

The cooperation of a doctor can also help to spell the difference between successful and unsuccessful home care. In fact, in some states physician participation in home care is required — you can't treat a person at home without the services of a doctor. And, again, Dr. Mather found that the physician's willingness to participate in home care was essential.

Although certainly physical factors and physician participation are important, probably the most important consideration in deciding for or against home care is whether or not family members and friends are available to act as a support network to take responsibility for the difficult and time-consuming tasks that accompany caring for an ill person.

In many ways, home care is a burden on the family that chooses it. No matter how much outside support is available, family members are still the ones who are going to be providing the primary care. That may require sacrifices; it may mean altering the way things are normally done in your family; it may force you to do things with which you're not familiar, and which may — at times — be some-what unpleasant.

Try to evaluate your situation and feelings as honestly as possible. Talk with the whole family about the problems you may encounter. Get the advice of professionals — doctors, nurses, therapists — to find out exactly what will need to be done, what equipment is required, and how many and what kind of support people will be available. Consider various options before actually making a decision.

If the decision is made to investigate the possibility of home health care, three basic areas need to be explored: what kind of outside services you will need; where those services will come from; and how those services will be paid for.

What Do You Need?

The term home health care encompasses a wide range of personnel and services. Generally, there are two kinds of services that can be provided: medical care or social services like housekeeping, Meals on Wheels programs, or transportation to appointments.

Direct nursing care is most often done by a registered nurse, who can be a graduate of a two-year community college, three-year hospital program, or four-year program. If an RN has a B.S. degree in nursing, she may be called a public health nurse. RNs with two- and three-year degrees are called professional nurses, and nurses with one year of special schooling are called licensed practical nurses (LPNs). Since the main difference between an LPN and an RN is that the latter can give some medication while the former cannot, in most cases you can employ either one for your home health care.

The RN may visit weekly or even daily for a limited period of time if the individual situation warrants it. She may do direct medical care like dressing changes, injections, blood pressure readings, enemas, urinary catheter changes, or treatment of bed sores; or, she may carry out such broader nursing functions as supervision, evaluation, teaching, and prevention. The nurse, through the agency with which he or she is affiliated, can also obtain certain equipment including syringes, bedpans, bandages, walkers, and chair lifts.

You may also need the services of a home health aid, who can assist with bathing, shampoos, and other personal care that's not considered to be medical or nursing care per se. The home health aid usually will visit for two to three hours several times a week. Check with the home health care agency to find out about training and references of the home health aids they employ. Many aids are certified, which shows they have completed certain course work, have had on-the-job training, and have attended inservice classes. The RN remains medically and legally responsible for the supervision of the home health aid.

Nursing agencies may provide physical, occupational, and speech therapy as part of their services, too. Therapists may make home visits, with the frequency of those visits varying according to the needs of the client and the availability of the therapist. Sometimes family members and/or friends are taught to assist and eventually carry out rehabilitative therapy. According to one home care recipient whose husband suffered a stroke, "The doctor said it would take months to recover the full use of his left arm and leg. The visiting nurse and physical therapist taught me how to exercise him twice a day, and I feel sure he recovered faster because of it."

Again, nursing, home health aid, and therapist services all are provided under the direction of the patient's physician. As one doctor explained, "Technically, home care is not difficult to do . . . but it does require a doctor who is interested and has some ability to call on certain resources." Treatment is evaluated and renewed as the home health professionals report changes in the client's situation. Careful records are kept by the nurse, aid, and therapist and are submitted for periodic approval by the physician.

Sometimes people don't need medical services, but an illness or injury prevents them from doing the things they normally would do in the course of a day to take care of themselves: cleaning the house, doing the grocery shopping, driving to take care of errands or to see the doctor. In that case, they need social services — services which are traditionally not considered health care, are not subject to physician approval, but may be delivered in conjunction with medical services, if necessary.

Homemaker services are the most popular. The homemaker may assist with housekeeping, chores, and help the family with meals. One family had a homemaker come to their house three times a week while the woman recovered from surgery. "The homemaker helped with light housekeeping, buying a few groceries at the store, and several times fixed a hot meal. It was a great help," the client commented. Often health aids will also do homemaker services, in which case they are called homemaker-home health aids.

Still other social services include:

Meal sites. Since 1972, Congress has provided funds for a program known as the Elderly Nutrition Program. The point of this program is to provide meal sites where older persons can gather for group meals. This means not only that the older person is guaranteed at least one nourishing and well-balanced meal a day, but that he or she also has other people to share that meal with in a friendly atmosphere. Meal sites are one defense against the need to put an elderly person in a nursing home.

Meals on Wheels. At the same time it was recognized that some homebound people also need hot meals. It was decided to use up to 15 percent of the funds allocated for meal sites for home delivery of meals or "Meals on Wheels." These programs are administered through each state and therefore vary greatly throughout the country. They are usually delivered through local social service agencies, the Department of Aging, or a local nonprofit agency. You may find them listed as Nutrition Programs for the Elderly or simply as "Meals on Wheels." Most programs provide up to one hot meal daily, five days a week. Often, arrangements can be made to have cold meals delivered for evenings and weekends.

Client advocacy. Many social service home care programs provide paraprofessional community workers who make home visits to evaluate a client's situation and advise her about available services. These workers serve as advocates for clients, many of whom are not aware of the services available to them or how to go about applying for them. As a director of one social service agency in New York City explains, "Client advocates are there to provide support, all the way from helping to fill out complicated Medicare forms to just holding someone's hand when they go to the Social Security office."

Transportation services may also be provided to get people to doctor's appointments, to the hospital for needed therapy, or for help in running errands.

In dealing with any and all personnel, you should of course know the qualifications of the person who is in your home. You'll also need to know how and when they'll be paid, and if you can get the same person to continue to care for the patient. These questions should be answered easily by the agency through which you contract for services — but you need to select that agency with care.

Providing the Services: the Home Health Care Industry

A wide variety of agencies is currently in the home health care business and finding the one that will provide you with the kind of care you want and need can sometimes be a difficult task. One place to begin your search is governmental agencies, including local public health departments and departments of welfare. Increasingly, some hospitals also have home health care programs; however, as of 1977 only 7 percent of the hospitals in this country provided this service to their patients.

In general there are three classifications of home health care agencies: public; nonprofit; and proprietary, or profit making.

Public home care providers include local public health departments and departments of welfare. They are funded entirely through state and local taxes and Medicare/Medicaid funds, and usually do most of their work with the elderly and needy.

Probably the most numerous nonprofit agencies are the visiting nurse associations (VNAs). First established in Boston in the 1870s, these organizations began to appear throughout the United States in the late nineteenth century. Today over 500 of them provide home health care.

There are a number of advantages of the VNAs. Approximately 30 percent of their nurses are public health nurses, who are usually good sources of information about other programs for the homebound. The VNAs also screen and supervise their employees well, and because the nurses are the associations' employees, you don't have to pay their Social Security taxes or fill out W-2 forms. Also the VNAs have prorated fees for people who don't have insurance coverage of some kind. "We wouldn't cut needed services because someone couldn't pay," said Bernice Rosner of the Visiting Nurse Service of New York.

Since VNA nurses are assigned cases by geographic area, you have some guarantee that you will be receiving care from the same person. But be forewarned: this is not always the case. One home health care patient complained about the constant shift in personnel. "It always happens this way," she said. "I just get used to my nurses and then they quit. I get attached to people, and then it's hard to see them go. I worry about who the next one will be." It's much more probable that you will have a switch in homemaker or home health aids, although a nurse should be keeping a detailed chart on your case for each aid to consult.

While social services as well as medical services may be provided by the VNAs, some private, nonprofit home care agencies provide only social services because the regulations for Medicare/Medicaid reimbursement for medical care are so stringent. Essentially, these voluntary agencies are taking over the work formerly done by the Department of Public Welfare by providing services funded by federal money to those who qualify under Medicare and the Older Americans Act.

Proprietary home health care agencies are private businesses. They seek to provide home health care at a profit. Probably the largest and most widely known is Upjohn Health Care Services, a subsidiary of the Upjohn Company of Kalamazoo, Michigan. Upjohn has over 200 offices nationwide. The next two largest firms are Medical Personnel Pool and Staff Builders.

Upjohn has a minimum charge for two-hour and four-hour visits with rates varying from state to state. (The VNA, however, charges on a per-visit basis.) The general pay for nurses is based on the pay rate for hospital nurses in each community. Upjohn also provides homemakers and home health aids.

Home health care is becoming big business. Upjohn reports that it supplied 20 million hours worth of services in a recent year, and assuming an average charge of $5 to $6 per hour, there is a potential to make at least $100 million a year.

But there is a hitch: in most states profit-making agencies are not certified by Medicare and thus cannot compete for Medicare/Medicaid dollars — a lucrative source of revenue.

In order to be certified for Medicare/Medicaid money, a home health agency must: (1) engage primarily in skilled nursing services and provide at least one other therapeutic service; (2) have policies which are developed by at least one physician and one registered nurse associated with the agency; (3) maintain clinical charts and records on all patients; (4) ensure that the professional personnel are licensed by their respective professional organizations; and (5) provide for regular review and evaluation of policies. Currently there are approximately 2,500 certified home health care agencies — of these only 81 are proprietary.

But in January 1976, new HEW regulations went into effect which allow public and nonprofit home health agencies to subcontract services from proprietary agencies. While this was done ostensibly to increase the availability of home care services, it promises to be a boon to the proprietary agencies.

In fact, subcontracting services is a fairly regular practice within the industry. Hospitals may subcontract from the VNAs, social service agencies which provide a number of services may subcontract from a single service agency, or providers of nursing care may subcontract from social service agencies. As will be discussed, this may well confuse you about which agency is providing you with what services. Sit down with a representative of the parent agency and learn where each of the services you are receiving is coming from. And you should know that the responsibility for control and supervision of subcontracted services still remains with that parent agency.

In choosing a home health care agency, then, you need to find out: What services does the agency offer? Does it offer a single service or a choice of services? If it does offer a choice of services, are some of them subcontracted? Are you able to select some and reject others? Are supplies available through the agency? Is the agency Medicaid/Medicare certified? Are the people it employs licensed? And, finally, what is the cost of the services and which, if any, are reimbursable either through Medicaid/Medicare or through private insurance?

Paying for Home Health Care

Whether or not you can get reimbursed for home health care services will, of course, play a big part in your decision about using those services.

Generally speaking, most commercial insurance policies do not cover home health care, although an increasing number are doing so. Some insurance companies include home health care as part of their major medical policies. Nursing, medical supplies, drugs, and laboratory services may be covered, but often there is a stipulation that the doctor must order the care. Most often, social services or home health aids are not paid for by these plans, and a limit is put on the number of visits which will be reimbursed.

As of now, about three-quarters of the Blue Cross plans offer home visits, but there are limitations. Blue Cross of New York, for instance, requires that you be hospitalized before you have home health care services, that your needs must be approved by a physician, and that the home health care agency must be certified. Other plans require that you lose one day of in-hospital coverage for each two or three home visits.

The Medicaid/Medicare programs enacted by Congress in 1965 provided federal support for "medical" home health care services.

If you are 65 years of age or older, part A of Medicare will pay for 100 home health visits each time you become ill, providing: (1) you are in the hospital at least 3 days before returning home; (2) your

A Day with a Visiting Nurse

Jean Hoover has worked as a visiting nurse for the county health department for two years. "I enjoy working in the community," she says. "Hospital nursing has given me good experience but I prefer to deal with people in their homes. The hospital setting is so unreal that it's often difficult to be aware of the patient's daily living situation. Besides, I like being on the road and having a more independent role as a nurse."

A usual day for Jean may contain as many as six home visits. She is responsible for a caseload of about 40 patients who live within the territory she covers. "We receive calls from just about anyone. Sometimes the family calls to ask for home care, other times it's the physician, friends, or even neighbors who call." Before leaving the office, she makes a detailed schedule. "I leave a copy of my schedule with the home care supervisor. That way I can be reached at a patient's home if something comes up during the day." Next, she gathers the necessary supplies: syringes, bandages, enema bag, and a catheter irrigation tray.

The first stop is to see a 74-year-old woman who has been bedridden for four years. The patient became paralyzed from the waist down and is cared for by her son and daughter-in-law. Jean visits her once a week. "She's a remarkable person. She wants to do as much as she can for herself. When she became paralyzed she lost bladder control. Now she has a catheter.

"Once a week I clean the catheter tubing, which is a sterile procedure. Every month we change the whole thing. Once a week the home health aid comes to give her a bath and change the linen. Twice a month I try to schedule my visit to coincide with the aid's. That way I

home care is planned by a physician within 14 days after you leave the hospital; (3) you are being treated for the same condition for which you were hospitalized; (4) you are in fact homebound; and (5) you require *skilled* care. Another part of the Medicare program, part B, may qualify you for 100 home visits during each calendar year even if you haven't been hospitalized. However, you have to register specifically for this program and pay a $60 deductible as well as be homebound and require skilled care. Eligibility for Medicaid is determined strictly on financial need, and medical costs will be paid by

can observe her work also." The patient seems to enjoy the visit. "Our visits give the family support and relief," Jean observes. "The patient doesn't need to feel that she's a burden to the family."

Next, Jean stops at the home of an older diabetic man. He is 80, his wife is 73. He has developed leg ulcers, a frequent occurrence in diabetics. "When he needs dressing changes I stop here two or three times a week. Sometimes, though, my schedule can't be too flexible. That's the most frustrating part of my job. I see so many things which should be done and I just don't have the time. Often, problems are related to having little money. Older persons receive such small incomes. These are people who have worked hard all their lives. They've had such rich experiences. But at a certain age, many of their friends have died and even relatives are unable to help. It's as though society abandons them."

Three visits later, on her way back to the office, Jean makes an unscheduled stop to check on the progress of a newborn infant with congenital complications. "Yesterday I thought the baby's mother seemed very tired. She's raising two other children alone. I told her I'd see about finding a babysitter and maybe some diapers and formula from the Red Cross. But it's hard even to help people get the things they're entitled to."

At the office, the paperwork begins. "I think it takes about 50 percent of my time," Jean complains. "There are so many forms and charts to fill out."

Then there are the telephone calls. Jean discusses one patient's progress with her physician. At 3:55 P.M. she receives a phone call from a school where she visits occasionally. "I think we have a lice epidemic. Could you come and help us do some head checks?" Jean is asked. She hangs up slowly. Tomorrow will be a very full day.

social service departments if you are qualified and registered for Medicaid.

(Remember only certain agencies are certified to receive Medicaid/Medicare reimbursement. Check with any agency you are considering using to see if they are certified.)

While a patient, or a patient's family, may purchase "social" services privately, federal funding is also available for these services for those who qualify under Medicare/Medicaid. Money for social services such as homemaking, transportation, and meals comes from sources other than those funding medical services, and the requirements for receiving these funds are not as stringent as those for medical care. Again, check with your department of social services to see if you are eligible for aid.

As a spokesperson for Upjohn commented, "Insurance companies will cover services which clients demand." If you have a choice in deciding which insurance company you will use, inquire about its home health care policies. If your company doesn't provide for home health care, now is the time to start asking for it.

The Pitfalls of Home Health Care

The home health care industry is still in its formative years — and that means it is far from being problem free. That, in turn, means that you, the consumer, must be particularly aware of these problems and make every attempt to protect yourself from them.

Fragmentation of services is one area in which you may run into difficulty. "First I thought I would only require a nursing visit once a week," began one home care recipient. "But before I knew it, someone else had to come in for my bath. And yet another person was coming in to bring me my meals."

This woman's experience is all too typical of the situation you may find when trying to contract for home health care services. Part of this is due to the Medicaid/Medicare requirements which narrowly define what are "medical services" and what are "social services." Based on these regulations, for instance, a homemaker is not allowed to touch the patient while the home health aid may not perform any services except direct patient care. In another case, an elderly woman could only get assistance with bathing by asking her doctor to write an order for it because her "personal care" had to be under medical supervision.

Duplication of services may also be a problem. One home health care patient in Indiana was visited by representatives of the VNA and a social service agency for several months before either became aware of the other's visits. And an RN who is employed by a home health care agency to supervise home health aids explained confidentially that she was really "unnecessary" because the public health nurses were doing exactly the same thing she was.

Fragmentation and duplication may well mean that you will have an intricate maze of agencies, requirements, and people to go through in order to get the kind of home health care services you need. We have tried to give you some general guidelines in this chapter — however, you should know that every state and every community has its own way of distributing home health care services. The best you can do is to continue making inquiries until you get what you want.

Another problem with home health care, as it exists now, is that it places too much emphasis on episodic and acute illnesses, and too little emphasis on the prevention of disease or the support of the chronically ill.

Ironically, it is the latter categories of care — prevention and maintenance — that home care is best designed to provide. As one chronically ill person commented, "It just doesn't make sense to wait 'till I'm sick from not eating right before I can get someone in here to help me get groceries." There doesn't seem to be any logical reason why a patient must be hospitalized prior to receiving home care, and some critics contend that this is the result of hospital economics. A New York State Health Services Administration report on home care states, "Inpatients requiring little medical care are profitable customers, and hospitals operating at less than full capacity are reluctant to part with such low cost for care patients. Transferring these patients to home care results in a loss of revenue. . . ."[8]

Quality assurance in the delivery of home care is one of consumers' and providers' greatest concerns. It is also the most difficult element to insure because of the particular characteristic of home care: that it is delivered in the isolation of the home.

Abuses in the home health care industry have occurred just as they have occurred in the nursing home industry. Agencies in Florida and California, for example, have been accused of using Medicare funds to buy personal items or finance enormous pensions. And in 1976, during regional public hearings, representatives of the Department of Health, Education, and Welfare heard about one homemaker who so intimidated a terminally ill woman that her husband begged the social worker for assistance in getting the aid fired. Another home attendant had other women working for her, paying them erratically and skimming off a small profit for herself.[9]

In fact, one increasingly important factor in the quality of home health care concerns the problems faced by home care workers. Edna, 82, and disabled by a stroke, worries about her housekeeper: "I can't tell you how important Patty's help is to me. She's a wonder. Still, she gives much more time than she gets paid for. She has her own family. But, she never complains. I ask her, 'Perhaps you're tired?' She says 'no', but I wonder to myself whether she is. I wonder whether I could make it alone. They don't pay her what she's worth."

A profile of a typical homemaker is that of a middle-aged woman, with several children, who wants to work part time while her children are in school. As a part-time employee she has few, if any, employee benefits; she receives minimum wage; and she has no vacations or health insurance. As a result, characteristically there is a very high turnover rate and clients lose continuity of care.

Small wonder then that many home health care workers are not happy workers. Home health aids carry out extremely difficult, often unpleasant work in isolation. They care for chronically ill patients for indefinite periods of time, at minimum wages, with no opportunity for job advancement. There is little incentive to do a good job. Add to this the fact that the supply of skilled health aid personnel is still inadequate to meet the demand, and the alienation of home care workers from their clients is easy to understand.

Several quality assurance mechanisms do exist which attempt to protect you the consumer. Licensing and registration are required of professional staff personnel such as physicians, nurses, and therapists. The professional staff, in turn, is responsible for the direct supervision of paraprofessional personnel, some of whom may be certified. However, the kind and amount of training varies so much among paraprofessionals that you would be wise to inquire about the background of any person whose services you retain.

You should realize, too, that practically speaking, supervision is difficult to enforce. "Supervision" of an aid by a nurse may be no more than a visit to a patient's home by both on the same day, every two weeks. Since the work is done in the home, adequate supervision is difficult.

A second mechanism deals with the certification of home health care agencies. Presently there are no uniform national standards. In general, the Medicare standards are considered a minimum basic standard for home health care services. Critics state that these, however, are ineffective and often unenforced. The standards used by groups such as the National Council of Homemaker-Home Health Aide Services, the Joint Commission for the Accreditation of Hospitals, and the National League for Nursing/American Public Health Association have been proposed as models for national standards. Observers agree that the problem of certification must be resolved before clients will be protected from having to operate under the "Buyer, beware" pretext.

Another Experience: Great Britain's Home Health Care System

A brief glance at the British home health care system will help show you how a good home care system can work. In Britain, the widespread use of home health care or domiciliary services, as they are called, reflects a general commitment to provide health care and social services within the community. Institutionalization is seen as a solution of last resort.

One of the most remarkable achievements of the British National Health Service is the level of integration of social and medical services in their delivery of home care and the priority which has been given to preventive care. In Britain, the basic health care unit is the district, in which local community health centers provide primary and preventive services virtually free to the area residents. The local health centers are the places where an individual enrolls for the care of a general practitioner. Local centers have access to the services of specialists in the district hospitals.

A wide range of services is available through the community health center. These include: maternity and child welfare, home health visitors, home nursing, domestic help, vaccination and immunization, ambulance transport, preventive services, day care, mental health services, and services and devices for the physically handicapped.

Health services are delivered in the home by several kinds of personnel, including health visitors, home nurses, and home helps. The health visitor, a public health nurse who has postregistration training as a midwife and additional health visitor preparation, is responsible for health education, prevention, and the early detection of disease. She does not, however, do actual nursing. This is the job of the home nurse who is responsible for rendering care under the direction of a general practitioner, performing such tasks as administering injections, changing dressings, and bathing patients.

The duties of the "home help" resemble those of our home-maker-home health aids. However, they are much more flexible in the duties they can do. As one expert explained, "We expect home helps to do whatever is needed. They are sent in to help. This means unlimited service except for those tasks which cannot safely be undertaken. It is far better to give unlimited services . . . at home, than to put people in hospitals or nursing homes."[10] A patient can have the services of a home help for as long as she needs it — the aim is to maintain the person in the home as long as possible. And, not surprisingly, the ratio of home helps per population is notably higher in Britain than in this country.

One young American couple, who were expecting their first child and were traveling to Scotland where they would be with her parents for the occasion, experienced the benefits of the British home health care system. While making a brief stop in London, the woman unexpectedly began labor, one week early. "It worked out wonderfully even though I hadn't planned it that way. I had a smooth delivery in a maternity hospital. All the medical care was free," she recalls.

"Then, after a ten-day rest, we went on to my mother's place. The day after we arrived, a public nurse came to the house. She said she had come for my postnatal check! 'Everyone gets one,' she said matter-of-factly. Imagine getting that kind of service here."

But in places across the country, we are attempting to provide that kind of care. New York City's Mutual Aid Project, for instance, has written a guidebook on how to set up informal neighborhood cooperatives and exchange projects for the purpose of helping elderly and disabled persons stay at home. They offer suggestions for food and medical delivery, library book delivery, and bill paying systems to be established and staffed by volunteers — and offer examples of how such systems are currently working in New York.

We still have a long way to go until we have turned our health care system around so that its primary purpose is to keep people in their own homes, to keep families together. We have the beginning of a home health care system and an ideal system for the future is not difficult to envision. We need to use what we have now while working to attain that ideal.

Notes

1. James L. Bischoff, "Home Health Care and the Insurance Industry," *Best's Review* 77(August 1976):4.

2. Ibid.

3. Ibid.

4. Upjohn Health Care Services, "Cost Analysis. Home Care as an Alternative to Institutionalized Care. A Compilation of Home Health Care Delivery Cost Studies Including Statistics and Examples of Alternative Use to Institutionalization" (Kalamazoo, Mich., 1976), p. 33.

5. Nancy H. Bryant, Louis Candland, and Regina Loewenstein, "Comparison of Care and Cost Outcomes for Stroke Patients with and without Home Care," *Stroke* 5 (January/February 1974):54.

6. J. D. Hill, Jr., J. R. Hampton, and J. R. A. Mitchell, "A Randomized Trial of Home-Versus-Hospital Management for Patients with Suspected Myocardial Infarction," *Lancet* 1 (April 1978):837-41.

7. "Homemade Heart Care," *Family Health/Today's Health* 9 (June 1977):54.

8. Office of Program Analysis, Planning and Budgeting, Health Services Administration, "Home Care — An Agenda for Action" (New York, 1974), p. 3.

9. U.S., Department of Health, Education, and Welfare, "Home Health Care, Report on the Regional Public Hearings" (Washington, D.C.: Government Printing Office, 1976), p. 55.

10. "Home Health Services in the United States. A Report to the Special Committee on Aging, U.S. Senate," (Washington, D.C.: Government Printing Office, 1972), p. 39.

For Further Reading

Boronson, Warren. "Getting Well at Home," *Money* 6 (October 1977):115.

"Connecticut Testing Home Care for Aged," *Aging* 223 (May 1973):8.

Martinson, Ida Marie, ed. *Home Care for the Dying Child; Professional and Family Perspectives.* New York: Appleton-Century-Crofts, 1976.

Nourse, A. E. "Can You Provide Hospital Care at Home?" *Better Homes and Gardens,* February 1972, p. 26.

Rossman, Isadore J. *The Family Handbook of Home Nursing and Medical Care.* New York: Random House, 1968.

Stolten, Jane Henry. *Home Care.* Boston: Little, Brown and Co., 1975.

Resource Guide

National Council for Homemaker-Home Health Aide Services, Inc.
67 Irving Place
New York, New York 10003
(212) 674-4990

This agency has published a new directory of homemaker and home health aid services throughout the country. The directory is designed for use by information and referral agencies, corporate personnel departments, governmental units, libraries, families, and individuals. Regular supplements will be issued to keep the volume up to date. Copies may be ordered for $10 by writing to the council.

Council of Home Health Agencies and Community Health Services
National League for Nursing
10 Columbus Circle
New York, New York 10019
(212) 582-1022

The council, a division of the National League for Nursing, assists agencies and communities in the development, improvement, and evaluation of services. It also represents member agencies in legislative activity and promotes research and demonstration projects in community health programs.

Upjohn Health Care Services
3651 Van Rick Drive
Kalamazoo, Michigan 49002
(616) 385-6851

Upjohn is one of the largest private corporations which provides home health care services. They have local offices throughout the country.

National Association of Home Health Agencies
426 C Street N.E.
Washington, D.C. 20002
(202) 547-1717

An association of agencies that provide home care services. They have liaisons with consumer groups. The association is involved in lobbying and educating member agencies about home care legislation through a newsletter and educational programs.

Center for Ambulatory Care
840 N. Lake Shore Drive
Chicago, Illinois 60611
(312) 280-6000

A division of the American Hospital Association, the center oversees policy development for hospital involvement in home care services. They sponsor educational programs geared to managers and medical and nursing staffs of home care programs.

Consumer Notes

1. Think about and discuss with other members of your family the advantages of home health care: comfort for the patient, the fact that relaxation and security can help healing take place faster, and the knowledge that family members won't be separated from one another.
2. Talk with the person who is ill — find out her feelings about being taken care of at home. Is she enthusiastic about it or is she afraid she will be a burden on the family?
3. Discuss the drawbacks and disadvantages of home care — it is always a big responsibility for the family that chooses it.
4. Assess the physical layout of your house. Is it conducive to taking care of a sick person? Find out the distance between your house and the nearest hospital in case of emergency. (You should acquaint yourself with emergency procedures as well.)
5. Do you have physician cooperation in your home health care plan? In some states, physician participation is required. Check with your local health department to find out the regulations in your state.

6. Do you have other members of your family (i.e., those not living with you) or friends who can form a support network to help you with home care? They can spell the difference between successful and unsuccessful home care.

7. Talk with professionals (doctors, nurses, social workers) to decide what your home health care needs really are. Do you need skilled nursing care? Personal care which can be handled by a home health aid? Or social services like homemaking help or transportation? Find out what kind of equipment you will need and if the patient requires some kind of therapy.

8. Remember hospitals, local health departments, and visiting nurse associations are good places to start your search for home health care help.

9. In hiring a home health care agency, find out the following information: What services do they provide? What services do they subcontract for? Whom do they subcontract from? How do they supervise personnel? Do they promise some continuity of care? Are they certified for Medicaid/Medicare reimbursement? What are their fees? Are they a public, nonprofit, or proprietary agency?

10. Before accepting any home health care professional into your home, find out the following information: What exactly are her responsibilities? Who supervises her? What is his training? Is he licensed? How many times a week will she come to your home? Who pays him — you or the agency? What is his fee?

11. Try to estimate how much home health care will cost you and compare it to other options. (In most cases, home health care will be your most economical choice.) Check with your insurance company to see if they reimburse home health care services (and what, if any, limitations they put on that reimbursement), or if the patient is qualified for Medicaid/Medicare.

12. Watch out for the pitfalls of home health care: duplication of services, fragmentation of services, the inability to provide preventive care.

13. Check into the credentials of the home health agency you hire as thoroughly as possible. There have been abuses in the home health care field similar to those in nursing homes. Until a national standard is set, you have to work on the philosophy, "Buyer, beware."

chapter four

Walk-In Surgery

Rebecca Christian

What could you have in common with a pregnant mother and her six-year-old son who needs minor surgery, an uninsured foreign worker with a hernia, and an executive who is torn between undergoing a surgical procedure and taking an important business trip? If you (or a member of your family) are faced with the possibility of minor surgery, you might, as these people did, decide to use an ambulatory surgery facility instead of a hospital. Ambulatory surgery centers not only can save you time and money, but they also can offer you care that is more personal and tailored to your particular needs.

What Is Ambulatory Care?

In the most general sense, ambulatory patients are those who are able to walk around — they aren't confined to their beds. Extending that idea, ambulatory surgery has come to mean minor surgery which does not require an overnight stay in the hospital; the patient walks in and walks out the same day. For the mother and her young son that meant avoiding a traumatic and exhausting three-day hospital stay; for the foreign worker it translated into a savings of hundreds of dollars; and for the business executive it spelled the difference between a trip that might have been medically hazardous and one that was taken in good health.

Born in the seventies, ambulatory surgery centers are for basically healthy people who need only minor surgery. In fact, according to David Seitzman, M.D., a Washington urologist and executive director of the Center for Ambulatory Surgery, Inc. (CASI), 20 to 40 percent of the surgical procedures done in this country can be done on an outpatient basis. However, as Dr. Seitzman points out, at the present time only 5 percent are done that way. When you think about the tremendous costs of health care today, and realize that one alternative that can be used to contain those costs is surgery on an outpatient basis, that discrepancy becomes even more important.

Ambulatory surgery can be performed in either a freestanding center designed solely for the ambulatory surgical patient, or in an outpatient surgery unit of a hospital. As long as your doctor approves and you feel satisfied with the facility's reputation and credentials, which of the two types of facilities you choose will probably make little difference in the medical outcome of your case. Prices are comparable, and although some hospital-affiliated Blue Cross and Blue Shield plans resist reimbursing the freestanding centers, most private insurance carriers encourage their members to go to either.

Going under trade names like Surgicenter® and Minor Surgery Center®, the freestanding units are privately funded and not affiliated with a hospital, regardless of the hospital affiliations of the surgeons who perform some of their surgery there. In this chapter, they will be called **freestanding ambulatory surgery centers.** The term will refer to centers where a variety of minor surgical operations is performed, as opposed to a one-procedure facility like a family planning clinic or plastic surgery unit.

Generally hospital based, and always hospital affiliated, the hospital facilities sometimes operate as separate cost-centers and are sometimes subsidized by the hospital. In this chapter they will be called **outpatient surgery units.** The term **ambulatory facility** will refer to either type of facility.

Is Ambulatory Surgery for You?

One-day, walk-in surgery and ambulatory facilities are particularly appropriate for:
   • patients undergoing diagnostic techniques;

- patients who can't afford the time off from work or
  away from home that hospitalization would require;
- patients who are uninsured;
- children or other patients who would be traumatized
  by being away from home overnight; and
- patients whose surgery is so minor that it does not
  require full hospital care.

Examples of procedures commonly done in the ambulatory setting include: diagnostic procedures like cystoscopy (examinations of bladder using a cystoscope); dilatation and curettage (or D & C, a stretching of the cervix and removal of material or growths from uterus); breast biopsy (removal and examination of breast tissue for diagnostic purposes); minor oral surgery (extraction, fracture correction); minor orthopedic procedures (such as removal of bunions); diagnostic laparoscopy (visual examination of the interior of the abdomen); tubal ligation (for voluntary female sterilization); and vasectomy (removal of the ductus of the vas deferens to sterilize men).

Ambulatory surgery is not for every patient. It is emphatically not for those who are dangerously ill and it is normally not for those who are high operative risks because of diabetes, hypertension, or other serious physical problems. An accredited facility will not allow a patient to be operated on without a referral from a doctor who attends the ambulatory facility. In order to remove the financial incentive for performing operations, physicians (except possibly a staff anesthesiologist) are not employed by the facility full time and have no financial involvement.

If you know, for example, that you want a growth on your foot removed on an ambulatory basis, but your podiatrist does not operate at the ambulatory facility in your community, call the facility for a list of podiatrists who do perform operations there. Even a referral to the facility from one of its attending doctors will not guarantee that the surgery can be performed at the facility. High-risk patients are not rejected out of hand, but they are very carefully screened by both the physician performing the surgical procedure and the anesthesiologist who monitors the patient preoperatively.

As Marian Kennedy, R.N., director of nursing for CASI explained, her patients are generally in good health except for the one problem that brings them to the facility in the first place. People who are acutely ill are not accepted for treatment. "Now that doesn't mean we will not operate on people who have problems," she explained further, "but they are people who have known problems and they are under the care of internal medicine specialists who consult closely with the surgeons." For instance, a diabetic and an 88-year-old man who, although elderly, was a "very healthy individual" were both operated on at CASI. Such patients are painstakingly monitored and backup systems (which are mandated by the society which accredits ambulatory facilities) exist for their protection.

You Can Save Time and Money

The biggest advantages of ambulatory surgery are that it saves time and money and provides the patient with streamlined, often more personalized care.

Estimates of savings for outpatient surgery versus hospital surgery range from $100 to $900* depending on where the surgery is performed and what type of operation is done.[1] Because the ambulatory facility will often assess you a lump sum regardless of your need for "extras" like intravenous feeding, fruit juice, phone calls, and bandages, you know in advance exactly what the procedure will cost. The lump sum, however, will *not* include your surgeon's fees or fees for the diagnostic procedures you undergo before admission to the facility. You will have to find out ahead of time from the surgeon what his or her fee will be. Administrators at the facilities expect their doctors to charge reasonable and customary rates, but they exert no direct control over the surgeon's fees and won't be able to tell you how much he or she will charge. The surgeon's fee is strictly between you and the surgeon. In addition to the actual dollar savings you gain from having ambulatory surgery instead of hospital surgery, you save time. Even a basically healthy person undergoing minor surgery at 8:00 A.M. in a hospital would probably be admitted the night before and discharged the day after surgery, resulting in a two-night stay. Patients undergoing diagnostic procedures such as breast biopsies are particularly inconvenienced by this overnight hospitalization. If the tissue is negative, they want to hurry home; if it's positive, they often need to make child care or sick-leave arrangements for their upcoming days in the hospital.

---

*The costs for a typical tonsillectomy and adenoidectomy are from $225 to $245 in an ambulatory surgery facility while the same operation would cost from $800 to $1,100 and include several days of hospitalization when performed on an inpatient basis in a hospital setting. In both cases, the prices do *not* include the surgeon's or anesthesiologist's fees.

Some hospitals retain patients for a standard amount of time after surgery regardless of the speed with which they recover. Sometimes "standard stays" are a matter of habit as much as medical imperative. As any mother of a 25-year-old can tell you, a generation ago women were hospitalized twice as long after delivery as they are now.

Even in the traditional hospital setting, doctors are beginning to realize the logic behind releasing patients after "right stay" rather than "standard stay."

A study of patients who underwent routine abdominal surgery in a British hospital showed that the 47 who were evaluated and discharged on a "right stay" basis were hospitalized an average of two days less than those discharged after the standard ten days. A follow-up report showed that the medical progress of the two groups was comparable. The time in which they returned to work did not differ significantly. The main differences were that patients in the "right stay" group complained less often about the length of time they spent in the hospital, and they were slightly freer of minor postoperative symptoms such as disturbed sleep. The report concluded that shorter stays, though often overlooked, can reduce demands on bed space and better serve the patient, who usually wants to be home as soon as possible.[2]

Although children and the elderly may be less concerned about time lost, for some patients, the old saying that "time is money" holds true. A study conducted by the National Bureau of Economic Research in Stanford, California, on who used surgery in 1963 and 1970 showed some interesting income and educational differences. People in the high-income brackets generally underwent more operations than the less affluent. But highly educated, prosperous men aged 20 to 64 were less likely to undergo surgery than less educated men in their income group.

The researchers speculate that doctors may recommend surgery less often for members of the high-education, high-income group because they think these patients will comply with alternate treatment in home conditions conducive to successful outpatient care. They added, however, that the patients themselves may avoid surgery because their time is too valuable to spend in the hospital.[3]

Similarly, money that might have to be spent on child care can be saved and often walk-in surgery means that a spouse won't have to leave work for a few days to take care of the home or be with the patient in the hospital. Lost time, surgeon's fees, and hospitalization charges are not the only costs of surgery in the traditional hospital setting. Indirectly, utilization of surgery also drives insurance premiums up.

Hospitalization doesn't necessarily expedite recovery either, according to CASI's Dr. Seitzman. Based on surgery experiences in both hospitals and ambulatory settings, it is his opinion that some of his patients in the hospital "tend to spend extra time there because they're confined. They have a tendency to feel ill because of this. Whereas, if you go home, although you may have the same degree of pain, you're at home. If you're home, you are ambulatory and you may not feel as sick."

The only other patients at an ambulatory facility will be ambulatory surgery candidates like yourself. That means you will not be bumped off the schedule by an emergency case, as you might be on the traditional hospital operating room schedule. (Administrators at the ambulatory facilities admit, however, that the doctors who perform surgery there may be detained at the office or hospital, but they say such a situation would only delay your operation, and only very rarely postpone it until the next day.)

With lower fees, fewer forms to fill out, the probability that you won't be bumped for an emergency case, no overnight stays, and often cheery, well-designed facilities, ambulatory centers present the consumer with a wealth of advantages.

Ambulatory Surgery and
Your Insurance Plan

Many people believe that one of the reasons health costs have become so exorbitant is that the comprehensive coverage insurance plans have made people lose touch with the prices of the health care they use. We tend to feel that our insurance will take care of everything, that we are shoppers with a blank check. If the patient has a decent insurance plan with a deductible, there's moderate concern about cost, but certainly not enough to make the patient count all the dollars or challenge a doctor or hospital if the total cost seems too high. If the patient has 100 percent coverage, where everything is covered from the first dollar spent, then both doctor and patient tend

A Good Experience

John I. Smith, a photographic manufacturer in Washington, D.C., is self-employed, uninsured, and committed to the care of his invalid mother. Although the type of surgery he had done, a hernia operation, is performed on an ambulatory basis very rarely, he wanted to avoid hospitalization for personal, financial, and business reasons. His experience is a good example of how outpatient surgery can be tailored to fit individual needs.

I stepped off my bike very hard into some guttering on the street one afternoon. I felt some warmth in my groin right afterward. It wasn't discomfort really, just a peculiar feeling of localized warmth. I felt it a couple more times and noticed a pouch on my groin. So I went to my surgeon. He said surgery would have to be done.

Going to the hospital just wasn't feasible for me. For one thing, I'm self-employed so I don't have Blue Cross. But more than money, it was a time problem. My mother is terminally ill and I take care of her. It just wasn't possible for me to go to the hospital for the six days it would normally take for the surgery I needed. Time was the overriding consideration. So my surgeon suggested I go to a nearby clinic that did surgery on a walk-in, walk-out basis. He thought I would find the doctor and the clinic attractive.

I wasn't really concerned about what would happen if there were complications. I felt the clinic was adequately equipped and I knew there were hospitals two blocks away. I was concerned, though, that I might have considerable discomfort.

When I went to the clinic, I thought it was more like an airline office or a good restaurant than a clinic, which was nice. I liked the color scheme very much. The recovery room's design made you want to get up and live again. I guess it was a little futuristic, a little 2001, but I liked that.

Everything was explained to me and I felt I was getting a lot of attention. I needed a lot of attention to be operated on and released in that amount of time. I was under general anesthetic for 40 minutes and on my way home in 2 hours. I was told not to drink alcohol for 24 hours after the surgery and to come back for a postoperative check in four days. I misunderstood, however, and thought they said a week. In four days they were back on the phone with me saying, "Where are you?"

When I got home after the surgery, mother and I had nurses eight hours a day, but I took care of us the rest of the time. I was able to handle both of us the first night after the surgery. After three weeks I was back on my ordinary schedule, which I worked up to gradually.

to relax and spend insurance money freely. But the sad truth is that, in the end, we all pay a price for our false security.

According to Dr. Seitzman, this attitude has kept many people from realizing the benefits of ambulatory surgery. "If you tell a patient that you can do something equally as well, equally as safely, but cheaper," he says, "the answer that you frequently will get is, 'But I pay my insurance, let them pay for it. I have insurance coverage, why should I bother or care?' We try to get across to the patient that he has to pay his premiums, and that those premiums are going up, but people don't think about that."

Similarly, because physicians are paid by third-party carriers, they don't necessarily concern themselves with cost. "A patient may go to one hospital or another," explains Seitzman, "depending on the physician's preference — not on the cost of one facility or another. The choice is done on the basis of 'Where am I going to be that day?' or who referred the patient."

While patients may be oblivious to costs covered by insurance, the insurance companies naturally are not. Douglas Hawthorne, assistant administrator of the Presbyterian Hospital of Dallas, said insurance companies have not reduced premiums even when costs to patients are less because of shorter overnight stays. Therefore, ambulatory surgery saves insurance companies more money than it saves hospitals, he said.

Joseph Clune, manager of the group claims division of Metropolitan Life Insurance, is enthusiastic about the savings involved for the patient, as well as the beneficial psychological effects of ambulatory facilities. "Use of the centers depends in part on surgeons' awareness of them and whether their patients know about them as an option," he said. "We've found that the patient saves 43 to 52 percent by having surgery done in a freestanding center." Having personally visited 170 facilities for ambulatory surgery and accepting only 53 of them for reimbursement, Clune admitted some facilities are substandard.*

---

*It's important to note that Metropolitan Life's standards are very high. Many of the facilities which Joseph Clune rejects are one-procedure facilities such as abortion clinics and plastic surgery units. In order to qualify for reimbursement the facility must perform a variety of surgical procedures. When evaluating a freestanding ambulatory unit, he checks not only for cleanliness and general organization but also for the number of fully equipped operating rooms; the emergency, laboratory, and sterilization facilities; patient flow; staff competence and training; and many other features.

When the facilities became popular, Metropolitan Life had to arrange a way for the privately funded centers to be approved because contracts between the company and the groups it covers mention only hospital reimbursement. The criteria Metropolitan Life follow in accepting a facility for full reimbursement are similar to those used by the Freestanding Ambulatory Surgical Association (FASA), the accrediting body for freestanding centers.

For example, FASA standards require that the physical and emotional well-being of patients and their families is provided for; that emergency services are available; and that careful statistics and medical records are kept. The standards also outline the need for a surgical review committee to review surgery performed at a center and a community advisory board, neither of whose members have a financial interest in the facility. General standards concerning matters such as fire codes, personnel policies, and sanitation and supportive services are also outlined.

It is up to you to find out which will be the safest, most economical way for you to have your surgery. Always call your insurance company before deciding on a facility to see if they will reimburse you for surgery done at an ambulatory center.

Ambulatory Surgery for Children

For children and their parents, the time and money saved by ambulatory surgery may not be as important as the trauma spared.

In a five-year study of over 5,000 children undergoing surgery on an outpatient basis at Children's Hospital in Jamaica, West Indies, there were no deaths or major complications. According to Mohammed El-Shafie, M.D., and Robert P. Shapiro, M.D., of the Medical College of Ohio, who reviewed the results of the surgery, in over 2,500 of the general surgical cases, the incidence of complications was 2.7 percent. The most common complication was superficial wound infections, which occurred in 1.58 percent of the patients, none of whom required hospital admission.

The researchers also noted that, "Parent cooperation played an important role in the program. Due to the shortage of qualified nurses, parents were encouraged to participate actively in looking after their children in the preoperative and postoperative periods, and did so with enthusiasm and competence."[4]

Even when nurses are plentiful, most parents are happy to be involved. Jo Anne Burka of Potomac, Maryland, was only too glad to help in the preoperative and postoperative care of her six-year-old son when he underwent ambulatory surgery for a minor urological problem. Mrs. Burka and her physician husband were allowed to stay with their child both in the preoperative holding area immediately before surgery and in the recovery room immediately after. Dr. Burka was in the operating room during the procedure. The Burkas' experiences with a freestanding ambulatory surgery center are described in the inset on the following page.

Dr. Robert C. Brownlee, writing in *Pediatrics* magazine, believes that much more pediatric surgery can be performed on an ambulatory basis than is currently being done. "One-third to one-half of all surgery cases in children can be done appropriately as outpatients," he writes. And he further believes that, "Perhaps after more experience with this approach, we can look forward to an even greater percentage falling into the day-care category."[5]

In Dr. Brownlee's opinion, the most important advantage of ambulatory surgery for your young child is the savings in emotional costs. The trauma of separation from home and from you that often accompanies hospitalization can be avoided. Usually ambulatory centers allow you to be by your child's side until the actual surgery is done, and to be there while she recovers. Then you can take her home to her familiar bed and room, brothers, sisters, and friends. Still another advantage of same-day surgery is a reduction in the risk of postoperative infection since the child won't be in the hospital. Of course, as with all medical procedures, you should explain to your child what will happen to him. But at least you can reassure him that you'll be with him all the time and that he can come home as soon as the procedure is over.

The types of pediatric surgery differ from facility to facility (as do the types of adult surgery), although generally any procedure the facility performs on adults — such as removal of warts or skin lesions — can be performed on children there as well. Some types of surgery usually performed only on children are also done at most ambulatory surgery centers. For example, you might want to check into an ambulatory facility if your doctor advises you to have your child's tonsils or adenoids removed, his umbilical hernia repaired, or the opening of

A Child's Surgery

Jo Anne Burka and her husband, Barrett, decided on ambulatory surgery for their son on the basis of previous experiences they had had with him in traditional hospital settings.

My son needed the type of surgery that could be performed in an ambulatory setting — enlargement of the opening of the penis. He had undergone surgery for an undescended testicle when he was three. He was hospitalized again for a tonsillectomy and adenoidectomy when he was five. His surgery at age three was especially traumatic because he was so young. He had to be hospitalized the night before, although he wasn't really ill. Of course, the nurses had to spend some of the night looking after him. I was pregnant and afterward I was exhausted from lost sleep while he was in the hospital. There were no facilities for parents to stay overnight. It was a 2½-day ordeal.

I know from experiences as a surgical patient in hospitals that the staff is often overworked. When you are not critically ill but are unable to care for yourself, you hesitate to make extra demands.

If the type of surgery needed can be performed in an ambulatory surgical unit, it's less traumatic for the patient. The family is better able to handle postoperative care. Having my son's surgery done on an ambulatory basis made everything much easier. Because of the large picture window in the preoperative room, we were able to see him as he was being wheeled out of the operating room. As soon as they had him ready, we went in to see him. I was the first thing he saw when he woke up. In fact, I was able to assist the nurse during his recovery.

I thought the ambulatory center was just fantastic. There was so much obvious concern for both the patient and his family. The staff works regular hours, they aren't exhausted from overwork, and their only job is to take care of people like you.

his penis enlarged. Surgeons at some facilities also perform plastic surgery on children.

Freestanding versus Hospital Affiliated

Currently, a battle about the merits of the two types of ambulatory facilities — hospital affiliated and freestanding — wages between

their administrators. Yet, not one of the freestanding or hospital proponents interviewed for this chapter argued that actual medical care
is better in the type of facility they prefer.

Drs. Wallace Reed and John Ford (who is no longer with the
facility) founded the first freestanding surgery facility under the registered name Surgicenter® in Phoenix in 1970. Why? Reed said:

> *Starting the Surgicenter® was an attempt to respond to criticism about
> doctors not being interested in the rising cost of medical care. I wanted to
> show that there are doctors who are interested. I put my reputation and
> money on the line to show it.*

> *We do not practice defensively [as protection against malpractice suits]
> — that's one of the ways we save money. We don't do extra X-rays —
> we accept them from other places. We do our own simple tests, but we
> don't charge extra for them; they are included in our lump fee. We've
> given ourselves a ceiling, in other words. We don't add on an extra
> charge for IVs, drugs, oxygen, and other items.*

After freestanding surgery centers came into being, hospitals
were quick to follow suit with their own outpatient surgery units,
built with the encouragement of the American Hospital Association
(AHA).

Since the Minor Surgery Center® of Wichita opened in Kansas
in 1974, for example, three other Wichita hospitals have begun to
offer ambulatory surgery. M. Robert Knapp, M.D., president of the
Wichita facility, welcomes the proliferation of outpatient care. He
said that in every instance he knows of where a freestanding center
was built, a hospital in the same area has created or enlarged an
outpatient surgical service soon afterward. "We do have evidence in
Wichita that more outpatient surgery starts to be done at the hospital
when the freestanding center is introduced," he explained. "But we
don't compete with the traditional system as much as complement it.
I do think, however, that the ambulatory center offers advantages
over the hospital outpatient facility."

One of the primary advantages, according to Knapp, is cost.
Although the charges are not necessarily lower at a freestanding facility, he pointed out that, "The overall cost of operating the freestanding center is less and ultimately the hospital is going to pass on that
extra cost to the consumer."

In fact, the main argument over freestanding versus hospital-affiliated clinics seems to center around the cost effectiveness of the latter. Proponents of freestanding centers maintain that because they are so small and simple, they have to be more cost effective. It is also argued that in many hospitals, costs are shared among departments. As Knapp explains, "The patient with a minor operation is helping to pay for the hospital laundry, medical school, the cafeteria, and sophisticated equipment."[6]

Hospital administrator Douglas Hawthorne disagrees. He maintains that fashioning an outpatient unit from an existing portion of the hospital makes good sense, and that such a unit is cost effective if operated as a separate cost-center of the hospital. In fact, Hawthorne's Presbyterian Hospital's Day Surgery Unit was created before a freestanding surgery center that eventually folded.

But Robert Williams, executive director of FASA, argues that hospitals know that, "there is more money to be made on the hospital inpatient than the hospital outpatient." With that knowledge, he asks, "How can a hospital, from a financial standpoint, be totally committed to a program which empties inpatient beds?" He charges that ambulatory surgical units are often expected to share services with other departments in the hospital to the detriment of the outpatient facility, which often does not receive top priority.

There are still other equally important factors to take into consideration when choosing one facility over the other. For instance, emergency backup facilities are right there if you go to a hospital-based center. "Complications like excessive bleeding or nausea develop in the operating room or recovery room in only about 3 percent of the cases," explains Hawthorne, "but it is nice to know you're right there for more extensive treatment if you need it."

On the other hand, freestanding centers often can give you more personal care. "We're concerned with the individual — not just another number coming down the line," says Knapp. A former American Hospital Association staff specialist in ambulatory care, Eugene Wood, flatly dismissed the arguments over the relative merits of the two types of facilities. "The difference is that the freestanding centers are not under the auspices of a hospital. Surgery is surgery. It doesn't matter where you have it," he said.

When asked how a patient can safeguard herself against facilities that are not up to par, Wood said he would trust his physician to make that decision. You may feel, however, that you would prefer more responsibility in choosing where you will have your surgery.

How to Get the Quality Care You Want

Not all ambulatory surgery facilities are created equal, nor are all of them run by dedicated people who smile lovingly at patient after patient, hour after hour, day after day. For that reason, you must step into your ambulatory surgery experience with a certain degree of awareness. Even if your surgeon is an old family friend you know you can trust, there are questions and comments only you can ask or make, to guarantee that you avoid unnecessary discomforts.

Ambulatory surgery facilities are open only during business hours, and every effort is made to discharge patients by the end of the afternoon. That doesn't mean that you will be kicked out into the street still woozy if you're physically unable to leave by 5:00 P.M. or your ride is late. It does mean that if the operation goes smoothly and your recovery is routine, you will be on your way home in at least a few hours.

Part of the reason that you are not retained overnight is that in an ambulatory surgery facility, you are not as heavily anesthetized as you might be in a hospital. According to Dr. Reed, just enough anesthetic to keep the patient pain free and provide suitable operating conditions for the surgeon is administered during surgery at his facility, thereby saving the patient time and money.

As past hospital surgical patients can testify, some hospitals administer enough anesthetic to keep you hazy for hours after reaching the recovery room. Using minimal anesthetic can backfire, however, according to one patient operated on at an East Coast facility. On an anonymous comment card returned to the institution after recovery at home the patient wrote: "As for the pain, the doctor said I absorbed the anesthetic very rapidly, so he had to inject more before the surgery was complete. So I was in great pain before I could get home and take medication."

Even so, the patient rated the service at the facility excellent, and added that she would return should she need a minor elective procedure again.

In the inset on pages 122-23, a well-educated and health-conscious woman went into a hospital-affiliated ambulatory surgery unit for laparascopy sterilization surgery. Although all the preliminary procedures went quite well, her overall impression of the experience has been tinged by her memories of recovery room disorganization, the lack of warmth among recovery room personnel, and terrible feelings of nausea. Learning from her experience, you may want to make special arrangements before surgery begins so that you will have at least an hour to lie flat on a bed in a quiet and peaceful area.

If the idea of being whisked in and out of surgery makes you anxious, ask to be posted early in the morning at a freestanding ambulatory surgery center or go to a hospital outpatient surgery unit so you can be admitted to the adjoining hospital should a problem arise. (Obviously, patients from freestanding centers can be admitted to hospitals, too, although they will have farther to go.)

Of course, if the idea of "in-and-out" surgery makes you very anxious, or if you would prefer full hospital care, then an ambulatory center is not for you. As Douglas Hawthorne explained, "We don't always admit patients [to the hospital] from our ambulatory surgery center because of a medical complication. It may be a case of patient apprehension. For example, parents might decide that they would feel more comfortable with their child hospitalized overnight rather than taking him home. That's fine with us." Be honest with yourself — you're the one who will have to undergo the experience.

If you are going to have an ambulatory surgery experience, you should be sure that the freestanding ambulatory surgery center you go to is accredited by FASA (Freestanding Ambulatory Surgical Association) or is at least a member of it and has applied for accreditation. Patients undergoing outpatient surgery in a hospital should make sure the hospital is accredited by JCAH (Joint Commission on Accreditation of Hospitals).

To locate ambulatory surgery facilities of either type within your community, call the county or regional health center, ask a knowledgeable doctor, or check at nearby hospitals. FASA claimed 65 member facilities in 1978. Marian Kessler from the AHA's Office of Research Affairs said in June 1978 that to their knowledge, no accurate tally of hospital outpatient surgery units exists, although such a study (by AHA) is under way.

After you have decided that ambulatory surgery is right for you temperamentally, checked with an insurance carrier, established that the facility is up to standard (by checking accreditation and licensure, asking the doctor, touring it), found an attending doctor, given your medical history, undergone the appropriate lab work for admission, and ascertained what you will be charged by *both* the facility and the surgeon, you should be ready for the procedure.

Problems with Outpatient Surgery

*After Jane Clossman and her doctor decided on laparoscopy steril-
ization surgery (an operation in which plastic rings are used to
clamp off the Fallopian tubes), she was told that it was now an
ambulatory procedure. She went to a hospital-affiliated center, and
was told to check into the hospital at 7:00 A.M. Friday and that she
would be released by noon or shortly thereafter.*

I was pleased that my surgery could be performed as an "in-and-
out" process. I wouldn't have to take time from work or need to explain a night in the hospital to my four-year-old. Also, I'm not too fond
of institutions and preferred to spend as little time in the hospital as
necessary.

The preliminaries to the surgery went quickly and well. On
Thursday afternoon, I reported to the in-and-out desk for tests. My file
was ready and there was no lineup at the testing station. In 40 minutes
I was back out on the sidewalk, electrocardiogram, blood, and urine
testing complete.

Friday morning directions were simple: "No eating or drinking
after midnight." My husband dropped me off, and went on to take our
son to nursery school. I signed a few consent papers, changed into a
hospital gown, and locked up my things in a locker. The in-and-out
surgery unit is complete with its own operating room, recovery, and
waiting areas. Like the ugly, wrinkled, green hospital gown, it was
efficient but dreary, located in the basement of the hospital.

Sitting in the area outside the operating room, I had a short talk
with the anesthesiologist about my medical history. He told me what
procedures he'd use and that the anesthetic would be sodium pento-
thol. Then my doctor walked in, brisk and cheerful, dressed in his
operating greens. We talked about the physical reactions I could expect after the operation. He mentioned some chest pains from the gas
used and the general tenderness of the incision. But I'd be ready for
normal activities by Sunday, he assured me.

An aid told me it was time to go into the operating room, so I
followed her in, climbed on the table, and chatted a bit with the
people in the room. I remember my doctor saying "good night" as I
got the anesthetic.

The procedure took about an hour. I woke up in the recovery
area feeling confused and drugged. My doctor was there and talked
with me twice as I was coming out of the anesthetic. I was grateful for
a familiar face and voice.

Then a nurse started to elevate the bed, announcing that I had to
get up soon in order to be able to sit up for an hour before I could leave
the hospital. The elevation felt awful. I started to get nauseated. I was

hardly adjusted to that when the nurse asked me to get up and move over to a chair.

With my mind intent on the fact that I did want to get out of there as quickly as possible, I moved to the chair with her help. For the next hour I sat there nauseated and feeling extremely uncomfortable. My lower back ached, making sitting in the uncomfortable chair an endurance test. When I mentioned the back pain, one nurse said that the operating table I'd been on had a peculiar slant and it tended to affect people's backs. No apology, just a fact. I got one antinausea tablet but that didn't seem to help.

I have bad memories of that recovery scene. The woman sitting next to me was also very nauseated. We were in an alcove separated from the recovery room by a small screen, so the sounds of other people coming out of anesthetic were in the background. An aid sat across from us reading some magazines. Staff in the area behind the screen were talking about their lunches, the weather, their weekend plans. I felt angry at their conversation, and just wanted a place where I could lie down and be quiet.

As soon as the required hour was up, I told the nurse I was ready to go home. Even though I didn't feel like standing up, I couldn't endure sitting there any longer. An aid helped me to the area where I got my street clothes back on and then walked me to the waiting area to meet my husband. I felt immense relief at being with him. Although he couldn't do much for the discomfort either, he did care about it.

We had an hour-and-a-half drive home, another time for endurance. Then in my own bed, I got a heating pad for my back and had quiet space for myself. By evening, I felt much better. On Sunday, I didn't feel normal, but was up and around the house.

Looking back at the experience, I believe the value of quick in-and-out surgery still rests in its ability to get the patient home — fast. In fact, the incision hadn't been a problem at all. But because of my strong reaction to the anesthetic and my sore back, I wish I could have slowed the process down a bit. I know I would have appreciated a quiet area and the chance to rest on my back a little longer. I think about the impersonality of the staff, and I wonder if the transitory nature of in-and-out patients tends to produce a lack of warmth.

For the future, I know it's important to have clear information about what aftereffects to expect, including possible effects of the anesthetic. I'd like to get a good picture of the postoperative procedure in the hospital and know if there are alternate options available if I felt that bad again. Could I slow the process down or get a bed space? For me it was very important to have a person I felt comfortable with for the trip home. Generally, I think being prepared for that physical low might make getting through the whole thing a lot easier.

It is important that you have an adult pick you up and drive you home and perhaps stay with you a few hours or all night. You should ask for postoperative instructions concerning food, drink, activity, return to work and follow-up visits. Know how to contact the surgeon should a problem arise.

With this preparation, a good surgeon, a good anesthesiologist, a basically healthy body, an eagerness to get well and no unexpected complications, your reaction to ambulatory surgery should be as enthusiastic as that of the patient who raved about his visit to an ambulatory facility:

"Excellent service, convenient location, pleasant surroundings, economical cost, and enthusiastic staff — an exciting concept whose time has come."

Notes

1. Robert C. Brownlee, Jr., "The Case for Day-Care Surgery," *Pediatrics* 60 (October 1977):650-51.

2. J. E. Simpson et al., " 'Right Stay' in Hospital after Surgery: Randomised Controlled Trial," *British Medical Journal* 1 (11 June 1977):1514-16.

3. Claire Bombardier et al., "Socioeconomic Factors Affecting the Utilization of Surgical Operations," *New England Journal of Medicine* 297 (29 September 1977):699-705.

4. Mohammed El-Shafie and Robert P. Shapiro, "Outpatient Pediatric Surgery in a Developing Country," *Pediatrics* 60 (October 1977):600-602.

5. Brownlee, "Case for Day-Care Surgery," pp. 650-51.

6. As quoted in "Now Surgery at 'Discount Rates,' " *U.S. News and World Report*, 18 July 1977, p. 73.

For Further Reading

Cooper, Ron. "Day-Surgery Centers Snip Away Red Tape, Put Clamp on Costs," *Wall Street Journal*, 23 January 1976, p. 1.

Crile, George Jr. *Surgery*. New York: Delacorte Press/Seymour Lawrence, 1978.

Graham, James, and Donald G. Cooley. *So You're Going to Have Surgery*. New York: Hawthorn Books, 1970.

Isenberg, Seymour, and L. M. Elting. *The Consumer's Guide to Successful Surgery*. New York: St. Martin's Press, 1978.

"New Centers for One-Day Surgery," *Medical World News*, 16 (27 January 1975):65–66.

O'Donovan, Thomas. *Ambulatory Surgical Centers: Development and Management*. Germantown, Md.: Aspen Systems Corp., 1976.

Resource Guide

American Board of Surgery, Inc.
1617 John F. Kennedy Boulevard
Philadelphia, Pennsylvania 19103
(215) 568-4000

Their "Booklet of Information" will tell you how surgeons are trained and certified.

Freestanding Ambulatory Surgical Association (FASA)
1040 E. McDowell Road
Phoenix, Arizona 85006
(602) 258-1521

If you call or write FASA, they will try to help you locate an ambulatory surgery facility in your area. They will also send you a copy of their "Facility Standards" upon request.

Your local or state health department might be able to help you find a nearby center, too. Try calling hospitals in your area as well to see if they do outpatient surgery on a regular basis.

Accreditation Council for Ambulatory Health Care and the Joint Commission on Accreditation of Hospitals
875 N. Michigan Avenue
Chicago, Illinois 60611
(312) 642-6061

This organization accredits not only freestanding ambulatory surgery units but *all* ambulatory facilities in the United States, including community health centers, HMOs, group practices, student health services and other ambulatory facilities which meet their eligibility requirements. If you want to know more about ambulatory health care, you can request a free copy of the Ambulatory Health Care newsletter and ask to be put on their mailing list. Their newsletter lists all accredited facilities. Also available by sending $7.50 to their Publication Department is their Accreditation Manual for Ambulatory Health Care which explains what the standards are for evaluating ambulatory facilities and how consumers can judge the quality of local facilities.

Consumer Notes

1. After you learn you may need surgery, find out about the procedure you must undergo. Ask the surgeon questions such as: How long will the operation take? What will happen if I don't have it? What kind of anesthetic will be used? How big and where will the incision be? How will I feel afterwards? How soon can I return to work, sexual relations, tub baths, sports, etc.?
2. Several consumer's guides to surgery are currently in print. (We've listed some of them in the "For Further Reading" section.) Check bookstores and libraries and read about your operation.
3. Ask the surgeon if your operation could be performed on an ambulatory basis and if he is authorized to perform ambulatory surgery at a local facility. If he isn't and you still think you want ambulatory surgery, call an ambulatory facility and ask for names of doctors who perform the operation you are going to undergo.
4. Check the credentials of the surgeon you choose. Find out how frequently he performs the surgery you are going to have. Talk to his former patients. Ask if he is board certified.
5. Call your insurance agent and see if you are covered for ambulatory surgery at any of the local facilities you are checking on.
6. Visit the ambulatory facility and ask questions. Some you might pose are: What if I don't feel well enough to go home when the facility closes? Will I have privacy during recovery? Is there a place for me to lie down in the recovery room? How close is the nearest hospital? What happens in an emergency? What is your standard fee? What does that include?

7. Ask if you can have references from other patients who have undergone surgery at the ambulatory facility.

8. Now you should be ready to make a decision. Do you feel comfortable with the idea of ambulatory surgery? Would you rather be totally "out" during surgery, even if it isn't medically necessary? What have your previous hospital experiences been? How have you reacted to surgery and anesthetic in the past? How many days would you have to be in the hospital if the surgery were not done on an ambulatory basis?

9. Find out from your surgeon what his fee will be. It is *not* included in the standard fee charged by the facility.

10. You will probably be asked to come in for routine tests a day or two before surgery. Find out if you will have any special instructions, such as overnight fasting, and how long the tests will take.

11. Ask to speak to the anesthesiologist *before* the day of the operation and find out what kind of anesthetic he thinks will be best for you. If you wait until the day of surgery, you may be too nervous to remember your questions.

12. Remember that all surgery, no matter how minor, is traumatic to your body. You'll be uncomfortable afterward, and possibly in pain. Plan to take it easy for a day or two, and find out what aftereffects to anticipate.

13. Make sure someone you are close to can take you home. You won't feel like driving or using public transportation.

New Options for Health Care at Critical Times

part three

chapter five

Having Your Baby — Your Way

Lori Breslow

For many years, there has been a standard scenario for birth in this country — a scenario which goes something like this: Upon hearing those three simple words, "This is it," from his wife, the expectant father proceeds to disintegrate into a mass of jangled nerves. In this somewhat useless state, he attempts to pack his wife, her belongings, and himself into the car to get them all to the hospital on time — a feat which often seems to be accomplished only with the help of divine intervention. Once at the hospital, the mother-to-be is wheeled off to her room while her husband is sent to the fathers' waiting room. There he paces nervously, smokes cigarettes, and drinks coffee until a nurse comes in to tell him at last that he has a new son or daughter, at which time he promptly faints. Once revived, the new family is finally united as mother and father happily beam at their new baby.

It was a scene that was repeated in hundreds of comic versions on television, in magazines, and on radio. But there was one problem: For many families the reality of birth according to this scenario was not at all funny. Unfortunately, this standard hospital birth robbed them of the vital experience of bringing their baby into the world the way they wanted to.

Changing the Scenario

Of course, the scenario described above wasn't always the norm. Prior to the 1940s, half the births in the United States took place at home. It wasn't until the 1920s and 1930s that the idea of giving birth in a hospital became popular.

Many women at first welcomed the changes that accompanied childbirth's move from home to hospital. But as birth became less a natural physiological event and more a complicated medical procedure, women began to voice some concerns. Today the entire process — from the time a woman enters the hospital until the time she leaves with her baby — is the subject of heated debate.

Problems with Hospital Birth

Many hospital births begin with a mandatory prepping — the lower pubic hair is shaved, the woman is given an enema, and she is hooked up to an IV. Prepping is supposedly done for medical reasons, but many women have complained that it is unnecessary and uncomfortable. They charge that this routine makes them feel more like a "thing" than a person and that it robs them of their individuality.

Often the next step in the process is to buckle the beltlike straps of a fetal monitor around the woman's abdomen. Originally developed to monitor babies of high-risk mothers during labor, the fetal monitor has become standard equipment for many births. (Fetal monitors can be worn externally as described above, or internal fetal monitors are inserted later in labor by literally screwing electrodes into the skin of the baby's scalp.) Some women have complained that fetal monitors are uncomfortable to wear and that they detract from the naturalness of the event. Moreover, if an internal monitor is used, the amniotic membranes, which serve as a built-in cushion for the baby's head as it descends the birth canal, must be ruptured.

In most hospitals the woman's husband or labor coach is now allowed to join her during the prepping and the hard work of labor begins. In most instances, they have to do that work without the support of a midwife or birth attendant, who, in other settings, sees to the couple's physical and emotional needs. Hospital staff, and in particular obstetricians (whose very training stresses the unusual or difficult pregnancy), have been accused not only of lacking warmth and understanding in dealing with laboring couples, but also of hindering attempts at natural childbirth.

Many women have been especially unhappy about the drugs that they are routinely being given during hospital births. It has been shown that any medication given the mother crosses the placenta to the baby, and, more importantly, that babies born to mothers who are given anesthetics during delivery are more apt to have physical and mental problems later in life. From early labor when tranquilizers, sedatives, and analgesics are given "to take the edge off of things" to regional anesthetics used to numb specific areas of the body during later labor and delivery, the birth process has become one that can be managed entirely by drugs.

Similarly, if labor doesn't proceed quickly enough, if the mother is overdue, or if the doctor and/or mother simply find it convenient to deliver at a particular time, labor can be induced. This is done by rupturing the amniotic membranes or by giving the woman Pitocin, a powerful synthetic hormone, to stimulate contractions. In a small number of cases, induction may be medically justifiable, but often it is done for the sake of convenience.

When she is ready to give birth, the woman is transferred to the delivery room — a cold, sterile, brightly lit place. Hospital policy may or may not let the baby's father go with her. With the mother flat on her back, feet in stirrups, and body draped completely with sterile sheeting, hospital delivery is a far cry from the nostalgic image of a woman giving birth in the comfort and security of her own bed.

In the majority of cases, the woman will have an episiotomy, a cut made through the perineum (the area between the vagina and the rectum), during delivery. Although episiotomy is supposedly done to prevent vaginal tearing and to keep the baby from needlessly battering his head, massage and manipulation can often prevent the former, and the fact that the baby's head is designed to withstand birth makes the latter reason untenable.

Finally, once the baby is born, he is frequently whisked away from his mother and placed in an incubator. That means that during those first precious moments of life, the baby can't be cuddled and held next to a warm, loving human body, and parents are deprived of the opportunity to communicate with their newborn. (Doctors have learned that the first minutes and hours of life are very important, for it is during this time that parents "bond" with their babies.) Mothers have also complained that hospitals are not supportive of breastfeeding, and that they and their babies are put on schedules that are convenient for the staff — but not for them.

Although, as will be discussed later in this chapter, many hospitals have made a concerted effort to move away from this kind of birth, the picture painted above has been all too real for too many families. And although women may have complained individually about the treatment they received in hospitals, their criticism was not heard. It wasn't until they — and their husbands — banded together that changes began to take place in American childbirth practices.

Creating Choices

In the late 1940s and early 1950s, Dr. Grantly Dick-Read in England and Dr. Fernand Lamaze in France began to offer women a way to deal with the pain of childbirth without using drugs.* Marjorie Karmel, an American, had used the Lamaze method in Paris, but when she wanted to use it again in America for the birth of her second child, she was unable to find a doctor who would support her desire for a nonmedicated birth. In 1958 she wrote about her experiences in a magazine article; the next year her book, *Thank You, Doctor Lamaze,* appeared. The book set off an avalanche of interest in the Lamaze method. This new interest in natural childbirth, as it was called, spurred the formation of the American Society for Psychoprophylaxis in Obstetrics (ASPO) in 1960. That same year the International Childbirth Education Association (ICEA) was formed. Both ASPO and ICEA (along with such organizations as the American Foundation for Maternal and Child Health and the National Association of Parents and Professionals for Safe Alternatives in Childbirth [NAPSAC]) began to pioneer programs in prepared childbirth.

But they also began to do something else. They began to demand something they called family-centered maternity care. Family-centered maternity care means a childbirth experience that puts the needs and desires of the family first. It promotes a process that allows

*The Lamaze method, or psychoprophylaxis, was actually developed by Soviet obstetricians based on Ivan Pavlov's work on conditioned reflexes. It is a set of exercises and breathing patterns which help women disassociate themselves from the pain of labor.

husbands and wives to become involved in their obstetrical care and in the decisions that affect how that care and the care of the newborn is handled. Childbirth is tailored to individual families within the bounds of medical safety.

One of the first innovations demanded under the family-centered maternity care concept was the right to have fathers in the labor and delivery rooms. This was helped considerably by the publication of a book called *Husband-Coached Childbirth* in 1965. Its author, Dr. Robert Bradley, advocated that couples should stay together during labor and delivery because, as Bradley explained it, the husband is his wife's natural labor coach.

Soon parents began to press for other alternatives: flexible rooming-in, beginning directly after birth (rooming-in simply means a baby can stay with his mother in her room rather than going to the central nursery); sibling visitation; breastfeeding on the delivery table; Leboyer births (named after the French obstetrician, Frederick Leboyer, who developed a method to welcome the newborn into the world "gently"); use of birth attendants; delay or avoidance of such routine procedures as the use of silver nitrate and vitamin K injections; fathers present for Cesarean births; allowing older children to be present for the birth of their younger brother or sister.

And when the medical establishment moved too slowly in adopting these changes, parents opted for returning to the old way — home birth. Still others sought a middle ground and thus the development of maternity centers, homelike institutions where parents not only could have their babies, but also could receive prenatal and postnatal care.

Now the decision is not only whether or not to have a child, but how to have it. An often bewildering number of questions needs to be answered by the pregnant couple: Which hospital should we go to? How flexible is our doctor? What options offered by the hospital do we want to take advantage of? Should we have a home birth? Go to a maternity center? Do we want friends or other members of our family present for the birth? Do we want our older children there? Should we use a midwife or birth attendant?

The childbirth movement has begun to offer expectant parents an ever-widening range of choices about the ways their child can be born, but each carries its own unique set of advantages and disadvantages which need to be carefully considered.

Home Birth

The number of home births is growing every year. Fed by consumerism, feminism, and the idea of self-care, home birth represents an effort by parents to regain control over their birth experience. But with that control must also come an increased sense of responsibility.

"I don't really know when or where I first heard the words, 'home birth', but once I did, I made up my mind. I knew that's how I wanted to have my baby," explained one home birth mother.

Some people are that sure that the only place they want to have their child is in the comfort and security of their own home. For others, however, it is a decision requiring that important pros and cons be weighed. Such considerations as safety, emotional satisfaction, parental versus professional control of the birth, how much time and effort can be put into preparation, willingness to take responsibility for the outcome of the birth, and whether or not home birth attendants can be found all come into play.

Are Home Births Safe?

Probably the most important question you'll have to answer for yourself is, "Are home births medically safe for both mother and child?" You'll have to answer that for yourself because the experts disagree. The answer to the question, "Are home births safe?" depends on which study you read or which expert you choose to listen to.

Dr. Lewis Mehl and his associates at the Center for Research on Birth and Human Development have done probably the most thorough testing to date on the safety of home birth. In a 1977 study conducted by Mehl, Lewis Leavitt, Gail Peterson, and Don Creevy, 1,046 hospital births in Madison, Wisconsin, were compared to 1,046 home births in northern California. Each hospital patient was matched with a home birth patient for age of the mother, number of previous children, income, education, state of health, and medical history. One hundred percent of the hospital births had physicians in attendance; two-thirds of the home births were attended by the family doctor, the rest by midwives. According to *NAPSAC News:*

The results were astonishing: In the hospital, the fetus had a 6 times greater incidence of distress in labor, babies were caught in the birth canal 8 times more frequently, and mothers were 3 times more likely to hemorrhage in the hospital than at home. Furthermore, 4 times as many babies in the hospital needed resuscitation, infection rates were 4 times higher, and chances of permanent injury at birth were over 30 times greater in the hospital. . . .

This and similar studies led NAPSAC to conclude, "Birth at home with a competent attendant and hospital backup is safer than the hospital for healthy mothers."[1]

Their conclusion is countered, however, by the American College of Obstetrics and Gynecology (ACOG), the official organization of board-certified obstetricians and gynecologists. In its official statement on home deliveries, ACOG maintained, "Labor and delivery, while a physiological process, clearly present potential hazards to both mother and fetus before and after birth. These hazards require standards of safety which are provided in the hospital setting and cannot be matched in the home situation." ACOG's executive director, Warren H. Pearse, a vocal opponent of home birth, has gone so far as to say, "Home delivery is maternal trauma — home delivery is child abuse!"[2]

Statistics and opinions like these characterize the home birth debate. Home birth proponents cite the good records of such organizations as the Chicago Maternity Center and Kentucky's Frontier Nursing Service, both of which have performed home births for a decade or more. Each side charges that its opponent has not conducted careful studies so that its results are inconclusive. And those in the middle believe that both pro- and anti-home birth forces have become so emotionally involved in the issue that they are influenced by preconceived notions.

The only thing that you, as a consumer, can do is to read and familiarize yourself with the studies, statistics, and arguments presented by both sides, and then attempt to make an intelligent decision based on them.

While it may be impossible to draw definite conclusions about the safety of home birth at this time, there are several things that can be said with relative certainty. First, not even the most ardent pro-home birth supporters believe that every birth should be a home birth. NAPSAC itself recognizes that hospitals are necessary for mothers who have serious medical problems.

Secondly, having a baby in a hospital cannot in and of itself guarantee a 100 percent safe birth. One doctor, who did home births both before and after a residency in obstetrics in a large Philadelphia teaching hospital said, "It was just horrible there. I saw doctors making all kinds of problems for themselves." One couple interviewed specifically chose a home birth for their second baby because their first child almost died of meningitis contracted in a hospital nursery. Still another Mehl study has shown that "the four principal hospital procedures accounting for a higher incidence of damaged babies are: (1) stimulating drugs to speed up or control labor; (2) pain-relieving drugs; (3) forceps; and (4) breaking the bag of waters."[3] As with the use of all drugs and medical equipment, there is always a chance that they may do more harm than good.

It can also be said with some certainty that there are things you can do to increase the chances for a successful home birth — the first of which is to decide whether or not you're committed to the idea of home birth.

Do You Really Want a Home Birth?

In an article describing the Maternity Center Association, a group of midwives and obstetricians who provide care for home birth couples, Janet Epstein and Marion McCartney write, "Potential home birth clients must expressly request a home birth and must give evidence of sufficient commitment."

In deciding for or against home birth, you need to spend time exploring your feelings about birth, family life, family responsibilities, and even death. Only by doing so can you decide if you have "sufficient commitment" for a home birth.

For instance, are you afraid that being away from a hospital could potentially put you or your baby in some kind of danger? Do you think that you might need drugs to get through labor? (Although some drugs can be given at home, many shouldn't be, and in practice, most aren't.) Or, do you believe that a hospital birth has psychological disadvantages and that increased use of medical technology can, in fact, lead to physical problems? And, perhaps most importantly, do you have an overriding desire to have a say in how your baby will be born?

Over and over again this desire for control is voiced by home birth families. (As one home birth mother expressed it, "We wanted our birth to be something we did together — not something that was done to us.") There is the desire not to submit to routine hospital procedures like enemas, shaving, or episiotomies. There is the desire not to be interrupted by unfamiliar hospital personnel, but rather to be supported and surrounded by caring birth attendants as well as family and friends.* There is a desire not to be separated from the baby, but to be able to bond with her immediately, nurse her, and welcome her into the family. Finally, there is the desire and the belief that childbirth can be a joyous experience that binds a family together and provides for a stronger base in the future — and that the hospital can rob a family of that experience.

At this point you may be thinking, "Yes, that sounds exactly like the kind of birthing experience I would like to have." But think again — for with this desire to control your birth must also come the conviction that you, not the hospital or the doctor, are responsible for its outcome. If a problem does occur during the birth that results in damage to or the death of your baby (assuming that you can't get to medical equipment that can help), it will be your burden to carry.

Many couples, of course, aren't willing to accept this responsibility and simply don't feel comfortable enough to give birth at home. Midwives sometimes tell stories of women who labored for hours at home, only to give birth minutes after they arrived safely at the hospital. Their nervousness made it impossible for them to relax sufficiently so that labor and delivery could proceed normally. As one mother-to-be who has ruled out home birth put it, "It appeals to me emotionally, but I want the assurance that there would be equipment close enough so that if there were some problem, the baby or I could get to it within minutes. I just don't think anyone can second-guess all the possible complications that can occur."

But you don't have to — and in fact, shouldn't — make this important decision solely on the basis of your feelings and beliefs. There are also some concrete factors which you need to take into account before you decide for or against home birth.

*You will need to give some thought to whom you would like present at the birth. Sometimes friends and relatives can provide you with wonderful support — other times they can take away from the intimacy of the experience or prove to be a distraction to a woman who is trying to put all her concentration and energy into delivering her baby.

Stella Weidner's Home Birth

Toni Weidner and her husband, Dave, had their first baby, Melinda, in a hospital three years ago. It wasn't a bad experience, but the idea of a home birth was much more appealing to them. Toni had been a patient of Dr. J. R. McTammany, an obstetrician from Reading, Pennsylvania, who brought three midwives into his practice shortly before Toni was due to give birth. Two of the McTammany midwives were present for Stella Weidner's birth in October 1977.

By 10:30 A.M. I was pretty sure I was in labor. My mom came by about 11:00, and I asked her to call Dave at work and tell him to come home. I really didn't want to admit I was in labor — I never do — so I just started cleaning up. I was really excited because I had waited so long for this baby and had been so tired and hot during my pregnancy.

When Dave came home I told him to call the midwives. He was so nervous when he called that they all started laughing. That was at 12:30 P.M. and they said to call back at 2:00, which we did. I talked to them then, and they said they would call back in an hour to see what was happening. So Dave and I went to lie down in bed while Mom took Melinda to the store to buy her and the new baby a toy.

When they got back we all got dressed and went outside for a walk. That did it. I walked over about an acre and then I told Dave that I didn't think I could make it back. We did manage to get back, though — it was about 3:00 then — and just as we got in the midwives called. I told them I was pretty sure they could come now and they said they were coming whether I said it was time or not.

Two of them, Esther and Sandy, got here at 3:15. They were excited. So was I. So were Mom, Melinda, and Dave. The midwives checked me and found out I was about eight or nine centimeters dilated.* I said, "Boy, I really am in labor," and that got a big laugh. I went to sit on the rocking chair with Esther and Sandy sitting close by

Other Factors in Making the Decision

If you do decide to explore the possibility of home birth further, the first thing you will need to check on is your physical condition. Many home birth proponents as well as doctors and midwives who actually do home births contend that it is possible to come very close

me. Everyone was gabbing, but I really didn't pay much attention to them.

Then they checked me again and found I was ten centimeters, but I didn't have an urge to push. The baby was upside down and sideways so they told me to get on my hands and knees and rock a little. That turned her right around. I knew if I pushed a little my waters would break, but I guess I just wasn't ready to do it. So I went to the toilet and my waters broke there. It felt like the baby was falling out, but Esther assured me I could make it back to the bed — which I did with Dave's help.

I told Melinda to come over because the baby was going to be born. I just sat right on the bed and within four contractions Stella was here. Dave had a mirror and he asked me if I wanted to look, but I told him I just wanted to watch Melinda's face. She was so thrilled when she saw the baby's face that she screamed, "My tiny baby."

Stella was wide awake when she was born — she was looking around and breathing as soon as she could. She was a little over six pounds and she didn't cry at all. I held her right away and she kept looking at me. Melinda was right on the bed and was kissing Stella all over. In fact, I held her and nursed her all the time — even when they cut her cord. They just took her away to examine and weigh her and that gave me a chance to put on some clean clothes.

Everything went so easily and it was all over so fast. There was almost no mess. Mom came out and made supper for all of us. Esther had to leave, but Sandy ate with us and then checked Stella and me before she left. It was strange because I realized I had already forgotten about being pregnant. Everything went back to normal almost immediately.

*The cervix is considered to be completely dilated when it reaches approximately ten centimeters.

to determining whether or not a woman will have a normal labor and delivery — and thus whether or not she's a candidate for home birth — based on the careful evaluation of her overall health.

Certain conditions and/or complications will "risk out" a woman from home birth. If, for instance, you have any of the following, you should *not* plan on having your baby at home: diabetes;

previous Cesarean birth or other serious uterine surgery; toxemia symptoms; previous history of hard-to-control hemorrhage; a first baby that is in the breech position; a baby of less than 36 weeks gestation; the possibility of Rh factor incompatibility; generally poor health including severe anemia or malnutrition; extreme overweight; and twins (sometimes). Check with your doctor or midwife about other possible problems that could make you a poor home birth risk. And remember that no one can *guarantee* that your birth will be problem free — all they can do is give you the odds.

Home births take an enormous amount of preparation, so another factor to take into consideration is whether or not you're willing to put in the necessary time and effort.

As in all pregnancies, prenatal care is extremely important. This includes a preliminary and thorough examination within the first trimester, periodic checkups, a good nutrition program, and regular exercise. In addition, classes in prepared childbirth, which train the woman and her coach to deal with the hard work of labor and delivery, should also be taken,* and you can enroll in classes in other areas relating to pregnancy, birth, breastfeeding, and childrearing as well. (The Association for Childbirth at Home, International [ACHI], for instance, offers a series of six classes covering: advantages of home birth, the normal birth, psychological issues, medical considerations, preparation for birth, and the newborn.) Finally, you would no doubt benefit from the advice of one pregnant woman who simply said, "I read everything I can get my hands on," for as another mother expressed it, "The more we learned the better we felt."

It will also be your responsibility to get your home ready. One midwife gives each of her home birth families a list of required supplies that includes everything from large plastic bags for trash and laundry to a small pile of newspapers, a roll of paper towels, a placenta bowl, Gatorade, heating pad, Fleet enema, flashlight, ear syringe, white shoestrings, and scissors. You probably will be given explicit directions for preparing your bed and you should have maps for your doctor, midwife, and/or birth attendants, extra food, and someone to watch your older child(ren) all lined up. You should arrange, too, to have a pediatrician see the baby within 24 to 48

---

*Besides the Lamaze method of childbirth, there is also the Bradley method, which advocates a "working with nature" approach. Bradley tells women to focus on their body sensations and only teaches a deep, slow abdominal breathing to bring about relaxation.

hours after birth and you need to become acquainted with emergency childbirth procedures.

Along with your own knowledge of what to do in an emergency, you must also have a plan for easy access to a cooperative hospital should the need arise. (The word "cooperative" needs to be stressed here since there have been horror stories of women in need of prompt medical attention who were turned away from a hospital because they had attempted a home birth.) It's your responsibility to prepare both emotionally and physically for the possibility of going to the hospital by attending the tour for expectant parents at the backup hospital, obtaining and filling out preregistration forms, and checking in advance to find out what kinds of financial arrangements may be necessary. Some attendants will not take families who live more than a certain number of miles (often 30) from a hospital.

Still another factor in deciding for or against home birth is whether or not you can find someone to help you. Often people who want a home birth have difficulty locating a competent birth attendant. Many doctors are reluctant to do home births, either because of a personal conviction regarding their danger or the fear of malpractice. (When Sue Morris broached the subject with her obstetrician, "He thought I was crazy. He went on about malpractice and very brusquely told me he wouldn't do it.") Often finding an attendant becomes a wild goose chase only accomplished by following lead after lead, usually passed on by word of mouth.

Just as often the search brings the couple to a midwife. Midwives, who are experiencing a renaissance today, fall into two groups: certified nurse-midwives who are registered nurses with additional training and experience in maternity care; and empirical midwives who are self-educated or educated by other midwives. (Since empirical midwives don't have formal training or degrees, in some states they have been charged with practicing medicine without a license. Thus, empirical midwives don't actively publicize their services, making it even more difficult to get in touch with them.) Sometimes, a midwife will also bring along someone to assist her. This person is usually called a birth attendant.

Whether certified or lay midwives, these women differ from obstetricians in several crucial ways. First is the simple fact that most are women and many women feel more comfortable being aided in labor by someone of their own sex. Secondly, the midwife's emphasis

A Home Birth That Ends Happily in the Hospital

Although Sue and Jim Morris had every intention of having their baby at home, it didn't work out that way. Sue and Jim were also patients of Dr. McTammany, and they used the hospital that he is affiliated with when it became apparent that the birth wasn't proceeding normally.

Sue Morris went into labor with her first child one morning in January. Her labor progressed normally throughout the morning and in the early afternoon she called her midwife, Kitty, who arrived shortly thereafter.

When Sue's legs began to shake after several hours, Kitty told Jim that she thought Sue was going into transition, the stage right before the baby is born. But when Kitty examined Sue, she found she wasn't dilated nearly enough to be in transition. Suspicious and concerned about what was happening, Kitty decided to take Sue's blood pressure, and found it to be high — so high, in fact, that she thought her blood pressure cuff might be broken. But after a second midwife arrived and they got another high blood pressure reading, they decided to take Sue to the hospital. That turned out to be a difficult task since it was snowing heavily by then and the ambulance drivers didn't want to risk transporting a patient in such bad weather. It was only after Kitty threatened to take Sue in her own car that the ambulance drivers agreed to pick her up. Sue labored for another 12 hours in the hospital (during which time the possibility of a Cesarean was discussed) and finally gave birth to a daughter.

Looking back on it, Sue feels that two things might have contributed to her high blood pressure. First, she may not have been getting enough protein, a classic cause of high blood pressure during pregnancy. Secondly, her mother had gone into the hospital the night before, and that, combined with the bad weather, may have made her especially nervous. In either case, it's important to realize that there hadn't been any trace of high blood pressure during Sue's pregnancy: it was something that developed during labor which no one could have anticipated.

is on normal pregnancy and childbirth as opposed to the obstetrician's training which focuses on the complications of the abnormal pregnancy and delivery. Finally, the midwife is willing to take time. She is willing to take time to listen, explain, and work with the couple. As one mother expressed it, "The midwives gave me so much attention. It's the one thing I really loved. They were so much different from my OB, from whom I got a four-second appointment that was usually interrupted by a telephone call. The midwives explained everything to me and to my husband." And the midwife is willing to let nature take its course. "If OBs were only filled with a little more patience," said one practicing midwife. "If they only had the ability to wait — even ten minutes — half our problems would be solved." (See chapter two for more information on midwives.)

Although cost may be the last factor in whether or not to have a baby at home, it is still worthy of some consideration. A 1978 study by the Health Insurance Institute estimates current hospital and obstetrician fees between $1,400 and $1,500. In comparison, one midwifery service charges $600 for complete prenatal care, labor and delivery at home, and postpartum care up to one year after delivery. Of course, there are additional expenses for equipment, laboratory fees, classes, etc., but it is reasonable to assume that these won't add up to $800 or $900. (However, hospital births may have one economic advantage: insurance companies will reimburse them. A spokeswoman for Blue Cross and Blue Shield of Philadelphia, for instance, said that the company would reimburse only the doctor's fee in a home birth — a midwife's fee, however, was not reimbursable.)

Again, it needs to be emphasized that deciding for or against home birth is often not an easy matter. The primary tradeoff seems to be access to emergency equipment and facilities at a hospital versus the psychological benefits of being in one's own home. For some, the perfect compromise seems to be a maternity center.

Birth in a Maternity Center

New York's Maternity Center Association (MCA) is headquartered in an old but still elegant townhouse on 92nd Street and Madison Avenue. The spiral staircase, paneled library, and spacious hallway are still there, but they are now filled with pregnant women, nursing mothers, and bulletin boards announcing the dates of the next prenatal classes. Where servants no doubt used to work, midwives, obstetricians, and childbirth educators now practice.

MCA began in 1918 and since then has been involved in a variety of projects designed to improve the care of pregnant women, fathers-to-be, and their babies. One of their most controversial projects is the Childbearing Center (CbC) begun in 1975 on the bottom floors of that elegant townhouse.

The Childbearing Center

Most simply, the Childbearing Center is a place where couples can come to have their babies in a homelike atmosphere. With two birthing rooms, a kitchen, living room, and garden available to laboring couples, it is a place that offers parents a satisfying, enriching childbirth experience. But since nurse-midwives are in attendance and some medical equipment is available, it is also a place that is more medically oriented than a private home. Its director, Ruth Watson Lubic, likes to call it a "halfway house," for it combines many of the advantages of both home and hospital.

The CbC was begun to satisfy a need. The proponents of the center were disturbed over the number of people who were practicing what they called "do-it-yourself" maternity care. Because these families were alienated from hospitals and the medical establishment, they were attempting to deliver their babies themselves in their own homes without the aid of competent medical assistance.* MCA's answer was to develop a place where low-risk births could be experienced in harmony with the psychological and human needs of the family and still provide safe care at a reasonable cost. CbC was devised as a test, and it is a test that so far seems to be successful.

Many different kinds of people use the center. There are married couples and unmarried women; first-time mothers and mothers who already have children; and women who range in age from 16 to 37 with anything from eighth-grade educations to graduate degrees.

Why are they coming? Perhaps the best reason is given by one CbC mother who simply said, "In the hospital it always looks like the baby is coming out of the sheets — I wanted my baby to come out of my body." Many people voice reasons that are similar to those for home birth: the desire for a bonding experience; the feeling that birth increases family unity; the desire to be delivered by a midwife. There is also the opportunity for self-care at the CbC. Patients are given

*MCA is not against home birth, per se, just unattended home birth. In fact, it provided care in the home for families in Harlem for 28 years. However, a decision was made against developing a full-fledged home birth service for two reasons: the expense involved, and the safety of the staff who would have had to travel throughout the city at all hours.

access to all their medical records and are taught and encouraged to do much of their own prenatal examination. And, of course, negative feelings about doctors and hospitals are also expressed. "I feel like this is a women's institution," said one mother whose baby had been delivered at the CbC six weeks earlier, "while hospitals are men's institutions."

But unlike home birth families, CbC parents have some reservations about giving birth at home. They may want to be closer to medical equipment or a backup hospital. (Experience has shown that patients can be brought by ambulance to the CbC's closest backup hospital in less than 11 minutes.) Or they may want to have the continued contact with and support of medical professionals. Whatever the reason might be, the Childbearing Center provides the perfect alternative for people caught in the home-or-hospital dilemma.

The Childbearing Center Experience

Once you make an inquiry about delivering at the CbC, you will be sent a package of information. This includes everything from a handbook on the center to a detailed medical and social history which you must fill out. All families are required to take a tour of the facilities and to have an orientation session before deciding for or against delivery at CbC. In fact, couples are asked to wait 24 hours before making a decision.

Even if you opt for a CbC delivery, MCA still has to make a decision as to whether or not you are eligible. A preliminary set of qualifications includes:

- Good general health;
- No more than 35 years old if having a first baby;
- No more than 37 years old if having a subsequent baby;
- Residence within the five boroughs of New York;
- No prior Cesarean sections.

In addition, you must enroll before the twenty-second week of pregnancy to allow time for required classes.

Even if you meet these preliminary requirements, you will be screened and rescreened during your entire pregnancy to make sure you maintain your low-risk status. A three-page, single-spaced typed list gives all the criteria which might prevent someone from delivering at the center. All entries carry a rating of one or two points, and it takes only two points for the patient to be referred somewhere else. Current estimates are that almost 50 percent of the families who come for the initial physical screening visit will eventually deliver elsewhere, although some families are referred or withdraw from the program for nonmedical reasons.

Besides labor and delivery facilities, MCA also provides its own prenatal care and classes. In fact, you must attend a series of classes which is given throughout your pregnancy and you'll be expected to do reading on your own. Early classes focus on nutrition and changes in pregnancy, while in the last three months the center offers a ten-week series on participation in labor and delivery, care of the new baby, and parenthood.

Regular prenatal examinations are conducted by nurse-mid-wives while the initial physical and 36-week prebirth evaluations are made by an obstetrician. (An obstetrician is available for consultation at all times, however.) Since labor and delivery are attended by the nurse-midwife on duty, an effort will be made to introduce you to each nurse-midwife. Many women prefer the nurse-midwife over the obstetrician.

"One of the main reasons I didn't want to go to an obstetrician," said one woman, "was because he would be an authority. By having various midwives, I didn't feel any one of them was actually managing my pregnancy. I really felt I was managing my pregnancy." Besides nurse-midwives and obstetricians, the CbC is staffed by pediatric physicians, nurse-midwife assistants, and various administrative and support personnel. You will be required to make arrangements with a backup obstetrician and hospital in case complications arise, and you will be asked to select a pediatrician by the twenty-eighth week of pregnancy.

The CbC is more than just a group of medical professionals, a series of classes, or a homey facility. An effort is made there to produce a community of people who both like each other and are committed to good birthing experiences. And judging by the smiling faces and happy parents and babies, that effort seems to be successful. "By the time we got through the whole thing," said Phil Bender, whose son's birth in the CbC is described on pages 150-51, "we felt we had made a connection. These people have given us a wonderful gift." And it was with some sadness that Phil and his wife, Dana Brooks, made their last visit to the center.

When labor begins, you will be instructed to call the center and your labor signs will be reviewed to determine whether or not you should come in. Generally, the staff encourages people to stay home as long as possible. When you do arrive at the center, the progress of your labor is evaluated, and you are free to use any of the facilities available: the family room complete with sofa, chairs, and a television; the kitchen; or the garden.

When active labor begins you'll be moved into one of two birthing rooms. You'll never be moved from this room (except, of course, in case of emergency) — this is where labor *and* delivery will take place. Both rooms, one orange and one blue, are furnished with a reconstructed hospital bed, a recliner for the support person, and a bassinet. There is also a sink and a wall of cabinets. The rooms are somewhat austere, but certainly not as barren as a standard hospital room.

Labor and delivery proceed as *you* want them to within the limits of safety. Women undergo no routine prepping, episiotomies are done only when absolutely necessary, medication is not routinely given, and delivery is in the position of your choice. (In fact, couples are asked to describe their desired birth plan in their charts in advance. The nurse-midwives make every attempt to follow those wishes.) Children can be present, although one other adult besides the woman's direct support person must be present to look after them. All this reinforces MCA's basic philosophy that "the system exists for the people and not vice versa."

You can remain with your baby during your entire stay, which usually lasts about 12 hours. The baby receives a complete pediatric examination before discharge. A public health nurse will visit you within 24 hours after you leave and again on the third or fourth day. There is a postpartum visit at the center approximately seven days after birth and then a final visit five or six weeks later.

Maternity centers may combine the best of hospital and home birth, but, as with all compromises, they have their drawbacks, too. Just as maternity centers do not have the sophisticated medical equipment found in hospitals, they also are not as comfortable or familiar as your own home. Considering these disadvantages against the advantages will help you decide if a maternity center birth is for you.

A Maternity Center Birth

Phil Bender and Dana Brooks had heard about the Childbearing Center from a friend of a friend. Although home birth was not an option they considered, Dana did know she wanted a midwife to deliver her baby. The center then was a good compromise. They attended an orientation program and according to Dana, "We really weren't very hard to sell on the place."

DANA: The baby was 13 days late and after my due date had come and gone and there were more and more days, I became very depressed. We had to go for blood tests to make sure my placenta was still functioning and that furthered my feelings of despair.*

Finally, on a Tuesday night, I began to feel something and by Wednesday morning contractions had started in earnest. By Wednesday night they were very strong. We called the center and one of the midwives suggested we go to a movie. At first that seemed like a pretty stupid idea, but it did serve its purpose — it got us through a couple of hours. When we got home the contractions were still coming, but we didn't call the center because we didn't think they were serious enough, although they were painful.

PHIL: We finally called at 1:00 A.M. because the contractions were very irregular — they would last over a minute and they might be five minutes apart or three minutes apart or eight minutes apart. When we called the center they told us to hold on and see what happened. We ended up sitting up until the TV went off and they continued to be sporadic all that time. We weren't at all sure what was happening.

DANA: We eventually went to bed and I remember being just desperate to find a position that would be comfortable. I had Phil lie on his side and I was kind of draped over him. Then in the morning I felt bad because I had been falling asleep and I hadn't really been on top of the contractions. We called the center again and said we were going to come in. The midwife saw us and said the baby would definitely be there that day and to go home.

PHIL: The reason that they didn't want us to stay there was because we live so close. And I think they were right. They said the baby wouldn't come until late that night and this was 8:00 A.M. We finally came back about 1:00 P.M. and by 2:00 Dana was admitted.

DANA: I remember the contractions were very strong and very long and I can remember being on the examining room table. Then I was brought into the birthing room and after that time became a blur. I also had a lot of back labor and I vomited several times just from the pain of moving, which took a lot of energy from me.

PHIL: That happened about 7:00 P.M.

DANA: At 8:00 the shifts changed for the midwives and a midwife came to be with me who was more the kind of person I needed. My first midwife was a little too distant. I remember being down on the floor when this woman came in — I didn't really know who she was because she's only at the center Thursday nights — and she just looked down at me and said, "May I help you?" It was like an angel had come. She brought me hot milk mixed with water which was the first thing I had been able to keep down. She was very good with her hands and she touched me and rubbed me and helped to relieve my back pain. I just felt she was really in there with me in a very physical way.

PHIL: I think it was at this point that I was beginning to understand the pain Dana was going through because it was just so long and constant. It had been going on for hours and hours and after awhile it just begins to wear you down. In some ways I had a helpless feeling because here's this person I love and I couldn't take her pain away.

DANA: But he was terrific. The thing that got me through it all was my breathing and holding on to Phil.

PHIL: At 9:00 P.M. Dana's water broke and towards the end, about 9:30 or 10:00, one of the midwives suggested Dana take a small dose of Demerol to help her relax.

DANA: I finally started to push, but I wasn't pushing correctly. I pushed for an hour and was soaked in sweat. I just had the feeling of burning and straining. Everything is so nice in the pictures, but it's different when you're actually doing it. At one point Phil told me how to push correctly and the midwife said, "Listen to him, he's right." That was really great because it helped to confirm us. It was really energizing.

PHIL: Finally, there he was — he looked a little yellow — and I said, "We have a boy." He was very clean, but there was some frantic suctioning there for a minute.

DANA: I was a little foggy after the birth and needed some time to recuperate. We ate some dinner and Phil fell asleep in the chair, I fell asleep in the bed, and Michael was in the bassinet. There was such a festive air about everything and the midwives helped me take care of the baby at first. The best thing was that he was never taken from us — I was even there when they did the footprint. We left 12 hours later in the middle of a snowstorm!

PHIL: I took off the first week Michael was home. That was great — I really felt part of what was happening.

---

*If a baby is more than two weeks late, CbC will not deliver it.

Maternity Center Pros and Cons

The Childbearing Center is one of a growing number of maternity centers being established across the country. Not all mimic the CbC, so if you do have the opportunity to choose a maternity center for your birth, there are certain questions you should ask and points you need to be aware of before making a final decision.

Again, the first consideration is one of safety. Although the CbC has shown an excellent safety record,* nearly all of the chiefs of obstetrics and gynecology departments of New York City's medical schools have voiced opposition to it on the grounds that it is dangerous to give birth there.

These doctors believe that births can be managed safely only within, or immediately adjacent to, a hospital. They feel that the MCA townhouse lacks the facilities and personnel to meet medical emergencies. Dr. Raymond L. Van de Wiele, chairman of obstetrics and gynecology at New York's Columbia-Presbyterian Medical Center, has charged that MCA chose their location, ". . . not because it is a good one but because they happen to own the building." (An accusation MCA, of course, denies.) Van de Wiele goes on to say, "There is no blood bank there; there is no facility for emergency Cesarean section. There should be a doctor there at all times, not just nurse-midwives. Any emergency will require transportation to a hospital, and the life of the fetus and the mother should not be dependent on New York traffic. . . ."[4]

MCA believes that with its strict screening policy, and with referral or transfer when needed, births can be managed safely in the CbC. "And the other side of this," says MCA's Martin Kelly, "is the implication that all births within the hospital are, by definition, safely managed. We disagree." Nevertheless, MCA makes sure that every prospective family receives a copy of the following statement:

We have taken every reasonable precaution to insure your safety, comfort

---

*There have been no maternal or infant deaths based upon data collected in the first two years of the CbC's operation. Nineteen percent of the families needed to be transferred to the hospital during labor or delivery. (Failure to progress in labor was the single largest reason for transferring.) Two percent of the mothers were taken to the hospital in the postpartum period and nine infants were taken to the hospital. To MCA's knowledge, there have been two infant deaths to families whose labor and delivery occurred in the hospital after transfer from the CbC.

and satisfaction. The Childbearing Center has on hand all the equipment, medication, and other paraphernalia we think necessary for normal childbearing in a homelike setting. We are not, however, a hospital. We do not have an operating room or intensive care unit for mother or baby, nor the highly specialized services and equipment which such units contain. Also, blood or blood fractions and general anesthesia are not administered here and the services of an anesthesiologist are not available. But all are available at the Center's backup hospitals in our service area. Nevertheless, some physicians and professional organizations have opposed our project because they feel there are certain inherent risks to mothers and babies in not being delivered in a hospital.

As with home birth, you need to read the statistics and listen to both sides of the controversy before deciding for yourself about the safety of a maternity center.

If you are comfortable using this type of facility, then you need to ask further questions about specific policies and procedures.

Find out how likely it is that some complication will keep you from actually laboring and delivering at the center. One of the fears many couples expressed about using the CbC was that they would end up having to go to the hospital after putting a good deal of time and effort into preparing for a CbC delivery.

Determine what other services are available at the center. One of the big advantages of the CbC is that it offers its own prenatal care and classes. Not only does that mean that parents don't have to go searching elsewhere for these services, but they also get to know the personnel and other families associated with the center better.

Ask about the staff and policies concerning labor, delivery, and postnatal care. Most CbC families don't stay longer than 12 hours. Many women appreciate the chance to go home right away, but others would rather stay in a hospital and rest for several days. Question emergency procedures that are used and find out exactly what your responsibilities are in the birth.

Finally, you'll need to talk about cost. CbC's fee is $885, which includes all initial laboratory tests and the two public health nurse home visits. MCA was awarded a Medicaid vendor number in March 1978, and as of this writing it is covered by Blue Cross but not Blue Shield. Talk to staff about payment plans, costs, and insurance reimbursement at any maternity center you are considering.

Hospital Birth

With the growth of the home birth movement and the development of maternity centers, some hospitals have been taking a second look at their own policies and facilities. Many institutions are making a concerted effort to institute family-centered maternity care in some form. Some hospitals, for instance, have unrestricted visiting hours for fathers while others have done away with routine prepping, are allowing breastfeeding on demand, or have 24-hour rooming-in available. All this is especially good news for families who want to combine a more personal, humanizing birth experience with the feeling of security they get from being in the hospital.

Two Important Innovations: Birthing Rooms and Sibling Visitation

At Phoenix's Memorial Hospital a two-room birthing suite was opened on September 1, 1976. According to hospital president Reginald Ballantyne III it was begun, ". . . to recreate the home environment within the hospital and to eliminate the need for an overnight stay." And, according to Mr. Ballantyne, the demand for the room is "unbelievable."

The Phoenix birthing suite contains a living room with sofa, chairs, and a television set, and a yellow and brown bedroom complete with such homey touches as a quilted spread, pottery lamps, and a beanbag chair. Between the two rooms is a viewing window with curtains that may be drawn shut. The woman labors *and* delivers in the bedroom, and relatives, friends, and siblings all may accompany the mother and father and be present for the birth. Mother and baby leave within 24 hours.[5]

At San Francisco General Hospital's Alternative Birth Center (whose birthing room one source describes as "a simulated bedroom that looks more like a room in a Holiday Inn, but which is still preferable to the regular labor and delivery suite. . . ."), the room is in some ways a symbol of the hospital's commitment to family-centered care. There is a nurse-midwifery service as well as an attached clinic for prenatal care. Childbirth preparation classes are offered and discharge is in as little as six hours. Again, as little medical intervention as possible is used. If a complication does arise, and the woman must be transferred to the regular labor and delivery wing, the experience is still kept as family oriented as possible.[6]

Needless to say, the advantages of birthing rooms, which are being incorporated into hospitals across the country, are many. Simply being allowed to labor and deliver in the same room is one of the biggest pluses. Their cheery, warm environments and the freedom to have more say in how you will plan your birth are also part of their appeal. About the only drawback is that many hospitals restrict the use of birthing rooms to low-risk deliveries, so inquire about the circumstances under which you may or may not be able to use your hospital's birthing room.

Birthing rooms signal another innovation in hospital childbirth: the opportunity to involve your other children in the birthing experience.

At Memorial Hospital, for instance, children are allowed to be with their parents in the birthing room provided there is one other person besides their father to take care of them. With the doctor's approval, children can actually be in the bedroom to watch the birth, or, if they or their parents prefer, they can wait in the living room and then be reunited with the family after the baby is born.

The question of whether or not you want your older child(ren) to be present at the birth deserves your special consideration. The general feeling among experts is that if the child is adequately prepared (and assuming, of course, that he wants to be there), it could be a beneficial experience. For instance, when the Center for Research on Birth and Human Development did a study comparing 20, 2- to 14-year-olds who were present at a birth with 20 who were not, they found that: "The children present at the delivery tended to have very accurate notions about where babies come from and tended to view birth in a positive, happy manner. The children not present found the idea of birth puzzling or inconceivable and did not seem to understand the concept or be able to relate it to their family." The paper concluded by suggesting some ways to incorporate children into birth, including: adequate prenatal preparation, an open-door policy in which the child can come and go at will, the presence of a well-known adult (other than the mother and father), anticipation of the child's concerns and fears, acknowledgment by the mother that she is all right, and opportunities for the child to be with the newborn.[7]

Although more and more hospitals are relaxing their rules about young children visiting their mothers and new sisters and brothers, many hospitals still don't permit siblings to be present at birth.

Family-Centered Cesarean Birth

Still other sought after, but not widely implemented, innovations concern hospital management of Cesarean births. C-sections, which are surgical procedures in which an incision is made in the woman's abdomen and the baby is lifted out of the uterus, are done for a variety of reasons — and their number is increasing.

They may, for example, eliminate the risk of a damaged baby from a particularly difficult birth. (Fetal monitors enable doctors to detect when a baby is in trouble.) Or, they may be done when labor doesn't progress satisfactorily and the mother seems fatigued beyond endurance. They may also be performed when there is a delivery complication such as the appearance of the umbilical cord before the head. However, some people maintain that many C-sections are done unnecessarily because doctors are afraid of malpractice suits. Critics charge that C-sections are performed at the slightest indication of a problem simply as protection for the doctor.

Whatever the reason for the C-section, the important point is that it is major surgery involving anesthetic, an incision, and all the aftereffects of a serious operation. Possible complications, affecting one-third of all C-section cases, range from hemorrhage, serious infections, and blood clots to injury to the bladder and intestines. The major risk to the baby is premature birth when a C-section has been scheduled in advance and the baby's due date is not correctly estimated.

There are several things, then, that can be done to make this an easier experience. First, you should be prepared for the chance that you will have a C-section. Make sure C-section is discussed in your childbirth class, even if you have to bring it up yourself. One C-section mother chastized her hospital for not including it in their classes. "They told me they didn't want to frighten their women. But I panicked when they told me they had to do an emergency C-section. I thought I was going to lose the baby. If I had known something about the procedure, I would have felt somewhat calmer."

Secondly, except in emergency cases, Cesarean sections are now being done under regional anesthetic, which numb the pain but will still leave you awake. When one woman, who was obviously uncomfortable with a regional, was asked if she wanted general anesthetic, her reply was simply, "I want to be awake for the baby. That's why I'm here."[8] Not being completely unconscious means that you will be able to hold and bond with your baby in the same way as a mother who has a vaginal delivery. Another woman who was put under general anesthetic remembers the first thing she said when she was brought her new daughter was, " 'Is that my baby?' I just don't think I had the same link with her that I would have had, had I been awake," she explains.

Perhaps the most important innovation is allowing fathers into the delivery room during a Cesarean delivery. A husband can offer support and comfort to his wife in those difficult circumstances. He can also be right there to hold his new baby, and being in the same room with his wife can help ease his mind. "Steve was so concerned about what was going on," said one C-section mother whose husband was not allowed to accompany her. "I think it would have made him feel better to be there."

At the University of Pennsylvania Hospital, one hospital where fathers are allowed in the delivery room, C-section mothers are also encouraged to breastfeed their new babies within hours after birth.

Be sure to discuss all your hospital's policies concerning family-centered maternity care, the use of birthing rooms, the right of older children to participate in the birth and/or visit, and how Cesarean births are handled *before* you actually enter the hospital for labor and delivery. As discussed below, this is one way to help guarantee that you will get the kind of hospital birth that you want.

Making Sure You Get Family-Centered Maternity Care

Even if the hospital you choose to deliver in does not specifically endorse family-centered maternity care, there are things you can do to insure a good birth.

Valmai Howe Elkins, whose book *The Rights of the Pregnant Parent* is concerned with how to get better hospital births, outlines 13 steps to help guarantee you get the kind of birth experience you want. She breaks her plan down into two parts, before the birth and during labor and delivery, and offers tips to follow if things go wrong.

Her basic instructions for before the birth are those that are

An Innovative Hospital

Booth Maternity Center in Philadelphia was originally founded and run by the Salvation Army as a home for unwed mothers. But in 1971, with the demand for that type of facility dwindling, it was decided to establish Booth as a "family-centered, patient-responsive" center.

Booth has all the options one expects from an institution devoted to family-centered maternity care: a nurse-midwifery service; prenatal care and counseling; prenatal classes; father support and involvement throughout pregnancy, labor, and delivery; continuous rooming-in; freedom of movement in early labor; and encouragement of sibling visits. It is the patient who is put at the "top of the pyramid" at Booth. That means it isn't the doctor who "directs" the birth experience; she only oversees parent-controlled birth.

High-risk patients are screened out, but among those who can use the facilities, satisfaction seems to be very high. Comments from mothers 24 to 48 hours after delivery included: "The nurse-midwives were really supportive"; "The care was very personal"; "I liked the fact that my husband could participate"; and "At Booth they discuss things with you, they give you the pros and cons of an option and then it's your choice." (In fact, patient involvement in and responsibility for

echoed over and over again by couples who have had successful births: Be prepared. Prepare yourself by reading, going to classes, and choosing your doctor, hospital, and pediatrician carefully. Discuss the kind of birth you want with your doctor and, if possible, members of the hospital staff well before your actual due date.

One midwife, who does both home and hospital births, has each of her parents send a letter off to their backup hospital outlining what they want should they need to be transferred. (She keeps a copy of the letter herself so that she can support their wishes.) As she points out, "More doctors are asking for such letters so they can be sure to give their clients what they want. Many of them feel it decreases the chance of malpractice suits as it shows that the client was (*a*) informed; and (*b*) taking an active part in her own care, thus lifting some of the weight from the physician's shoulders."

Perhaps Elkins offers her best advice when she writes, "It's cru-

self-care is one of the guiding principles at Booth.)

There are two other principles at Booth which distinguish it from other hospitals. The first is the attempt to create a place "where . . . parents can have power in making decisions that affect them. . . ."[9] To that end, two members of Booth's Management Task Force, which is the hospital's decision-making body, are patients. Secondly, there is the feeling at Booth that birth is a beginning, not an end, and thus there are many resources available for parents after the baby is born. For instance, a buddy system puts new parents in touch with experienced parents. There is also a drop-in center where parents can leave their children for a period of time and parent-child groups are arranged that meet on a weekly basis. This is all done in the belief that parents can help each other and don't necessarily need to consult professionals to guide them in their child raising.

Yet for all its innovations, Booth looks like — in fact is — a hospital. Standard equipment like fetal monitors can be found there. The two delivery rooms are basically hospital operating rooms and Cesarean sections are performed in them. Rooms look like rooms found in any other hospital. But the care patients receive is very different from care they receive in other hospitals, and thus Booth is a perfect example of what can be done to provide family-centered care within a hospital setting.

cial that you clear everything in advance: Find out what you can and cannot have before labor. Don't wait until you're hiccuping and fiercely concentrating on the all-absorbing beat of 'Yankee Doodle' in the hour before birth to ask about the way birth is to be managed — you won't feel like discussing things then at all! The last thing either of you will feel like at this point is explaining your philosophy of couple-oriented childbirth!"[10]

At the time of the birth, there are basically two things to do: first, explain to the staff what you're doing ("We're practicing Lamaze breathing and would appreciate it if you wouldn't talk to us during a contraction." Also, assuming you have cleared things with your doctor, you'll be surprised what a simple, "Our doctor said it was all right" will do); and, secondly, use the tactic of informed consent.

Informed consent basically means that nothing can be done to you without a specific explanation of the procedure, and without your specific consent to it. Informed consent can be guaranteed by adding the following statement to the general consent form which you are given at the time of admission, "All procedures to be carried out only with my complete understanding of the need for such." This will prevent hospital personnel from administering Pitocin or an epidural without your knowledge.

If things do go wrong, Elkins suggests first to "act at the time." She rightly points out that the hospital and hospital procedures can be intimidating, but since you will probably only have the experience of childbirth several times in your life, you must be assertive. At the same time, she counsels that you should be as diplomatic as possible with the staff since it may be your "demands" that are creating friction. If all else fails, try to find the top person (the head nurse or obstetrical supervisor) to see if you can enlist her help. If you don't get what you wanted, be sure to write a letter of complaint to the hospital afterward, and equally as important, write a letter of thanks if your birth goes just as you planned.

This brings up the final point: there are things you can do, as a consumer, to help bring about family-centered maternity care in your community. Hospitals are sensitive to consumer demands and criticisms — especially from an economic point of view. According to one nurse-midwife who is responsible for many innovations at her hospital (many changes have been made through the efforts of hospital personnel), "Consumers have to take the initiative. They have to say, 'Look, I want X, Y, Z in maternity care.' And they have to be willing to do what I call 'voting with your feet.' If they don't like the treatment they get at one hospital, they should go to another one." Besides that, she says, "They need to take the time to give hospital administrators feedback. Rational, reasonable letters carry a phenomenal amount of weight around here." Let your hospital know about the innovations you would like to see — not only for yourself, but for all the families in your community.

Making the Decision Easier

Perhaps the bottom line concerning childbirth is this: birth, by its very nature, will always carry a set of risks, so that the choice, as Ruth Watson Lubic points out, "is really based on which risks are most palatable to you." Do you prefer the set of risks which come from being away from sophisticated medical equipment at home or in a maternity center? Or, do you prefer the risks that are inherent in hospital birth — possible psychological and physical damage which can come from the overuse of medical technology. It is your responsibility to inform yourself of the risks — and benefits — each choice carries with it and then to decide which you are most comfortable with.

And we can hope that in the future, parents won't be faced with such a difficult decision. As hospitals become more willing to allow parents to have the kind of family-centered birth they want, the decision will be easier. As maternity centers grow in number, the decision will be easier. And, as home birth proponents work with medical technicians to develop support systems that will help nonhospital-birth families avail themselves of medical aid, the decision will be easier. Then parents can truly have births — the way they want them.

Notes

1. "Home Birth Controversy Rages. Experts Take Opposing Stands. Mothers and Babies Caught in Dilemma," *NAPSAC News* 3 (Winter 1978): 10.

2. American College of Obstetrics and Gynecology, Chicago, Ill., *ACOG Newsletter,* May 1975 and July 1977.

3. As cited in *NAPSAC News,* "Home Birth Controversy," p. 10.

4. Francine Pollner, "Homelike Delivery Center Opens Amid Controversy," *Ob. Gyn. News* 10 (November 1975):44.

5. Athia Hardt, "In Phoenix Hospital, Birthing Room Offers Home-Style Delivery," *New York Times,* 12 July 1977, p. 34.

6. Chuck Fager, "Having a Baby. A Guide for Prospective Parents," *San Francisco Bay Guardian,* 25 August 1977, p. 11.

7. Lewis E. Mehl, Carol Brendsel, and Gail H. Peterson, "Children at Birth: Effects and Implications" (Paper presented at the annual meeting of the Eastern Association for Sex Therapy, 1977), pp. ii, 8-9.

8. Joel N. Shurkin, "A Family Affair Right There in the Delivery Room," *Philadelphia Inquirer,* 29 January 1978, p. 1H.

9. Eunice K. M. Ernst and Mabel P. Forder, "Maternity Care: An Attempt at an Alternative," *Nursing Clinics of North America* 10 (June 1975): 241-49, as quoted in Rebecca Rowe Parfitt, *The Birth Primer* (Philadelphia: Running Press, 1977), p. 171.

10. Valmai Howe Elkins, *The Rights of the Pregnant Parent.* New York: Two Continents, 1976, p. 239.

For Further Reading

Arms, Suzanne. *Immaculate Deception.* Boston: Houghton Mifflin Co., 1975.

Bing, Elizabeth. *Six Practical Lessons for an Easier Childbirth.* New York: Grosset & Dunlap, 1967.

Bradley, Robert A. *Husband-Coached Childbirth.* Rev. ed. New York: Harper & Row, 1965.

Brooks, Tanya, and Linda Bennett. *Giving Birth at Home.* Cerritos, Calif.: Association for Childbirth at Home, International, 1976.

Dick-Read, Grantly. *Childbirth Without Fear.* 2d rev. ed. New York: Harper & Row, 1970.

Elkins, Valmai Howe. *The Rights of the Pregnant Parent.* New York: Two Continents, 1976.

Fager, Chuck. "Having a Baby. A Guide for Prospective Parents," *San Francisco Bay Guardian,* 25 August 1977, pp. 11-16.

Gaskin, Ida May. *Spiritual Midwifery.* Rev. ed. Summertown, Tenn. The Book Publishing Co., 1978.

Haire, Doris B. *The Cultural Warping of Childbirth.* Milwaukee, Wis.: ICEA, 1972.

Hazell, Lester Dessez. *Commonsense Childbirth.* New York: G. P. Putnam's Sons, 1969.

Karmel, Marjorie. *Thank You, Doctor Lamaze: A Mother's Experience in Painless Childbirth.* Philadelphia: J. B. Lippincott Co., 1959.

Kitzinger, Sheila. *The Experience of Childbirth.* 3d ed. Baltimore: Penguin Books, 1972.

Klaus, Marshall H., and John H. Kennell. *Maternal-Infant Bonding: The Impact of Early Separation or Loss on Family Development.* St. Louis: C. V. Mosby Co., 1976.

Leboyer, Frederick. *Birth Without Violence.* New York: Alfred A. Knopf, 1975.

Lipnack, Jessica. ". . . Birth," *New Age,* 3 (October 1977):35, 37–39, 86–89.

Parfitt, Rebecca Rowe. *The Birth Primer.* Philadelphia: Running Press, 1977.

Sousa, Marion. *Childbirth at Home.* Englewood Cliffs, N.J.: Prentice-Hall, 1976.

Stewart, Lee, and David Stewart, eds. *21st Century Obstetrics Now!* Chapel Hill, N.C.: NAPSAC, Inc., 1977. 2 vols.

Ward, Charlotte, and Fred Ward. *The Home Birth Book.* Washington, D.C.: INSCAPE, 1976.

White, Gregory J. *Emergency Childbirth: A Manual.* Franklin Park, Ill.: Police Training Foundation, 1958.

Resource Guide

American Academy of Husband-Coached Childbirth (AAHCC)
P.O. Box 5224
Sherman Oaks, California 91413
(213) 788-6662

This organization was begun to promote the Bradley method of childbirth. It runs childbirth classes, trains instructors, and does consumer advocacy work.

American College of Home Obstetrics (ACHO)
664 N. Michigan Avenue, Suite 610
Chicago, Illinois 60611
(312) 642-7472

This group is primarily interested in setting standards for training home birth attendants as well as getting home obstetrics recognized as a separate medical specialty.

American Foundation for Maternal and Child Health
30 Beekman Place
New York, New York 10022
(212) 759-5510

A research group that holds an annual conference on maternity care.

American Society for Psychoprophylaxis in Obstetrics (ASPO)
1411 K Street N.W., Suite 200
Washington, D.C. 20005
(202) 783-7050

ASPO, a coalition of parents and professionals, trains and certifies instructors in the Lamaze method of childbirth.

The Association for Childbirth at Home, International (ACHI)
6840 Orangethorpe Avenue, Suite E
Buena Park, California 92060
(714) 994-5880

ACHI is a good source of information on home birth. It trains childbirth class leaders, runs a series of classes, holds conferences, and publishes a home birth manual.

The address of their supply center for publications is: R.D. 9 Fair Street, Carmel, New York 10512; (914) 225-7763.

Home Oriented Maternity Experience (H.O.M.E.)
511 New York Avenue
Takoma Park, Washington, D.C. 20012

H.O.M.E. offers support and information to expectant parents doing home births or homelike births. It runs childbirth education classes as well as publishing an excellent booklet, *A Home-Oriented Maternity Experience* ($3.75), and a quarterly newsletter, *News from Home*.

International Childbirth Education Association (ICEA)
P.O. Box 20852
Milwaukee, Wisconsin 53220

ICEA is an international, volunteer organization representing groups interested in promoting family-centered maternity care. Local groups often run childbirth classes and the organization sponsors conventions.

The address of their supply center, which mails publications on a number of different subjects relating to childbirth, is: P.O. Box 70258, Seattle, Washington 98107; (206) 789-4444.

La Leche League International
9616 Minneapolis Avenue
Franklin Park, Illinois 60131
(312) 455-7730

One of the best sources for information on breastfeeding. It trains leaders and has groups to assist women who want to breastfeed as well as maintaining a 24-hour telephone service. Also publishes pamphlets, bulletins, newsletters as well as their manual, *The Womanly Art of Breastfeeding*.

Maternity Center Association (MCA)
48 E. 92nd Street
New York, New York 10028
(212) 369-7300

Besides running the Childbearing Center, MCA also distributes information in a variety of ways to educate the public about childbearing.

National Association of Parents and Professionals for Safe Alternatives in Childbirth (NAPSAC)
P.O. Box 267
Marble Hill, Missouri 63764
(314) 238-2010

NAPSAC is an organization designed to promote family-centered maternity care. It holds an annual conference and produces a number of publications, including a new 1,500-entry list of alternative birth services and consumer guide, which you can get for $4.50 by writing to the organization.

Although the addresses of the national headquarters of these childbirth groups are listed here, many have local chapters throughout the country. You can write to the national organization for the address of its local group, look in your phonebook (under the name of the group, "Childbirth Education," or "Social Service Organizations"), or ask your doctor or hospital for the name of childbirth leaders in your own area.

Consumer Notes

Home Birth

1. Acquaint yourself with the literature on the safety of home birth; remember that some studies have shown home birth to be safer than hospital birth, while others have proven the opposite.

2. Discuss your feelings about home birth. Some questions you might want to consider are: are you afraid of being away from emergency medical equipment; do you believe labor is hard work, but not something to be feared; would you be unhappy with the constraints imposed on you in a hospital; do you want to have a large say in how your baby will be born; have you checked out other alternatives and decided they're not for you?

3. If you do opt for home birth, you must be willing to take responsibility for the outcome of your birth.

4. Childbirth classes will help to insure a safe home birth. There are basically two kinds of childbirth preparation methods: Lamaze, which teaches you to disassociate yourself from labor, and Bradley, which advocates a "working with nature approach." In addition, you might want to take classes on pregnancy, breastfeeding, and childrearing.

5. You should also have periodic prenatal checkups as well as good nutritional and exercise programs.

6. You will be responsible for getting your home ready for the birth. This may include anything from having certain things on hand to preparing maps and food for your birth attendants.

7. You should determine if you are a safe distance from a hospital. (30 miles is often the limit given by childbirth experts.) You will need to make arrangements with the hospital in case you need its services.

8. Make sure a pediatrician will see your baby within 24 to 48 hours after birth.

9. Acquaint yourself with emergency childbirth procedures. One of the best sources is Gregory White's *Emergency Childbirth: A Manual.*

10. The services of a competent birth attendant are also necessary to help insure a safe home birth. This person may be a doctor, nurse-midwife, or lay midwife. Check on the qualifications of the person you choose, including how many home births she or he has done. If possible, talk to other clients.

11. Decide whom you would like present at the birth: simply the mother and father, the immediate family, siblings, close friends.

12. Determine the cost of your home birth, including equipment needed, birth attendant's fees, and hospital costs, if necessary.

Maternity Center Birth

1. Visit the maternity center and talk with the people there. See the facilities that are available for your use and find out about the center's personnel, procedures, and policies before making a decision.

2. Find out how likely it is that you will be "risked out" before your birth. Make alternate arrangements in case you are "risked out."
3. Determine what other services are available at the center, such as childbirth preparation classes, prenatal care, or parents' groups.
4. Determine who actually will be taking care of you prenatally, during labor and delivery, and postnatally. A doctor? A nurse-midwife? A lay midwife? A combination of people?
5. Find out who actually will be delivering your baby. If personnel rotate (meaning that your birth attendant will be whoever is on duty at the time), try to meet everyone at the center at least once.
6. Discuss the procedures once labor begins. How early should you come to the center? Are you confined to one room? How freely is medication given? Can your other children come with you? Can other members of your family and friends come with you?
7. Talk to the people at the center about how emergencies are handled. What emergency equipment, if any, is available at the center? Does the center have a standing arrangement with a hospital? How far is the center from that hospital or from the hospital the center is closest to?
8. Discuss the center's postnatal policies. Do you have to be separated from your baby? Can breastfeeding begin immediately? How soon after the birth can you and your baby go home? What arrangements need to be made to have a doctor and/or other medical people see you and your baby following birth?
9. Determine the cost of your maternity center birth. Find out if your insurance company will reimburse you for any or all of the cost.

Hospital Birth

1. Find out what the policies are at your hospital regarding family-centered maternity care. Some of the areas you should explore are: fathers present in the labor *and* delivery rooms; routine use of drugs (including Pitocin) and fetal monitors; routine prepping and/or episiotomies; labor and delivery in different rooms; separation of baby and family after birth; breastfeeding immediately after birth and breastfeeding on demand; use of midwives in the hospital; siblings present for birth or sibling visitation after birth; length of stay after birth.
2. See if your hospital has a birthing room, a special homelike room set aside for labor and delivery. Find out if you qualify for the use of the birthing room and check the policies concerning its use against the criteria listed above. If you can use a birthing room, find out the

conditions under which you might need to be transferred to regular labor and delivery rooms.

3. Prepare yourself for the possibility of a Cesarean birth. Find out the hospital's Cesarean rate, and if it has risen dramatically in the last several years, ask your doctor why.

4. Find out the hospital's procedures for Cesareans, including whether local anesthetic is usually used, if fathers can be present, and if breastfeeding can be done shortly after birth.

5. In order to insure that you will have a family-centered birth, you will need to prepare yourself well in advance of the event. Discuss the kind of birth you want with your doctor and hospital personnel. One possibility is to send the hospital a detailed letter, which is to be part of your permanent record, outlining the kind of birth you want.

6. When you get to the hospital, explain to the staff what you're doing. Be diplomatic, but assertive. (This is especially true for the labor coach.)

7. In order to guarantee that nothing can be done without a specific explanation of the procedure (including its pros and cons) and without your specific consent to it, use the tactic of informed consent.

chapter six

Dying a Comfortable Death

Sara Ebenreck

When someone in your family is dying, the difficult health care decisions you make will shape the quality of that person's last moments of life. Will he or she die in pain or in peace? Accepting death or fighting to the end with the aid of tubes and lifesaving machines? As a transient in a hospital bed or in the warmth of his own home? With or without the support necessary for sorting through the thoughts and emotions that come with the end of life?

Until the last few years, our health care system had not looked very seriously at these questions. Medical professionals could offer highly skilled hospital care to prolong life, but less attention was given to the quality of care when the goal was no longer curing disease but helping a dying person make the most of the remainder of life.

Now a new health service called "hospice," which is designed to be a center of care and support for the dying and their families, is spreading across America. Hospice teams know that good health care for the dying means freedom from pain with as little loss of mental and physical ability as possible, personalized help in treating symptoms, and support in choosing a place of death and way of dying that affirms the worth of the dying person. Hospice care reaches out to the patient's own home, helps with psychological as well as physical pain, and gives support to the whole family.

In their concern for the total well-being of the dying person, hospices are part of a larger movement in America aimed at learning how to provide better care for the dying. Volunteer community groups are beginning to reach out with support services to families caring for dying members. Self-help groups of seriously ill cancer patients are getting together to share their feelings about impending death and to give each other practical help. Hospitals and health care professionals are beginning to look for better ways of caring, some starting "death and dying" programs aimed at helping both patients and hospital staff deal better with the crisis of death.

We do need to look for better ways than we've had in the past. For decades America has been a death-denying society and our health care has reflected that denial. We are achievers, putting our energies into building homes, careers, and human welfare programs. We've asked our health professionals to focus on curing disease, and they've responded with wonder drugs and treatments that have extended our average life span by 23 years since the turn of the century. But death is the limiter of all those medical miracles, the point at which cures fail. Its presence points to our ultimate vulnerability, coming to strike not only the elderly, but also small children, young parents, or adults at the beginning of their careers. Death is hard to accept.

So often we've chosen not to look at death. Thinking it best, we take our dying to hospitals or nursing homes and turn their care over to professionals. (Whereas at the turn of the century, 70 to 80 percent of deaths took place at home, today the majority of deaths happen in institutions, primarily hospitals.) We feel inadequate, not sure of what to say or do for a dying person. Professionals often don't know either. Because we are uncomfortable with our emotions, especially with our tears, both professionals and family find it hard to sit quietly with a dying person. And not being able to listen and understand the personal needs of the dying has been one of our basic problems.

Where We've Been; Where We're Going

Hospitals provide the concentrated medical skills needed to save lives, but they can be cold, lonely, and frightening places to die. Too often, writes Dr. Melvin Krant, a physician experienced in the care of dying cancer patients, "the fright, impotence, and loneliness of the patient remains unattended although his body fluids, temperature, and blood pressure are carefully monitored."[1] Separated from the familiar warmth of home and family, a dying person ekes out life in an antiseptic atmosphere from which children are excluded. Drugs administered only when the level of pain is already rising may leave the patient in constant anxiety about expected pain.

Hospitals are not geared to individual freedom, so the patient may spend his last days lacking any important control over his nursing care, his pain, his food — over his life and death. Hospital staff, trained to cure disease and rewarded for healing, may quietly forget patients for whom "nothing more can be done." And even if the patient is not ignored, death is too often a topic that is shushed away, a taboo word that is hidden just as the dead body will be hidden from patients and visitors — a symbol of failure in medicine.

The alternatives to hospitalization have not been easy choices either. Nursing homes and long-term centers are also institutions, places where it is easy for a patient's personal needs to go unnoticed. And in cases where a family has wanted or needed to bring their patient home, the burden has been heavy and the cost high. The warmth of familiar rooms and care by a family member are achieved at the cost of running against the prevailing social pattern.

Much needed medical care has been organized around hospital use, not home care. Few doctors make regular home calls and visits to a physician's office may be difficult, if not impossible, for a bedridden patient. Night and weekend service is often available only at a hospital clinic from personnel who don't know the patient. Help from visiting nurses may be too expensive, for unless the patient has been recently discharged from a hospital, insurance plans often don't cover home care expenses.

Hospices and community support groups want to turn this dismal situation around, and the growth of their movement shows that a turnabout may in fact be happening. The impetus for change is coming from many directions, from psychologists and doctors as well as families coping with death. An initial push came in 1959 when Herman Feifel, a Los Angeles psychologist, startled the health community by his charge that concern about death had become a taboo in America. "We avoid thinking about death," wrote Feifel, "yet life itself is not really comprehended or lived fully unless we grapple honestly with our ideas of death."[2]

In 1969, Dr. Elisabeth Kubler-Ross, a Chicago psychiatrist who had spent four years listening to dying patients in hospitals, began giving some directions for better ways to deal with death. Dying patients often want to talk, she said, if we will take the time and have the openness to listen. If we ask them simply what it is like to be seriously ill, they can become our teachers.

Patients taught Dr. Kubler-Ross about the process of facing death, about their denial of it, and their anger. They shared with her their attempts to bargain with God and their depression when bargaining failed. They sorted out with her some of their unresolved business. And sometimes they offered her in words or symbols their final acceptance of the passage into death. If we try, Dr. Kubler-Ross concluded, both we and the patient are offered an important human experience: the sharing of a basic human crisis.[3]

While Dr. Kubler-Ross was listening to dying patients to learn their psychological needs, important developments in comfort care were happening in England. In 1967, Dr. Cecile Saunders founded a center for the dying in London which got international attention for its work in controlling pain and its spirit of personal care. Her center was named St. Christopher's Hospice, evoking the image of a place of solace for wayfarers. There she trained a staff to focus on symptom control, relief from the stresses of final illness, and loving care which flowed from recognizing the importance of this final phase of life.

From Dr. Saunders came a firm and positive philosophy. "We can control the symptoms of the uncontrollable disease," she said, "and help the patient do the most with the time and space left in life." That may mean keeping a diary to record what you are learning as you face death. It may simply mean being in a place where you can share important last moments with your children. "It is better to have your family and a cup of tea on your last day than all the apparatus and stress aimed at curing," says Dr. Saunders. Surrounded by a positive atmosphere, Dr. Saunders's patients gave witness. "Maybe we don't know what is at the end of our lives," said one, "but we are not afraid."[4]

Medical visitors, concerned about the inadequate care of the dying in America, traveled to St. Christopher's and brought the vision of hospice back to Connecticut, California, and Wisconsin. Here, joined with insights from psychologists such as Dr. Kubler-Ross, the idea took root. In 1973, New Haven's Hospice, Inc. opened a home care program under the direction of Dr. Sylvia Lack, a physician who had trained at St. Christopher's. In 1978, the map at the National Hospice Organization in New Haven shows more than 150 circles representing hospices across the United States. About 25 are in operation — the rest in stages of planning. The growth has been fast because the need has been great.

Hospice: A Center of Support for the Dying and Their Families

What exactly is a "center of support for the dying"? One way to understand is to look at a hospice in action.

Riverside Hospice

The Riverside Hospice in Riverside, New Jersey, opened in 1977 with a home care program and in 1978 added an inpatient center. A spacious, converted brick home, with flowering chestnuts in front and ponds in back, affords work space for staff and 16 beds for patient care. The hospice team includes a doctor as medical director, nursing staff, social worker, psychologist, clergy, and volunteers. A dietician, physical therapist, and psychiatrist are consultants to the center.

Support for home care is central to the program, with the hospice beds seen as a backup. Supportive services are tailored to individual family needs. They include medical visits by the doctor, although Riverside encourages the family physician to continue active care for the patient. Special medical attention is given to control of pain so the patient will be comfortable and able to use her energies to live. "We can almost always promise the patient he'll be pain free," says Dr. Donald Wernsing, Riverside's medical director.

Pain control may involve doses of a morphine mixture. The goal is to break the "cycle of pain," the patient's knowledge that even with medication, the pain will always be coming back. In hospitals, drugs are given when the patient asks, often when pain has already built to a peak past tolerance. Then there is a time lag in getting the drug and waiting for its effect. In a hospice, you know you can get the relief you need before pain develops and still not be in a stupor.

Because pain is often an accumulation of symptoms which may include constipation, nausea, anxiety, and depression along with the chronic pain of a disease itself, the hospice approach treats each symptom. Psychological and physical elements interact in pain so that anxiety about impending death, fear of disfigurement by disease, or worry about family matters can intensify physical pain. Hospice success in pain control flows from combining strong medical pain relief methods with a highly supportive and comforting environment.[5]

"Worry that patients would need an ever-escalating amount of drugs just hasn't been borne out," says Dr. Wernsing. With careful monitoring of pain control, patients tend to plateau at the level which gives release from pain while allowing maximum alertness.

Even if the patient doesn't need extensive pain control, access to medical help in emergencies can be a vital aid. Riverside staff can be contacted 24 hours a day, seven days a week. This commitment is so complete that a doctor in another hospice, New Haven's, skied her way to an emergency during a snowstorm that had immobilized the city. For patients and families who are anxious about what to do if medical problems erupt on weekends or during the night, this service is crucial.

Riverside nurses visit homes to help move and bathe the patient or do dressing changes. Encouraging self-reliance, they're teachers as well as doers. If you need to learn how to give injections or sterilize bandages, for instance, hospice nurses are there to demonstrate. The nurses may also act as mediators with a family doctor or help a patient formulate questions to ask during the next doctor's visit. Since a busy or abrupt doctor can stifle the patient's desire to ask questions, the hospice team fills this gap.

Social workers can help you get proper insurance coverage or find support services such as Meals on Wheels. A psychologist and clergymen are on call for their counsel. Religious ideas aren't pushed at Riverside, but access to religious leaders may meet a deep spiritual need for a dying person and family members.

Volunteers are central to the Riverside support system. With a 20-hour training course on care of the dying, they're a select group of people. They'll take shifts in a home to provide relief for the family, get patients to medical appointments, help with shopping or babysitting, and just plain share.

A wide variety of people take advantage of the hospice. The

youngest patient in Riverside's program was 17 months; the oldest 94. Some get in contact only a few days before a death; others participate in the program for many months. What participants had in common was a final illness, completion of cure-oriented treatment, and a projection of months or weeks to live. The only restrictions are living within 30 minutes of the hospice so team members can respond quickly to crisis and having one person in the home responsible for the patient. Riverside is fairly flexible about the last requirement, Dr. Wernsing said, because it's often difficult to have someone in the house around the clock. A neighbor or member of a church group can be a substitute primary care person for periods of time.

Hospice care doesn't end with the patient's death. Whether support means sharing tears or cheerfully helping a lonely family member get back in touch with an active social life, bereavement care is also an integral part of the hospice program. Before a patient dies, someone on the hospice team is asked to be the "bereavement person." This contact person will aid with funeral arrangements if necessary and stay in touch with the family for up to a year.

Often it is several weeks after the death before family members can ask needed questions about the dying experience or begin to explore their own deep emotional reactions. And there is a high rate of death among spouses in the first year after a partner's death, a probable sign of delayed shock. Hospitals and medical helpers aren't usually on the scene once the patient has died, but at hospice centers, where family care is a key concept, the support continues through the entire process of meeting death, a process that includes the stage of grieving.

Inpatient Care at the Hospice Center

Riverside's inpatient center is a backup for their home care program. It's a place to bring a patient for closer observation to help doctors get pain under control, to provide nursing care for vomiting or respiratory problems, and to deal with other symptoms that may cause the family concern. It's a place for the patient to come while her family takes a break from the stress of home care. And the hospice is also a place where the patient may choose to come for the last stages of dying.

As a place of refuge for the dying, Riverside and other hospices play a unique role. They're not hospitals with emergency equipment

The Death of Crosby Fassett

When Crosby Fassett's hospital exam returned a diagnosis of stomach cancer and gave him only a short time to live, it came as a shock. Crosby was 78, actively enjoying his retirement years with his wife, Hilma. They had a warm family life, three children and several grandchildren, and a home full of color and creativity. Years of gardening had produced flower beds with blooms from April to October. With his camera Crosby had recorded the growth of tulips, daffodils, and roses. And his hands were skilled at woodwork: repairing antique chairs and carving a wild pintailed duck that hung in the dining room.

So although the New Jersey hospital had efficient and supportive staff, Crosby wanted to go home for the brief time left to him. His daughter Lorraine, a nurse, wanted him home, too, but had many questions. She couldn't be there to help since her own family and work were in Maryland. How would her mother at 72 manage home care as the illness progressed? A visiting nurse could be hired to come several times weekly. But who would help her mother if there was an emergency between those times — during the night or on the weekend?

Lorraine had heard of Riverside Hospice, so she called there to explain the situation. The response was immediate. The hospice would provide free home care help, sending a nurse who would supplement the visiting nurse by being on 24-hour call for emergencies. A doctor trained in pain control would back up care by the family physician. A social worker could aid in working out financial or insurance problems. Volunteers would help them get to doctor appointments or come in to

or an intensive care unit. In fact, says Dr. Wernsing, "We don't do anything here that couldn't be done at home." But they are a community of support, a staff of health care professionals committed to providing comfort and aiding in quality of life choices as a patient moves on his unique journey toward death.

Hospice centers are designed to look like home. At Riverside, comfortable two-bed rooms shine with color: flowered draperies, seashells in a bowl on a bedside table, paintings, and a view out to gardens and ponds. Yellow sheets and nurses in gingham aprons help dispel any sense of being in an institution. Patients are encouraged to

stay while Mrs. Fassett took a nap, went out shopping, or visited friends.

So Crosby Fassett came home. It was early spring and he could see the gardens coming to life outside his windows. Grandchildren stopped by after school with pictures to pin to his wall. As it became harder for him to move around, the family had Sunday picnics up in his room. On a family anniversary, Crosby was there to drink a tiny sip of champagne.

Hospice workers came regularly during the weeks before Crosby's death. "The nurses got to know us like family," says Mrs. Fassett. "It's a terrible thing to see someone strong wasting away, and they helped me to talk about my feelings as I went through the process. That's important, and something they don't have time for in the hospital."

At the very end, with Mr. Fassett failing fast, his wife decided to take him back to the hospital in the hope that something could be done to shore up his strength. He died there, soon, quietly. Hospice workers stayed in touch with the family, providing continuity of support. The nurses and volunteers who had cared for Mr. Fassett were at the wake and funeral.

And the hospice staff understood Mrs. Fassett's feeling that "afterwards is hardest." They called and visited, providing an outlet for shared memories and gropings toward a new life. They invited Hilma to share in Thursday morning socials at the hospice center: a gathering of hospice workers, friends, and patients which often centered around a play or talks by community groups. People there understood Hilma's grief. "I could cry there," she said, "and it was all right."

bring in books, plants, or other special objects. Families are welcome to bring in food and eat with patients. At Green Bay's hospice, patients have their own kitchen "so someone can get up to have sardines and a can of beer," said a staffer there.

Hospices shatter any expectation that they're places of gloom. Genuine sorrow and the tears that come with honestly meeting human pain and loss are there, but not gloom and depression. The prevailing belief is that life is still to be lived. There's the helicopter ride that Hillhaven Hospice of Tucson, Arizona, arranged for a lively 63-year-old patient dying of cancer. Someone at hospice had asked her what her wish would be if she could have anything in the world. The answer: a helicopter ride. So she got to fly all over Tucson, even buzzing the hospice.[6]

There are quieter scenes from hospice life. Two small boys wearing baseball hats and reading comic books sit in chairs next to the bed of their granny at Green Bay's hospice. A visiting cat meows in the hall while patients, family, and staff mingle around a coffee pot in the community kitchen of another hospice. There is the special breakfast cooked for a patient who had to be out early for a doctor's appointment, and the meat loaf cooked for the staff by a patient. And there is the image of a nurse with her arm around a woman whose forehead rests on the hand of her husband who has just stopped breathing.[7] Hospice is a place for the passage of death to be met with as much care as human hearts can gather.

Differing Services

Hospice programs do differ from community to community, each growing out of a local situation and relating to community attitudes, available facilities, and money. Knowing the specific services of programs close to you will help with your decision about whether to use them. (You can find out if there is a hospice near you by contacting the Virginia office of the National Hospice Organization listed in the resource guide at the end of this chapter.)

Some programs are open to all patients with terminal illnesses. Others have been funded by the National Cancer Institute and work only with cancer patients. Some programs offer only a home care support team while others focus on inpatient care. A few offer both phases of care. Hillhaven Hospice in Tucson has a unique program for day or night care which allows working families to alternate care with the hospice. That is a vital aid to two-career families or any home where patient care can't be managed for 24 hours at a time.

Riverside and New Haven both have freestanding hospices, away from hospital grounds. They believe that a homelike atmosphere and independence from a hospital are important factors. In Green Bay and Indianapolis, hospice units are part of the hospital structure. Patients can come to the hospital hospice unit before going home to be reoriented from an intensive care regime of aggressive therapy toward a more natural lifestyle.

At St. Luke's in New York City, a hospice team oversees the care of dying patients throughout the hospital. Their approach was born of financial necessity, but has had an unexpected bonus in what its chairman, Carleton Sweetser, calls the "rub-off effect": the hospice approach to dying patients is catching on with other staff and patients. Hospice patients at St. Luke's have special rules allowing visitors of all ages around the clock. They have easy access to a cathedral park across from the hospital. The team works hard at creative support. When one patient, an organist, returned to the hospital for a final bout with his illness, the hospice team helped him plan a last organ recital in the hospital chapel for friends and family.

What It Costs

Hospice costs vary. At Riverside, present costs are being picked up by a grant from the National Cancer Institute and all care is free to patients. The New Haven Hospice also first operated under a grant. It now charges for services, estimating that a home visit costs $29 and a day of inpatient hospice care about $100. At Green Bay, inpatient costs run about $130 a day; there is a one-time-only charge of $50 for home care visits from the physician; and there is no charge for bereavement contacts. At those rates, hospice care is a bargain compared to a hospital. Home care with a hospice team costs less than either a hospital or nursing home.

Based on successes in Connecticut and Wisconsin, insurance underwriting for hospice care will probably be coming. Green Bay's hospice care is covered by Blue Cross and Blue Shield as a test for cost comparisons. Connecticut's model legislation mandates that all insurance policies for Connecticut residents must cover home health care and medical social services for the terminally ill. The National Hospice Organization is working hard for such insurance coverage across the nation.

Knowing the current status of insurance coverage in your state and your specific insurance plan is important because obstacles to coverage for hospice care are built into some. Insurance may cover home care only if it follows hospitalization or it may cover only a limited number of home visits, sometimes only visits by a nurse. Bereavement visits to the family usually aren't covered, but hospices usually don't charge for them. If your patient is eligible for Medicare or Medicaid coverage, you'll need to check on how much hospice care is paid. Right now, says John Abbott of the National Hospice Organization, if a person can go outdoors, Medicare says he is no longer "homebound" and isn't covered. Such a distinction is absurd for terminal patients who need care and the right to whatever outdoor trips they can manage. The National Hospice Organization is working to eliminate that provision and open up Medicare for the dying patient.

Why Not Hospice?

Not everyone wants hospice care. In the first place, linking up with a support center for the dying means accepting the fact that a person is in the final phase of the movement toward death. One couple in their mid-sixties, referred to a hospice after the husband's surgery and chemotherapy, saw being part of the home care program as acceptance of death and withdrew. And some physicians highly trained in aggressive approaches to disease resist placing their patients in hospices.

But hospice workers are quick to emphasize that their centers aren't "death houses," but places to live well in the time left. Green Bay's hospice staff estimates that 50 percent of the patients there leave for home. One woman, for example, came in after intensive chemotherapy, expecting to die. With encouragement, physical therapy, and the joy of learning to work on a loom, her spirit slowly revived. She left the unit after volunteers built ramps at her home so she could walk with canes and her walker.

Like any new program, hospices can be seen as a threat to the established system, implying by their very existence that previous health care was inadequate. Because conventional medical approaches focused almost entirely on treatment of physical illness, doctors asked to cooperate with hospices may be overwhelmed by the demand to relate to patients as whole persons. Dealing with social, spiritual, psychological, and financial aspects of the patient's life may sound like a social worker's role and not "medicine."

Established hospices have been able to answer these objections too. As Don Gaetz of Green Bay summarized, "We've been able to show our hospice isn't a way to encourage people to give up hope. Nor is it a place where we're going to undermine the role of the family physician. We simply say to the medical profession, 'In your zeal to eliminate human disease, remember we all shall die. We need to face that and maximize the life that is left.' So resistance has waned substantially," Gaetz continued. "That's important, because when people have a terminal disease, you don't want to cut lifelines, you want to build them."

Although there hasn't been any controversial public questioning of hospice standards or medical procedures, hospice workers themselves point to possible pitfalls in the future. They worry about charlatanism, the growth of places called "hospices" operating without adequate medical staff or training. Most present hospices are nonprofit organizations. What will happen if hospices become for-profit ventures is still an open question. Hospice leaders are aware of the funeral industry's ability to play on our emotions in the choice of expensive services and are concerned about whether the hospice concept could be used to exploit people. Will hospitals or nursing homes with empty beds rush to establish hospices without embodying the central concepts of care?

To provide some protection for consumers and insurance companies, both the National Hospice Organization and the federal government are formulating standards for hospices. Since the word is a dictionary term, it may be hard to restrict its use, but standards would let a family judge care offered by any particular program. At the minimum, says Don Gaetz of Green Bay's hospice, a good program needs proper medical staffing and the resources to deal with problems in human relations.

There are still other concerns you should be aware of. Hospital-based hospices may be subject to utilization reviews that limit the time a patient can stay. And despite their commitment to personalized care, hospices themselves are institutions and can develop a set of assumptions about patient and family needs that don't work for your situation. Clarifying your needs and setting goals to negotiate with staff are important. Expectations about care should be checked out by a hard look at the particular hospice: its medical care plan, staffing, and atmosphere — including rules. Calling a care plan "hospice" may not make it best for you.

Even with those qualifications, however, hospice care programs clearly have immense promise for families hard pressed by presently inadequate care for the dying. They offer us a lifeline from the past to a more hopeful future.

Community Support Systems:
A Second Model for Caring

Total hospice care gives one ideal for support of the dying, but in many situations the financial demands, long-term planning, and professional personnel needed can become obstacles in the way of building such a program. So caring activists are organizing other community programs. These programs assume that you will seek physical care from the conventional medical system while they provide needed support.

Haven

When Dorothy Garrett of Annandale, Virginia, began thinking about a "neighbor helping neighbor" support program for families with a seriously ill member, she and nine volunteers wrote volumes of letters trying to find a group to serve as a model. Finding none, the core group in Virginia set about creating one. What emerged in 1976 was Haven — an all-volunteer organization which provides free home help, aid in finding community health resources, and group support sessions for people involved in a life-threatening illness. By 1978, new Havens were being organized in New York, Florida, and Pennsylvania.

Unlike a hospice, Virginia's Haven does not have an inpatient center or a full medical home care team. What it does have are 200 volunteers who include doctors, nurses, psychologists, psychiatrists, social workers, clergymen and trained "ordinary people," who are prepared to share themselves and their skills. From its center in a warmly informal home, Haven staff members take phone calls and match volunteers to needs. An initial contact with a family may show they need a nurse to teach home care methods and Haven finds a volunteer to meet the need. That may mean demonstrating how to give injections of pain medication or showing how to move a patient to and from a wheelchair — simple processes that once learned can give patient and family new independence and flexibility.

Another family may need help dealing with insurance plans and financial pressures. Haven finds a volunteer to do financial counseling. A fatigued mother of four caring for a baby with cystic fibrosis needs a chance to escape and relax. Haven locates a volunteer to come in for four hours each week to give the mother a break.

Built on the concept of a network of community helpers, Haven found it natural to foster self-help group sessions for people who could share their difficulties and insights with each other. A distraught widow, upset by her unconscious habit of setting a table for two and listening for her husband to come home at 5:30 p.m. came to Haven to talk. She ended up forming a group for widows to share experiences, grief, and provide support for each other.

Seeing the success of the widows' group, Haven began initiating other groups. Parents of a child who dies especially need support after the death, says Gerry McGrath, who leads Haven's sessions for parents. Gerry knows from experience since she cared for two of her own children dying from a kidney disease. She still feels the pain of her three-year-old daughter's death, alone in a strange hospital in a new city. And despite the weeks of warm attention she gave her son, Brian, Gerry suffers from knowing that he too died at night in the hospital, just after she left in exhaustion from her long vigils. She wonders if Brian might have awakened before he died and found himself alone.

From those experiences, Gerry knows the two major topics that parents of children who've died need to talk about: anger and guilt. Parents may be angry at doctors, hospitals, friends, themselves, and each other. They need to work through this anger. Guilt feelings may be strong — about what they failed to do, about their relief that the crisis of illness is over, and even about their happiness as they move on to more life. "Parents need to work through their feelings at their own pace," says Gerry McGrath. "There is a time for giving toys and clothes away, but it will come differently for each family." In the Haven group, parents can choose to share their feelings about these moments of the grieving process.

"When babies die," said Peg Cauley, another Haven volunteer leader who has coped with death in her own family, "people resent the fact that others act as if the baby had never been or suggest that they can have another." In a misguided attempt to treat the parents' feelings carefully, friends and relatives may choose not to mention the baby's birthday or the anniversary of its death. One woman, said Peg, brought a coffee cake to the Haven group to celebrate the first birthday of her baby who had died at seven months. It was the only place where she could share her feelings, the woman explained.

Along with their present group for grieving parents, Gerry and

Peg are talking about forming a group to provide support for those people who are primarily responsible for the care of the ill patient. There is an immense sense of shock and loss that comes with the diagnosis of a life-threatening illness, and thus the primary care giver needs a great deal of support. Often this person is already seen as the strongest one in the family and not only is supporting the sick patient but also giving psychological strength to other family members as well. "Sometimes," says Gerry, "it's the little things that get to the person doing care. You are committed to the process, and your mind says it's OK to give up the family vacation. But on another level you hate it. Having someone to listen can help you put mind and feelings together and decide where you want to go from your deepest level."

Another function of the group is to help identify alternatives. When you're under stress, you may see only one way to handle a problem. But a group can help open up other paths. "Also," says Gerry, "it really helps to come to the group and just laugh."

Despite the occasional laughter, Haven and its volunteers can't take away the pain of meeting with death. But they're not frightened by looking at the pain, and so they can help people slowly work through their agony to get to its other side — toward a life lived more deeply because it has come through an embrace with death.

The Shanti Project

A slightly different community support program, California's Shanti Project ("Shanti" means "peace"), operates by pairing a trained lay volunteer with a dying person who makes a request for support. The program's founder, Dr. Charles Garfield, a psychologist at the University of California's Medical Center, sees these volunteers as "client advocates" who can work with a client wherever he is, doing what the volunteer and client decide is needed.

"The dying person is grappling with the outrageousness of not being around any more," says Garfield. In the face of that, the person may realize that there are lots of things that haven't been done, precisely at the point when disease creates a boxed-in feeling. The volunteer can provide some emotional nourishment and help the person work out options when she may be experiencing a sense of fewer choices.

In one case a dying mother was coping with the grief of leaving behind her young children, too young to understand what she wanted to say to them. The Shanti volunteer suggested a solution — to make a tape of her thoughts for the children to hear when they are older. In another case, a young woman studying to be a music therapist was diagnosed as having terminal cancer. The volunteers helped her wrestle with her emotions as she went through treatments and in and out of remissions. They also helped with the practical tasks involved in fulfilling her desire to live by herself in an apartment next to, but separate from, her parents' home.

Ultimately Garfield sees the Shanti Project as part of a larger human task: the work of coming to understand and live our humanity deeply. In this, the living have much to learn from the dying, he says. For those who have faced openly the hard insight that their life is limited often grow to a new honesty and clarity in their own relationships.[8]

The Growth of Peer Groups

As hospice and community support workers know, naming fears about death can help the process of coping with them and expressing anger can free energy for living. Yet traditional medical professionals can leave patient and family stranded when it comes to dealing with the personal pressures of meeting death. So across the county, thousands of people are learning new ways to cope by joining or organizing peer support groups which provide a place to talk with other people who suffer the same problems, to share insights and practical help, to laugh together, and to feel the strength that comes from being needed. Sharing a hard-won insight about death can blend its pain with love and give the experience of loss a meaning.

In Chicago, Rabbi Robert Marx, a father who lost his 15-year-old son in 1973, leads a group called Parents United by Tragedy. Gathering together once a month, they share stories rooted in their own experience of losing a child and reach out to each other for support.

In Washington, D.C., social worker Mila Tecala of St. Francis Institute leads group sessions for seriously ill cancer patients. "Some of the most difficult topics to discuss started with a macabre joke," she says. One day a young woman who had had major breast surgery and was losing her hair because of chemotherapy treatments came in and announced that she had a lot to say and was going to "let her hair down." In the laughter that followed she could sense support and empathy, and for the first time she was able to verbalize what it meant to her to lose parts of her body and face the final loss of death. "She died at 32," says Mila Tecala, "but she had learned how to live well, how to be open with her feelings."

Imagining Death

In Fort Worth, Texas, Dr. Carl Simonton and Stephanie Simonton work with patients' fears about death as part of their broader work in helping patients recover. Cancer patients often fear the prospect of a lonely, painful death in a hospital. And they suffer from their families' attempts to avoid the subject of death. A square look at the real facts about cancer and an understanding of how to relieve pain can help eliminate false fears. But the fact of death still remains to be faced.

The Simontons developed a mental imagery process to help patients confront the possibility of their deaths. The relaxed person is asked to picture being told that he is dying and to experience the inner response to this information. He is asked to visualize his moment of death, his funeral service, and what happens to his consciousness after death. In each step he takes sufficient time to allow feelings and thoughts about the moment to surface for reflection. Next the patient is asked to place himself in the presence of whatever he believes is the source of the universe and to review his life. And finally, he tries to visualize coming back to earth with a new plan for life, in a renewal that is an image of the death-and-rebirth process of life.

The Simontons report that patients gain valuable insights about what changes they want to make in the time they have left and often the power to make those changes.[9]

Some of the peer groups are organized by health professionals or associations long concerned with health issues. In Washington, D.C., Susan Keating, a nurse, and Marcia Weiss, a social worker, led a family discussion group sponsored by the local chapter of the American Cancer Society. "The family of a person with serious illness is going through their own personal crisis," says Susan Keating. "They need a chance to express feelings like anger that they don't get out with the patient present."

Other groups are organized by community programs like Haven or the Centre for Living with Dying in Santa Clara, California. The Santa Clara group has special sessions for survivors of suicide and homicide victims as well as people facing death or experiencing grief. Survivors of a suicide have particularly hard questions to deal with, says the program coordinator at the Centre. "Was it my fault? What could I have done to stop it? Does everyone blame me? Why did she do this to me?" are all questions that a peer group can help survivors deal with.

The most phenomenal growth on the national level has been in two networks of peer support groups organized by people themselves coping with death: Candlelighters and Make Today Count (MTC). Candlelighters was formed almost simultaneously in Washington, D.C., Florida, and California in 1970 by local groups of parents who had children with cancer. The name of the organization comes from the proverb, "It is better to light one candle than to curse the darkness," expressing the conviction that taking action is better than complaining about inadequate medical care. Candlelighter groups meet locally, bringing in medical speakers, psychologists, and insurance people to help supply the vital information that is difficult to get in the brief time most parents have with family physicians. Self-help discussions are supplemented with social activities as the bridge of friendship is built between families who share a common bond. And Candlelighters has an organized legislative program, working for federal funding for psychological support groups, physician education, and public information.[10]

Make Today Count got its start in 1974 when a cancer patient in Iowa, Orville Kelly, wrote a piece in a local newspaper about how it would help if people with incurable diseases could get together and talk with each other about ways to work through their problems. Kelly was a journalist, ex-army man, and a cancer patient who had moved through despair to a vision of the beauty of each day of life. He hosted a group at the local Elks club and Make Today Count was born.

In 1978, there were more than 135 groups across the United States — places where seriously ill persons, their families, and friends, can get together to discuss their concerns. A typical meeting starts with people introducing themselves and then saying, "And I have this problem." Eighty percent of the problems are about communication difficulties, says Kathy Roche, director of Maryland's MTC chapters. Friends or relatives can't talk openly about the disease and possible death. Or a person can't talk freely with a doctor about treatments or surgery. The chance to speak out, to say, "I may die and I am afraid," or, "I have cancer and I don't know how to tell my parents . . . or child," is a vital step in getting hold of life again.

Make Today Count groups also bring in resource people to talk about nutrition, home care, biofeedback, doctor-patient relationships, aggressiveness training for cancer patients, making out wills. But the deepest thing the groups provide is a knowledge that, "Others too have been told they may die — and they are learning to fight for life and live with joy. I can too." Although in a broad sense we're all terminally ill, no healthy care giver can give that insight — it is a gift reserved for those confronting death to share with each other.

Linking Up with a Support Group

Most of the community support services are free. Haven and the Centre for Living with Dying operate with volunteers, for example, and are funded by donations, not fees. Most peer-organized groups are also free, but some professionally led sessions like those at St. Francis Institute in Washington, D.C., do charge a fee. Often that is based on a sliding scale adjusted to your ability to pay.

There are several ways to find out if there are support groups near you. Make Today Count and Candlelighters both have national offices listed in the resource guide at the end of this chapter. You may also find local groups listed in your phonebook. Local chapters of the American Cancer Society often know about support services for terminally ill patients, as do social workers who are on hospital discharge teams. Both Haven and the Shanti Project (listed in the resource guide) give help to other groups organizing similar projects and they may know if a new group is getting started near you.

A conversation with group organizers should help you decide if you want to participate in their activities. It's hard to imagine a reason for not wanting to utilize services such as Haven of Northern Virginia offers. But if you're in the lucky position of choosing between a volunteer-based support system and a hospice-type group, you would want to know about such factors as reliability of volunteer help and whether the same people will work with you over the period of time you need. With their medical team and inpatient centers, hos-

What Does It Mean to Be "Terminal"?

This essay was written by Sheryl Baker, a former member of Make Today Count in Montgomery County, Maryland.

After participating in several meetings of the Montgomery County Make Today Count chapter, I would like to share what was a learning experience for me. The word "terminal" used by each of us left me uncomfortable enough to explore its uses further.

The most commonly accepted definition of the word "terminal" is the end or ending of something.

A terminal is also a passageway; a connecting place through which we pass on our way to somewhere else. At a terminal, people never stay, they arrive and depart; they begin new journeys even as they complete old ones. It goes both ways, commencing as we end, perhaps because we end; like living even as we are dying.

Terminals are also meeting places where people gather in off the streets to wait for the next thing or place in their lives.

Used as a noun, the terminal in a car battery is the conductor through which the current flows to run the engine.

In botany, the terminal forms the apex of a stem or shoot bearing a flower. The terminal bud is responsible for continuation of the stem's growth in its original direction.

All these additional meanings have one thing in common: a continuing on; none of them are ends in themselves. Each is either a connecting agent or part of a larger ongoing process.

We are all terminal in the sense that we must often die to find growth. And so that which promotes continuity through change also applies to the content of our lives. From infant to child-adolescent to adult, each stage of development requires an experiencing and a passing through and then a letting go, to begin the next phase (birth through death through birth cycle). To the extent that we all share death, each differently, living is a terminal disease; dying is the change agent; and all that's in between is our humanness played out.

pices offer different services from peer groups or even community support centers, so the ideal might be to use them both.

Group discussions will be helpful as long as the group and leader are prepared to be open and sharing about issues you face. It's hard to go wrong with an attempt to meet with others who share your pain and problems. You're not going to be exploited for money and you can judge for yourself after a session or so whether they are really right for you.

If you're aware that your emotional problems are deep and that you want intensive attention from a professional, you may want to choose a group — or even individual sessions — led by a mental health professional. While peer groups discuss common problems, professionally led therapy sessions are designed to help members through individually deep and difficult emotions.

How Hospitals Respond to the Dying

At least some hospitals and health care professionals have not been left behind by the growing movement toward better care for the dying. At Albert Einstein Medical Center in Philadelphia, a new program is designed for crisis patients as well as those dying after a long-term illness. A patient who has a heart attack while in the hospital for appendicitis or another who enters for open heart surgery both may need help in coping with their fears about death and plans for continued life, yet they are not likely to be part of a hospice program. The support team reaches out to them in their stress.

The Einstein team of three nurses, on 24-hour call, often helps handle emergencies. On a recent weekend, an ambulance brought in a policeman wounded as he fatally shot a young man in a gun battle. A team nurse stayed with the policeman as he worked through his feelings about shooting the man. She was also there to give support to family members of the dead young man when they arrived at the hospital emergency room. Another nurse was present to support the parents of a baby born dead, helping them through the moments of seeing and touching their dead child and working through feelings and practical decisions.

With dying patients who are in the hospital for a longer time, the team can help by acting as patient advocates: somebody who can see patient needs and make contact with the right people to get action. The team nurse can call a physician to suggest pain prevention techniques or recommend changes in diet or movement. The nurse on the scene knows how important it is for a man to walk his wife to the elevator and kiss her — even if he needs to rest in bed for

most of the day. She can work with the dieticians to find ways to
spruce up an otherwise tasteless diet.

There are signs that programs based on such an awareness of the
special needs of the dying are growing in hospitals across the country.
At Harrisburg Hospital in Pennsylvania, nurse Joy Ufema has set up
a one-person program for helping the dying. At Providence Hospital
in Detroit, social workers attached to department teams are trained
to be alert to the unique situations of dying patients and their families. At Fairfax Hospital in Virginia, a special room is set aside for
the family of a dying person to talk with their doctor or simply to
grieve. In Tampa, Florida, a social worker does art and music therapy with dying children in a pediatrics ward. Other hospitals are
quietly making exceptions for bringing in children to visit with dying
relatives.

Because hospitals are where we go in emergencies and are still
our primary choice for care in the last hours of chronic illness, such
programs are an important supplement to the growth of hospices.
Ordinarily, they aren't an additional cost to the patient. So if you
choose a hospital for care, you'll want to check on available programs.

When, for whatever reason, you do decide on a hospital for a
dying patient's care, the time may be ripe to push for more personalized care programs even if your hospital isn't a hospice. Knowing
what elements of good terminal care are important to you and discussing them openly with the staff can lead to sympathetic support for
what you want. More physicians are becoming aware of pain prevention as a philosophy for dying patients, for example, and your doctor
may respond if you talk to him about it.

Some of the intimacy of home can be provided even in a hospital
if you work at it. Hospitals can turn up an extra cot for sleeping over
in a room if you ask persistently. Along with bringing in a few plants,
you might be able to hang a favorite painting or poster and bring
colored pillowcases or a bedspread from home.

In a moving article which provides a model for other families of
dying patients, Carolyn Driver describes her struggle to break hospital conventions and provide a freer living atmosphere for her husband
as he died of leukemia.[11] She brought their FM stereo to her husband's private room, along with books, posters, and some wine kept
chilled on top of the air conditioner. Bob Driver posted their living
schedule on the door, including times when no hospital personnel

could walk in. They brought their children in, explaining their need to have that sharing.

Their struggle for these rights wasn't easy. Nurses and doctors often resisted before they yielded to the determined couple. (Their fight was helped by their professional experience in breaking through communication barriers through work in a group encounter movement.) But they proved an important point: concentrated pressure for more personalized hospital care can yield fruit right now.

Carolyn Driver emphasizes the fact that the staff members weren't "bad" people. It's just that they were afraid of breaking conventions to reach out on a human-to-human level. So you may need to break some rules, especially the silent ones never written down. Does your hospital have a "rule" against bringing in home-cooked food? Against lively posters on the wall? More often than not it will turn out to be a matter of unquestioned convention, and you may get some support for overturning those conventions as the effect on the patient's life becomes apparent.

Nursing homes can be approached with the same attitude. Instead of assuming you have to fit their patterns, begin by defining what you would like to see happen there for your patient, and work step-by-step toward that goal. Robert Bainum, owner of an innovative nursing home in Fairfax, Virginia, suggests that it's important for the patient to have control over visitors; to be able to see her chart, to be able to decide on bed, meal, and bath times; and to be able to have privacy in her room when wanted.

Institutions too often tend to organize schedules and patients' lives around the needs and optimal schedules of staff, to give care "for the good of patients but at the convenience of staff," as one hospice person put it. What is needed is care that considers the patient's convenience and personal desires. A basic approach, then, is to define your own patient needs and negotiate them. Remember that for you, and probably for all the other patients, it's going to be a better institution if the patient comes first.

Making a Choice for Home Care

Hospice, community support, and hospital programs giving special care to the dying are opening up new options for health care in the final phase of life. Working your way through these options means directly facing a basic question: do you want to do care at home or do you need an institution?

Both medical professionals and the public are becoming convinced that the person with final illness should be allowed to choose his environment as death approaches. Some also argue that home may be the very best place to die. "Home care is the direction of the future," says Lee Green, director of Georgetown University Hospital's home care program in Washington, D.C. Backing her statement are several recent studies which show that, with good medical support, almost any complication can be handled at home and that the advantages to patient and family are enormous.

At the University of Minnesota's School of Nursing, Ida Marie Martinson, R.N., Ph.D., is completing a study of 29 families who cared for their dying children at home with the support of medical teams. The data and her reflections on it are deeply moving. "A mother awakened at night to the faint cry of her six-year-old son who was terminally ill," Dr. Martinson writes. "She went immediately to his side to comfort him. As she responded he asked, 'Will it be long now?' She whispered, 'No, it won't be long anymore', and carried him to her bed where he lay between her and his father. Together the family fell asleep. When the parents awoke a couple of hours later, they found their son had died quietly in his sleep. Because the parents had the courage to cope with the difficult experience at home, they gave their child the sense of security he needed to die in peace."[12]

Out of her experience, Dr. Martinson argues that hospitalization of dying children may be costly, traumatic, and unnecessary. Pain can be controlled at home as well as in the hospital if parents learn to watch for its symptoms and nursing help is available. The security and love they have at home can give the children happiness and peace. Other children in the family seem to handle death better when they are part of the final days. And parents have a strong feeling of satisfaction that they are able to fulfill the child's wish to be at home. There are also economic benefits: compared to an average hospital cost of $12,000 per child, the average cost of care for the 11 children who died at home was less than $700.[13]

A Vancouver hospital study showed that nursing care of adults at home can also equal the care given in a hospital. Of the 47 families in the program, only a few were unable to cope with the care. Most continued the care until a few days before death, and 14 of the families continued care until death at home. And families who did the care were happy with their choice.[14]

Vancouver's program stressed the importance of involvement by the family doctor, who needs to be aware of emotional and physical needs, supervise changing equipment requirements, and be available to nurses for advice. The hospital team supplied nurses for home visits, which were often made daily. Physiotherapist and homemaker services were also available to families.

Results of such studies openly challenge the assumption that the

Dying at Home

Betty Laresche of Vienna, Virginia, is a nurse who cared for both of her parents as they died at home. In 1977 her mother, who was terminally ill with cancer of the pancreas, was with them for ten days. A year later, her father, diagnosed as having inoperable tumors of the liver and colon, also came for the last months of his life.

The Laresches had a downstairs bedroom adjacent to living areas which made it fairly easy for grandparents to be part of family life as long as possible. Betty's husband, a dentist who'd been a male nurse, shared in the care. With ingenuity, he rigged up a small button system for the bedroom that turned on the television or the lights and also rang a buzzer if help was needed. Michael, at 17, was good at lifting the patient, and Susan could stay home briefly while her mother ran errands. Three of Betty's sisters who lived in the area came over to help. And in the last six weeks of care for her father, Betty linked up with the Georgetown Hospital home care program which provided nursing visits.

For Betty, the value of her choice is clear. "If it's not an unbearable burden, I believe that home is the place to die," she says. "Any death hurts a lot, but at home you know you're cared for with warmth."

When her father's cancer began to worsen, the family gathered together with him for a home Mass. From his daughter's home, he supervised the disposition of furniture and things from his apartment — seeing that each child had the special things he or she wanted.

Betty's father was self-reliant, wanting the family to go about their business — until the last week when he fell and hurt his head. Then his care became a demanding round of day-and-night vigils

hospital is the best place to die. But does that always mean that home is best?

Often families who have experienced a member's death at home, especially those who've had help from support programs, speak warmly about their choice. Being at home means a last family party together, quiet games played with a dying child, or the struggle through a period of pain together. Sharing the final moments of life is an affirmation of love at the point of final human loss.

When they're caring at home, the family can directly control the

whose pitch left Betty exhausted after five days. A call to another out-of-town sister, also a nurse, brought relief for the last two days. Death finally came to her father quietly as he simply stopped breathing in the downstairs bedroom where his family was gathered, reading the Bible.

"It's important that the person wants to be at home and trusts in your care," says Frances Quigley, a competent executive secretary who, with her mother-in-law, cared for her husband through months of illness. Her husband hated hospitals and was content with the care she gave him. "I always got a thank you and a kiss," she said.

Frances went on working while her husband was at home. His mother stayed with him during the day and a hospital home care nurse came for regular visits. The team doctor also came for checkups and was on emergency call.

Some of the days were hard, since Eugene Quigley's cancer of the tongue and throat led to hemorrhaging. One evening the bleeding was bad, splattering over their bedroom. At that point, continuing home care was a decision made purely by his staunch refusal to be carried into the ambulance for the hospital. They endured through the bleeding, which finally stopped by itself. All during the episode, Frances said, her husband prayed for strength and kept telling her she could make it.

Her choice had its final reward in knowing she had given him the gift he wanted most: staying home. She sat with him during his last restless night, reading some prayers from his book. The following day he was awake to say good-bye to the nurse and social worker who came to check his condition. Frances was with him in their bedroom for the last hours, there holding his hand when he quietly stopped breathing.

quality of nursing care and assure that a patient has adequate attention. Because they can learn to give pain-relief injections or the hospice liquid pain-relief mixture, they'll be sure a pain prevention method is practiced. Taking responsibility for care in sickness and death lets the care giver embrace the whole life of a person he or she loves.

But it's also important to take a square look at the exhausting pressures of home care. Such care means learning how to do nursing procedures and giving hours of bedside attention, sometimes day-and-night vigils. So having a support group in your family or community is vital. A connection with a hospice or hospital home care program is ideal, making the choice of home care feasible if you're unsure about your own nursing skills. Whether the family doctor will make home visits and whether you can afford nursing help must also figure in the decision.

The type of illness and need for quick emergency skills and equipment is still another factor that plays into a decision about home care. So are the physical and mental condition of the patient and the length of illness projected. A ten-day process is very different from the strain of a three-year progression toward death. Care for a generally mobile or alert person is simpler than care of the completely bedridden or mentally disturbed patient.

If crucial factors in the support system are missing, there may be painful results from a choice for home care. If you lack medical information and can't get home visits by a doctor or nurse, your patient might suffer more pain than necessary. Or without understanding support, the task of care may become overwhelming for you, leading to exhaustion, frustration, or resentment. That, in turn, increases the painful sense of being a burden for the patient.

Simply because home care means someone being at home to care, its basis is a tough requirement for two-career families. One woman in Boston gave up a career in mid-life to care for her mother at home, and found that the slow illness lasted for six years. It took immense faith and stamina to survive the social isolation she experienced — and at the end it meant reentry into a career field at a lower level. This woman was single and open to a radical change in her life. If you are the head of a household or involved in a career vital to your life, you might find such a choice impossible. Day care programs, like the one in Tucson's hospice, can help immensely with this burden, allowing the compromise of home-based care with strong hospice assistance.

In short, a balanced look shows that home care is often medically feasible and has many personal rewards. Yet what is right for you is going to be the result of weighing many complex factors. You'll need all the information you can get about support care programs and other alternatives in your area. And then you still need to balance the rights and needs of caring people along with those of the dying person.

Looking to the Future

What is emerging in America's health care is a new vision of how to care for the dying. From hospice, Shanti, and Einstein's program come a strong commitment to care for the dying person as a whole being, not simply as a conglomerate of symptoms and medical problems. These groups see that a diagnosis of a life-threatening illness is a crisis not just for the patient but for everyone involved: husbands and wives, parents, children, and close friends. Their vision is one of ways to care and places of caring that help people meet death as they would choose, making it indeed a last affirmation of life. They see we have much to learn ourselves by looking at death. They have given us the insight that right care for the dying is right care for ourselves as well. "If I am going to make sense out of life, I have to make death my adviser," says Charles Garfield of the Shanti Project.

Along with their vision, professionals in the movement point to areas we need to learn more about: better ways of pain control, clearer knowledge of when to switch from aggressive treatment to comfort care (and if we should switch back again), ways to help with the changing sexual needs of dying persons.

And the vision of possibilities also makes us see our needs more clearly: for more hospices or more hospital home care teams; for more programs giving day or night care that lets working families have the chance to give some care at home. Looking at the personal warmth of hospice care, we can see that these new concepts need to reach nursing homes, long-care institutions, and general hospitals. So the vision of new ways to care is ultimately a call to action.

With strong optimism, Dennis Rezendes, administrator of New

Haven's hospice, projects that in ten years everybody in the health field will be sensitive to the care of dying patients and their families.[15] The gap between our present care and this goal is still wide, but programs such as hospice are showing a path. They tell us we can meet death openly, calmly prepared, free from pain, and surrounded by people we love. We can find that each death holds its own meaning both for the living and the dying, a meaning to be found as we learn to meet death well.

Notes

1. Melvin Krant, *Dying and Dignity* (Springfield, Ill.: C. C. Thomas Co., 1974), pp. 3, 10.

. 2. Herman Feifel, *The Meaning of Death* (New York: McGraw-Hill, 1959), pp. xii, xv.

3. Elisabeth Kubler-Ross, "The Dying Patient's Point of View," in *The Dying Patient*, eds. Orville Brim et al. (New York: Russell Sage, 1970), pp. 156-70.

4. Cecile Saunders, "Standards and Accreditation" (Lecture presented at the Fifth National Hospice Symposium, Washington, D.C., 5 October 1978.)

5. R. Melzack, J. G. Ofiesh, and B. M. Mount, "The Brompton Mixture: Effects on Pain in Cancer Patients," in *Psychosocial Care of the Dying Patient*, ed. Charles Garfield (New York: McGraw-Hill, 1978), pp. 386-95.

6. Joan Libman, "Death's Door," *Wall Street Journal,* 28 March 1978, p. 1.

7. Sandol Stoddard, *The Hospice Movement* (New York: Stein and Day, 1978), p. 81.

8. Charles Garfield, "On Caring, Doctors, and Death," in ed. Garfield, *Care of the Dying Patient*, p. 7.

9. Carl Simonton and Stephanie Simonton, *Getting Well Again* (New York: J. P. Tarcher, 1978), pp. 225-28.

10. Grace Powers Monaco, "Candlelighters: Self Help Legislative Ac-

tion" (Reprint from National Candlelighters Office, Washington, D.C., 1977), p. 1.

11. Carolyn Driver, "What a Dying Man Taught Doctors about Caring," in ed. Garfield, *Care of the Dying Patient*, pp. 72-77.

12. Ida Martinson, "Why Don't We Let Them Die at Home?" *RN* 42 (January 1976):58.

13. Martinson, "Taking the Dying Child Home," *The Journal of the American Medical Association* 237, no. 24 (13 June 1977):2591-93.

14. S. Malkin, "Care of the Terminally Ill at Home," *Canadian Medical Association Journal* 115 (17 July 1976):129-30. The same sort of results were found in another American home care study at the Vermont Regional Cancer Center involving 180 patients. Marie G. Kassakian, "Revival of an Old Custom" (Unpublished study, 1977).

15. Stoddard, *Hospice Movement*, p. 123.

For Further Reading

Garfield, Charles A. *Psychosocial Care of the Dying Patient.* New York: McGraw-Hill, 1978.

Kelly, Orville. *Make Today Count.* New York: Delacorte Press, 1975.

Kubler-Ross, Elisabeth. *Death: the Final Stage of Growth.* Englewood Cliffs, N.J.: Prentice-Hall, 1975.

Kubler-Ross, Elisabeth. *On Death and Dying.* Englewood Cliffs, N.J.: Prentice-Hall, 1969.

Lack, Sylvia. "I Want to Die While I'm Still Alive," *Death Education,* 1 (1977):165-76.

Mount, Balfour. "Use of the Brompton Mixture in Treating the Chronic Pain of Malignant Disease," *Canadian Medical Association Journal* 115 (17 July 1976):112-24. (May be ordered from Dr. Mount at Palliative Care Service, Royal Victoria Hospital, 687 Pine Avenue W., Montreal, Canada PQ H3A 1A1.)

Stoddard, Sandol. *The Hospice Movement.* New York: Stein and Day, 1978.

Resource Guide

The National Hospice Organization
1750 Old Meadow Road
McLean, Virginia 22102
(703) 734-0818

　　and

765 Prospect Street
New Haven, Connecticut 06511
(203) 787-5871

This is the central place for hospice information in the United States.
From the Virginia office you can get a directory of hospices ($5) or a
name of one near you. They'll also send you a list of hospice publications,
including a book on the New Haven hospice and articles from journals
which capture highlights of hospice care. Membership in the organization
is $25 for individuals and includes the directory, a quarterly newsletter,
and discounts on hospice seminars around the country. The New Haven
office is connected with the New Haven hospice and is the central place
for information on medical or more personal questions about hospice.

Haven of Northern Virginia
7300 McWhorter Place
Annandale, Virginia 22003
(703) 941-7000

Each Haven group is independent and there is no national organization or
formal directory. Haven of Northern Virginia, the first such group, does
answer inquiries about starting similar projects and has contacts with
Havenlike groups.

Candlelighters
123 C Street, S. E.
Washington, D.C. 20003
(202) 544-1626

This is the national organization for local groups of parents who have
children with cancer. The national group does lobbying, has newsletters,
keeps a list of local groups. You can find local groups by checking the
phonebook under "Candlelighters" or asking at the nearest chapter of the
American Cancer Society.

The Shanti Project
1314 Addison Street
Berkeley, California 94702
(415) 849-4980

The Shanti Project will send descriptions of its program and answer questions about organizing similar groups.

Make Today Count
Box 303
Burlington, Iowa 52601
(319) 754-7266

This national organization has a newsletter and overview of Make Today Count activities. Local groups may be listed in the phonebook. If they aren't, ask at the local chapter of the American Cancer Society for information about a support group near you.

Consumer Notes

If you need to care for a dying person, it's important to do a full check on community resources available to you. Hospice and other support services may be new and your doctor won't necessarily refer you to them.

Often discharge teams at your local hospital will have a fund of information on community resources. Because cancer is a long-term illness, local chapters of the American Cancer Society often know about support services. And you can get information on nearby hospices or support groups from national offices (see resource guide for addresses). Knowing your options and the support available is the first important step in making a decision about care.

The following notes summarize some important questions to ask as you consider the options of hospice, home care, or hospital care. A fourth option, use of a nursing home or long-term care center, isn't covered here, although some of the questions about hospitals would also apply to those places.

Hospice Care

1. If you do find a hospice, you'll need to ask about the services since each hospice is unique. Find out who is on the staff (doctor? nurses?

social worker? counselor? physical therapist? clergymen?) and what care you can expect. Get a clear picture of what you will be responsible for yourself. If there's a social worker on the team, see if she will help you go over plans to open up options and explore all angles for help.

2. Be frank in talking about expenses. Some hospices are receiving government grants and give free services. Others have arrangements for payment through insurance plans. But not all hospice care may be covered by your insurance, so you should get clear estimates of your cost in using their services.

3. Check on the relationship between the hospice doctor and your family physician or specialists. Will they be in touch with each other and share information? Whom should you call for emergencies if you're doing home care? If the hospice offers only home care, which doctor will follow your patient into the hospital for care should that be necessary?

4. If the hospice has an inpatient center, find out how you can use it. Can you check in your patient for short periods while you get rest from home care? Can you use the hospice during the day or night, alternating care? How long a time can a patient stay in the hospice center?

5. Since the key to good care isn't just what the care giver wants but what's right for the patient, arrange for a meeting between hospice staffers and your patient before you make arrangements final. The patient needs to be comfortable with the team for the care plan to work.

6. Hospices support the ideal of a natural death, not using extraordinary means to prolong life. How do you feel about emergency measures to save life? Determine what is available through hospice, through hospitals near you.

7. Talk directly with the hospice team about your feelings in approaching the death of the person you're caring for. Encourage your patient to talk about the best ways to spend the time remaining. Both of you may want to talk about the actual meeting of death. Do you want some of the hospice team with you? Do you want simply family together? Whom do you want with you for support after the death?

8. Hospices are new and for now there isn't any record of exploitation. But you may want to ask for names of other people who have been served by the group to get a sense of whether the care has been what's promised.

Home Care (without a hospice team)

1. Find out if any hospital near you has a home care team that will

provide support nurses, social workers, doctors. Check on how often nurses or social workers will visit, what they will do, and what additional support care you'll need. Social workers on such a team can be really helpful in evaluating this and helping you link up with other community programs. The social worker on a hospital discharge team can help also if your patient is coming home after a hospice stay.

2. If you do connect with a hospital home care team, talk about the relationship of the team doctor to your family doctor. See if either will make home visits. Find out who should cover emergencies and where. If your patient is in pain, ask if either is willing to use the hospice pain prevention approach.

3. If you need supplementary home nursing care, check on alternate groups who may provide this. Find out if nurses and doctors will give you instructions on care treatments you'll need to handle yourself.

4. Work out a support system with other family members, friends, and neighbors. Even a completely dedicated care giver needs breaks for relief during what can be a long caring period, and openly discussing your needs with others can lead to some good practical arrangements. Do you need someone to come in while you shop? go to church? during the night? simply to get away for a while?

5. Work out your system for handling emergencies. Will you take your patient to a hospital? How? Can you get a doctor to make home calls?

6. Make arrangements for how you want to handle the home death itself. Whom do you want to be with you? How will you interact with nurses or a doctor who may be present? Do you want only family with the dying person? Who will be there to give you support after the death?

Hospital Care

1. Find out if there is any special hospital program for care of the dying. Even a single nurse or social worker from the staff who is aware of the special needs of dying persons can help you immensely in getting person-centered care for your patient.

2. Ask about methods of pain control. See if your doctor is willing to explore pain prevention techniques such as hospice teams use. If he isn't, see if a doctor on the hospital staff might.

3. Talk with the nursing staff about diet and care procedures, working toward getting what is best for your patient. You might, for example, want to have some times of the day when no staff will interrupt you. Or you might want to work out ways to supplement a hospital diet with food brought from home.

4. Explore ways of creating a personal environment for your patient.

Can you bring in posters, paintings, or pictures? record player? Can the people who are important come to visit, including children? Base your discussions with the staff on the point that hospital time for a dying person is very different from time for other patients who will be getting well and going home. You want to make final days as beautiful as possible.

5. Find out what the usual procedures are for emergency treatment as death approaches. If you or your patient want to choose a natural death without emergency lifesaving procedures, discuss this with your doctor and the hospital staff. If you want to be alone with the dying person for some time, make this clear.

6. Find out about the usual procedures after death. If you want time to be with the body, say so. Recognize your own need to cry and grieve and try to locate some space where you can let it happen.

Finally, a note for the care giving people, no matter what physical arrangements you work out. Caring people, as well as the dying person, need to meet death as openly as possible, experience its loss, and move through that grief. You may need some help in looking at death. Books like Elisabeth Kubler-Ross's *On Death and Dying* may help you feel more comfortable with your emotions. Being part of a support group of care givers or dying persons and friends may help you share the struggles you'll face as you live through this time of deep human growth.

Conclusion

What You Can Do for Yourself

We began by telling you what this book could do for you: that is, describe the new health care options which you can use to get better health care for yourself and your family. We'd like to conclude by telling you about what you can do for yourself to help insure better health and health care. Our reason for doing this is very simple: many health care experts maintain that the next major improvement in our health care will be what the individual does for himself.

With all the miracle drugs, equipment, and techniques medical science has developed in the last decades, we still suffer from a number of serious diseases. The main threats to our health as we approach the 1980s are heart disease, cancer, and strokes. (Together, heart disease and strokes account for about 50 percent of the deaths in this country; cancer claims another 16 percent.)

There are several things which these diseases have in common. For one thing, a large percentage of the deaths that are caused by cardiovascular disease and cancer are premature deaths — their victims are not the elderly, but the middle aged. Secondly, these diseases are chronic, which means there really isn't any cure for them, and they are degenerative. Finally, and most importantly, it has been shown that each of them is at least in part caused by the individual's habits and lifestyle. And that means they are preventable.

It is also true that there is often very little a doctor can do to help with many of the more minor diseases which bother all of us. It has been estimated that 80 percent of all our trips to primary care physicians are for problems that will simply get better with time. Thus, many office visits to the doctor are a waste of time, money, and effort because the medical practitioner is really as helpless as you are to do anything to "cure" or even improve your ailment. The old adage, "Drink plenty of liquids and get some rest," is as good advice for dealing with a cold as any doctor can give you.

These two facts about our health — that many diseases are preventable to an extent, and that many health problems are really untreatable or can be treated just as well by a layperson as a medical practitioner — point to two of the newest ideas in health care: self-care and prevention.

Self-Care:
On Becoming Your Doctor's Partner

In 1970, Dr. Keith W. Sehnert began a course at the Center for Continuing Health Education at Georgetown University designed to produce what he called "the activated patient." Combining a series of classes with home study, the course's aim was to teach people about common health problems and emphasize self-help and preventive medicine.

What is an "activated patient"? According to Sehnert, she is simply a person whose medical knowledge makes it possible for her to become an active partner in her own health care, rather than a passive recipient of health care that is being doled out by a physician.

In order to produce "activated patients" Sehnert taught his students how to: get and use a "black bag" of medical tools, including a stethoscope, blood pressure cuff, otoscope (a device used to examine ears), a tongue depressor, dental mirror, and thermometer; listen and interpret messages the body was sending back, like headaches or a lack of energy; know and use drugs wisely; get and understand their own medical records; practice yoga; decide on a doctor; question a doctor; and decide what to do about common illnesses and emergencies in a logical, rational manner. In addition, he dealt with nutrition and other preventive medicine techniques, and talked about such problems as drugs, alcoholism, and mental illness. Underlying it all was the conviction that people had to become their own primary sources for good health care. (Sehnert has since published a book entitled, *How to Be Your Own Doctor (Sometimes)* [New York: Grosset & Dunlap, 1975.], which includes much of the same information found in his course.)

Since then the idea of patient education and responsibility has spread. Throughout the country people are combining forces with one another and with doctors and nurses to gain some of the skills and knowledge which have been the special province of the medical profession for too long.

In Boise, Idaho, for example, consumers and professionals began to think about ways for the layperson to gain a better understanding of health care problems. What evolved was a series of self-care education classes, called the Healthwise Workshops, which attempt to teach people (especially parents with young children) how to cope with their most common health problems. Using videotapes and a handbook (*Healthwise Handbook*, [New York: Doubleday & Co., 1979]), the workshops focus on checkups, abdominal pain, headaches, backaches, upper respiratory problems, skin problems, minor injuries, and emergency procedures.

In Inverness, California, Tom Ferguson, a Yale medical school graduate, began *Medical Self-Care* magazine to give people concrete advice on managing their health. In it, Ferguson writes about current and worthwhile medical books, health care skills, how lifestyle can affect health, information on how to use the medical literature that is available, news of the self-care movement, and classes on self-care that are being held.

The Maternity Center Association began what they call the Self-Help Education Initiated in Childbirth (SHEIC) program in 1976 in New York City. The purpose of the program is to incorporate pregnant couples in their own prenatal care. Each couple does their own prenatal examination, including weight, urine analysis, blood pressure reading, measurement of the abdomen, and listening to the baby's heartbeat and locating its position. The couple's nurse-midwife serves as guide and helper as they assume responsibility for their pregnancy.

Also in New York City, the Center for Medical Consumers has gathered together a health and medical information library which may be used by any resident of that city. The center also has a newsletter and by calling a special number, people can hear tapes prepared on a variety of health care subjects. "We want people to take control, to have power over their own health care," says the center's director, Arthur Levin. "The way to do that is to make information available to the laity."

Still another way the desire for self-care is being implemented is in the spread of a technique known as cardiopulmonary resuscitation (CPR). CPR, which can be administered by any person who has taken a course in it, is an emergency procedure designed to keep the brain supplied with oxygen until a heartbeat can be restored by medical personnel. In Seattle, Washington, over 120,000 people know CPR and within a five-year period more than 600 people in that city have been saved from death from a heart attack or stroke by their fellow citizens.

Self-care can also be as simple as monitoring your own blood pressure, an especially important exercise since high blood pressure is virtually symptomless. Since 1976 thousands of blood pressure machines have been installed in shopping malls, supermarkets, drugstores, and hotels — still another manifestation of people's willingness to become responsible for their own well-being.

Finally, many self-help groups have sprung up around the country. In groups such as Reach for Recovery (for women who have had mastectomies), Mended Hearts (for people who have undergone heart surgery), and Make Today Count (for people who have had or do have cancer), people are gathering together to give each other the kind of information, mutual support, and psychological uplifting that health professionals, who are not usually intimately affected by the problem, could never give.

Is the kind of self-care that is being advocated medically safe? As with many other innovations we have discussed, the experts disagree on just how far self-care should go. But most everyone does agree on two things: that some self-care is good and that self-care doesn't mean "going it alone." It does mean working in partnership with health care providers, making decisions as to when you need to consult with them and use their services — and when you don't. (One method that's been devised to help you make the decision is called clinical algorithms. These are charts which lead you through a series of step-by-step questions, the answers to which will help you decide if you need a doctor. For example, if you have a sore throat, one question might be, "Do you have a rash?" If you answer yes, then you'll be told to see a physician immediately. If you answer no, you'll go on to the next question, which might be, "Are your tonsils inflamed?" The answer to that will then lead you to the next step until you finally know if you should see a doctor quickly, eventually, or not at all. A book entitled, *Take Care of Yourself: a Consumer's Guide to Medical Care* [Reading, Mass.: Addison-Wesley, 1976] by Drs. Donald M. Vickery and James F. Fries contains clinical algorithms for 68 common medical problems.)

People who have gone through self-care courses or who have done reading and studying on their own often say that the most tangible byproduct of their work is that they can talk to their doctors intelligently. They're no longer intimidated by medical professionals, they understand what the diagnosis of their condition is, and they have input concerning the course of their treatment. (This is not to say that self-care advocates aren't also enthusiastic about their increasing feelings of self-reliance and their decreasing medical bills!)

If you're interested in self-care, talk to your doctor, hospital, or local public health department about setting up a class or check sources like *Medical Self-Care* to find out if a course is being given near you. And, finally, if you really want to take care of yourself, you need to adopt a healthy lifestyle.

Prevention: The Most Effective Cure

John H. Knowles, who was president of the Rockefeller Foundation until his recent death, perhaps said it best when he wrote in his book, *Doing Better and Feeling Worse*, "The health of human beings is determined by their behavior, their food, and the nature of their environment."

In the last years we have come to learn more and more about the relationship between the way we live and our health. If we eat the wrong foods, eat too much, smoke, drink alcohol, live with stress, and don't exercise, we contribute to poor health — and early death. And in our society of instant rewards and gratification with our constant demand for fun and stimulation, we are prime targets for the degenerative diseases which are in part caused by these bad health habits.

But just as we are witnessing improvements in the health care system per se, we are also becoming more aware of what it means to have a healthy lifestyle. We are beginning to eat sensibly, we are starting to exercise regularly, we are cutting down on our consumption of alcohol and drugs. In a study of nearly 7,000 adults over a 5½-year time span, it was shown that life expectancy and health are intimately related to the following seven health habits: (1) three meals a day and no eating between meals; (2) breakfast every day; (3) moderate exercise; (4) seven or eight hours of sleep every night; (5) no smoking; (6) near correct weight; and (7) no alcohol or alcohol in moderation.*

The options and alternatives we've described for you in this book can certainly help you improve your own health care. They can help you get care that is more personal, less expensive, and tailored to your individual needs. On a broader scale, they can make vast improvements in our primary health care system; they can help cut hospital costs; and they can help us reestablish the connection between ourselves and the two experiences each of us encounters, birth and death. They can help show us how to stay healthy and, perhaps, even how to achieve a state of wellness beyond mere absence of illness.

But in the last analysis, they are only our aids. In the last analysis it is we who must manage our own health care and produce good health for ourselves and our families. It is encouraging that we are beginning to have the support of programs and people who will help us in this. But ultimately, the responsibility is ours.

---

*N. B. Belloc and L. Breslow, "The Relation of Physical Health Status and Health Practices," *Preventive Medicine* 1 (August 1972):409-21 as quoted in John H. Knowles, ed., *Doing Better and Feeling Worse* (New York: W. W. Norton & Co., 1977), p. 61.

Glossary

Health Care Terms

acupuncture — an oriental healing technique which uses needles inserted at key points in the body to balance the flow of energy within the body.

adolescent medicine — the medical specialty which focuses on the health needs of teen-agers.

ambulatory — able to walk.

ambulatory surgery facility — a place to which a patient comes for minor surgery in the morning and returns home in the afternoon.

anesthetic — a substance which either numbs a certain part of the body (local anesthetic) or which produces unconsciousness (general anesthetic) for surgery.

biofeedback — a technique or device which allows biological monitoring and thus helps in healing.

birthing room — a homelike room set aside for labor and delivery in hospitals.

Blue Cross and Blue Shield — independent nonprofit corporations providing protection against the costs of hospital care (Blue Cross) or doctors, surgery, and other items of medical care (Blue Shield).

board certified — a physician who is board certified has passed exams given by the professional association that regulates his specialty.

bonding — the psychological attachment between parents and newborns which takes place in the first minutes and hours after birth.

Bradley method — a childbirth preparation method named after Dr. Robert Bradley which advocates a "working with nature" approach.

Brompton mixture — a morphine- or heroin-based pain relief mixture given to terminally ill patients.

cardiopulmonary resuscitation (CPR) — an emergency procedure, which can be administered by a lay person, to keep the brain supplied with oxygen until a heartbeat can be restored by medical personnel.

Cesarean birth — birth in which the fetus is taken surgically from the uterus rather than being delivered vaginally.

chiropractor — a medical practitioner who seeks to bring about improvements in health through the manipulation of joints.

chronic — a long-lasting illness; in most cases there are no dramatic treatments to help chronic illnesses.

clinical algorithm — a series of step-by-step questions, the answers to which help you to decide whether you need to seek medical help for a health problem or whether you can treat it yourself.

episiotomy — a cut made in the perineum, the area between the vagina and the anus, during childbirth.

family-centered maternity care — a concept which emphasizes the needs and desires of the family during their birth experience.

family practice — a medical specialty which focuses on providing primary care within the family setting.

fetal monitor — an instrument used to check fetal heartbeat during childbirth; may be worn either externally or internally.

freestanding ambulatory surgery center — an ambulatory surgery facility which is privately funded and not affiliated with a hospital.

gynecology — the medical specialty which focuses on the female reproductive system.

health maintenance organization (HMO) — an organization which agrees to provide medical, hospital, emergency, and preventive health care in return for a prepaid membership.

holistic health — a concept which stresses the interrelationship among mind, body, and spirit, and which believes that all three must be well and in harmony for the individual to be truly healthy.

home health aid — a paraprofessional who comes into the home to do personal care (for example, shampoos, bathing) for a homebound patient.

homemaker-home health aid — a home health aid who also does homemaking tasks (for example, food preparation or cleaning).

homeopath — a medical practitioner who believes diseases should be treated by giving a patient small doses of an agent which, if given in a much larger dose, produces symptoms in a healthy person similar to those of the disease under treatment.

hospice — a place or service designed to be a center of care and support for the dying and their families and which allows a more personal, meaningful death.

inpatient — a person who is receiving medical care in a hospital or other institution.

interdisciplinary health care team — a group of health professionals (for example, a doctor, therapist, nutritionist) who work together to provide health care that focuses on the whole person.

Lamaze method — a childbirth preparation method that consists of a set of exercises and breathing patterns which help women disassociate themselves from the pain of labor.

Leboyer birth — a philosophy of childbirth which seeks to welcome the newborn into the world "gently" with soft lights, low voices, a warm bath, etc.

maternity center — a homelike institution physically separated from a hospital which provides family-centered maternity care.

Meals on Wheels — a program which delivers hot and cold meals to the homebound.

Medicaid — a federally sponsored program to provide health care to the needy.

Medicare — a federally sponsored program to provide health care to the elderly.

meditation — a technique which brings about an altered state of consciousness between waking and sleeping and which brings with it profound relaxation.

midlevel health practitioner (MHP) — a physician's assistant, nurse practitioner, or nurse clinician who is capable of doing many of the basic tasks usually performed by a doctor.

midwife — a person trained to help families with *normal* pregnancy and childbirth; certified nurse-midwives are registered nurses with a year or two of training in midwifery; empirical, or lay, midwives are self-taught or have apprenticed with another midwife.

osteopath — a medical practitioner who has had a four-year training program in osteopathic medicine, served a hospital-based internship, and performs basically as an MD.

outpatient — a person who is receiving medical care outside of the hospital or any other institution.

outpatient surgical unit — a hospital-affiliated ambulatory surgery facility.

paramedic — a person with extensive training in handling medical emergencies and who is involved in some system that provides rapid emergency treatment.

participatory examinations — a medical exam in which the patient takes an active part, learning about the human body in the process.

pediatrics — the medical specialty which focuses on babies and children.

practical nurse — a nurse with one year of special schooling.

preventive health — health care which stresses ways to prevent illness from occurring.

primary care — basic care that one receives from a family practitioner for minor illness, health preservation, prevention of illness; implicit in the idea of primary care is the notion that health care should treat the whole person rather than just the body, and that people should receive continuity of care.

professional nurse — a nurse with a two- or three-year degree.

public health nurse — a nurse with a B.S. degree in nursing.

registered nurse (RN) — a nurse who is a graduate of a two-year community college, a three-year hospital program, or a four-year college.

self-help — a concept which stresses that the individual can and must manage and be responsible for much of his own health care.

Tai chi — an oriental martial art which is composed of a series of slow movements.

wellness — a concept which maintains that there is a state beyond mere absence of illness characterized by "optimal health."

yoga — in the most limited sense, a series of stretching and toning exercises accompanied by certain breathing patterns and meditation; in the broadest sense, yoga means being at one with whatever you are doing.

Index

cost of, 153
experience at, 150-51
other services at, 153
procedure at, 147-49
resource guide for, 163-65
safety of, 152-53
May, Jan, example of MHP, 43-44, 48-49
Meal sites, for elderly, 91
Meals on Wheels, 91-92
Medex program, to train MHPs, 45, 51
Medicaid
coverage for home care, 93, 94, 95-97
coverage for hospice programs, 179-80
coverage for maternity centers, 153
coverage for MHPs, 52
Medical insurance. *See* Insurance
Medical Personnel Pool, 94
Medicare
coverage for home care, 93, 94, 95-97
coverage for hospice programs, 179-80
coverage for MHPs, 52
HMOs accepting, 11
Medic I, 67-70
Memorial Hospital, Phoenix
birthing suite at, 154
sibling visitation at, 155
Mental health services, in HMOs, 8-9
Metropolitan Life Insurance, standards for
ambulatory surgery centers, 114-15
MHPs. *See* Midlevel health practitioners
Midlevel health practitioners, 43-54
consumer notes on, 75
cost effectiveness of, 52-53
cost of, 51-52
medical establishment's attitudes
toward, 53
need for, 44-46
questions about, 50-52
regulation of, 46
resource guide for, 74
services of, 46-50
training for, 45-46, 50-51
Midwives, 61-64. *See also* Nurse-midwife
certified, 62-63, 65
consumer notes on, 76
empirical, 63
for home births, 143-45
opposition to, 62
questions about, 63-64
resource guide for, 74, 75
Minor Surgery Center, 108, 118
Morris, Sue, home birth for, 144
Mount Sinai's adolescent center, 22-24
Mutal Aid Project, New York City, 102
National Association of Home Health
Agencies, 105

National Association of Parents and
Professionals for Safe Alternatives in
Childbirth, 165
National Cancer Institute, funding for
hospice programs, 178, 179
National Council for Homemaker-Home
Health Aide Services, Inc., 104
National Hospice Organization, 173, 200
formulating standards, 181
National League for Nursing, 104
National Midwives Association, 75
NC. *See* Nurse clinicians
Neble family, HMO services for, 7
Neighborhood Health Centers, 34-35
New Haven Hospice, 173, 178, 179
NP. *See* Nurse practitioners
Nurse clinicians, 44, 46, 51
Nurse-midwife, 62-63. *See also* Midwives
in an HMO, 4-5
Maternity Center Associates as example
of, 65
resource guide for, 74
Nurse practitioners, 44, 45, 51
Nursing agencies, nonprofit
for home health care, 90-91, 93
resource guide for, 104-5
Nursing agencies, profit-making, 94-95
resource guide for, 104-5
Nutrition, for home health care, 91-92
Nutrition counseling
in adolescent health centers, 23-26
in HMOs, 9
in holistic health centers, 29-32 passim
by orthomolecular therapists, 71
by wellness doctors, 66
Orthomolecular therapists, 71
Osteopaths, 71
Outpatient care. *See also* Ambulatory
surgery centers; Home health care
HMOs and, 6
Oxygen therapists, 71
PA. *See* Physician's assistants
Paramedics, 67-70
consumer notes on, 77
Parents United by Tragedy, 185
Participatory exams, at women's health
centers, 14-15
Pediatric surgery, 115-17
Physician's assistants, 44, 45, 46, 51
resource guide for, 74
Pitocin, 133
Planned Parenthood, 34
Poetry therapy, 71
Pregnancy
adolescent problems with, 21
screening for, at women's health centers,
16